T0329518

Swing and Day Trading

Founded in 1807, John Wiley & Sons is the oldest independent publishing company in the United States. With offices in North America, Europe, Australia and Asia, Wiley is globally committed to developing and marketing print and electronic products and services for our customers' professional and personal knowledge and understanding.

The Wiley Trading series features books by traders who have survived the market's ever changing temperament and have prospered—some by reinventing systems, others by getting back to basics. Whether a novice trader, professional or somewhere in-between, these books will provide the advice and strategies needed to prosper today and well into the future.

For a list of available titles, visit our Web site at www.WileyFinance.com.

Swing and Day Trading

Evolution of a Trader

THOMAS N. BULKOWSKI

WILEY

John Wiley & Sons, Inc.

Published by John Wiley & Sons, Inc., Hoboken, New Jersey.
Published simultaneously in Canada.

For general information on our other products and services or for technical support, please contact our Customer Care Department within the United States at (800) 762-2974, outside the United States at (317) 572-3993 or fax (317) 572-4002.

Wiley publishes in a variety of print and electronic formats and by print-on-demand. Some material included with standard print versions of this book may not be included in e-books or in print-on-demand. If this book refers to media such as a CD or DVD that is not included in the version you purchased, you may download this material at http://booksupport.wiley.com. For more information about Wiley products, visit www.wiley.com.

Library of Congress Cataloging-in-Publication Data:
Bulkowski, Thomas N., –
    Swing and day trading : evolution of a trader / Thomas N. Bulkowski.
        p. cm. – (Wiley trading series)
    Includes bibliographical references and index.
    ISBN 978-1-118-46422-9 (cloth); ISBN 978-1-118-51696-6 (ebk);
ISBN 978-1-118-51697-3 (ebk); ISBN 978-1-118-51699-7 (ebk)
    1. Investment analysis. 2. Portfolio management. 3. Electronic trading of securities. 4. Day trading (Securities) I. Title.
    HG4529.B85 2013
    332.64–dc23
                                                                2012033910

Printed in the United States of America
10 9 8 7 6 5 4 3 2 1

Contents

Preface

Are you like John?

He learned early in life to save his money for a rainy day. Instead of putting it into the bank, he put it into the stock market. He bought Cisco Systems in mid-1999 at 35 and watched the stock soar to 82 in less than a year.

"I'm looking for my first 10-bagger," he said, and held onto the stock.

In 2001, when the tech bubble burst, the Cisco balloon popped, too, and it plunged back to 35. He was at breakeven after seeing the stock more than double.

"It'll recover," he said. "It's a $200 stock. You'll see."

The stock tunneled through 35 then 30, then 20, and bottomed at 15, all in *one* month. When it hit 10, he sold it for a 70 percent loss.

"I should have sold at the top. Buy-and-hold doesn't work." But it did work. Cisco more than doubled, but he held too long.

Next, he tried position trading to better time the exit and chose Eastman Chemical. He bought it in 2003 at 14, just pennies from the bear market bottom, and rode it up to 21 before selling. He made 50 percent in a year. Was he happy?

"I sold too soon." The stock continued rising, hitting 30 in 2005. He disliked seeing profits mount after he sold, and wanted to profit from swings in both directions.

He switched to swing trading in 2005 and tried his old favorite: Cisco. The stock bounced from 17 to 20 to 17 to 22 over the next year, but he always bought too late and exited too early. He made money, but not enough.

He took a vacation from his day job and watched Applied Materials wave to him on the computer screen, inviting him to come day trade it. So he did. He made $400 in just 15 minutes. "If I can make $400 a day for a year, I'll make"—he grabbed his calculator and punched buttons—"$146,000! No, that's not right. How many trading days are there in a year?"

He redid the math and discovered that he could make $100,000 a year by nibbling off just 40 cents a share on 1,000 shares every trading day. "Wow. Count me in."

After paying $5,000 for a trading course and more for hardware, software, and data feeds, he took the plunge and started day trading full time.

It took a year to blow through his savings. Another three months took out his emergency fund. He moved back in with his parents while he looked for a real job.

Now, he is saving again and putting it to work in the market. "After reading the manuscript for this book," he said, "I found a trading style that works for me. I'm a swinger—a swing trader. And I'm making money, too." He handles not only his own money but his parents and siblings as well, providing them with extra income and building a nest egg for their retirement.

EVOLUTION OF A TRADER

John represents an amalgam of traders, a composite of those searching for a trading style that they can call their own. He suffered through many failed trades before finding a trading style that worked for him. I wrote the *Evolution of a Trader* series to help people like John.

Evolution of a Trader traces my journey from a buy-and-hold investor to position trader to swing trader to day trader as I searched for styles that worked best when markets evolved. However, these are not autobiographical. Rather, they are an exploration of what has worked, what is supposed to work but does not, and what may work in the future.

This series dissects the four trading styles and provides discoveries, trading tips, setups, and tactics to make each style a profitable endeavor. I have done the research so you do not have to. I show what is needed to make each style work.

CONTENT OVERVIEW

The three books in the *Evolution of a Trader* series provide numerous tips, trading ideas, and setups based on personal experience and that of others.

Easy to understand tests are used to confirm trading folklore and to illustrate ideas and setups, and yet the books are an entertaining read with an engaging style that appeals to the novice.

Each section has bullet items summarizing the importance of the findings. A checklist at chapter's end provides an easy-to-use summary of the contents and reference of where to find more information.

At the end of each book is a topic checklist and reference.

Trading Basics

The first book in the series begins with the basics, creating a solid foundation of terms and techniques. Although you may understand market basics, you will learn from this book.

How do I know? Take this quiz. If you have to guess at the answers, then you need to buy this book. If you get some of them wrong, then imagine what you are missing. Answers are at the end of the quiz.

From Chapter 2: Money Management

1. True or false: Trading a constant position size can have disastrous results.

2. True or false: A market order to cancel a buy can be denied if it is within two minutes of the Nasdaq's open.

3. True or false: Dollar cost averaging underperforms.

From Chapter 3: Do Stops Work?

1. True or false: Fibonacci retracements offer no advantage over any other number as a turning point.

2. True or false: A chandelier stop hangs off the high price.

3. True or false: Stops cut profit more than they limit risk.

From Chapter 4: Support and Resistance

1. True or false: Peaks with below average volume show more resistance.

2. True or false: Support gets stronger over time.

3. True or false: The middle of a tall candle is no more likely to show support or resistance than any other part.

From Chapter 5: 45 Tips Every Trader Should Know

1. True or false: Fibonacci extensions are no more accurate than any other tool for determining where price might reverse.

2a. True or false: Only bullish divergence (in the RSI indicator) works and only in a bull market.

2b. True or false: Bullish divergence (in the RSI indicator) fails to beat the market more often than it works.

3. True or false: Price drops faster than it rises.

From Chapter 6: Finding and Fixing What Is Wrong

1. True or false: The industry trend is more important than the market trend.

2. True or false: Holding a trade too long is worse than selling too early.

3. True or false: Sell in May and go away.

The answer to every statement is true.

Fundamental Analysis and Position Trading

This book explains and describes the test results of various fundamental factors such as book value, price-to-earnings ratio, and so on, to see how important they are to stock selection and performance.

The Fundamental Analysis Summary chapter provides tables of fundamental factors based on hold times of one, three, and five years that show which factor is most important to use for those anticipated hold times. The tables provide a handy reference for buy-and-hold investors or for other trading styles that wish to own a core portfolio of stocks based on fundamental analysis.

Chapters such as "How to Double Your Money," "Finding 10-Baggers," and "Trading 10-Baggers" put the fundamentals to work. The chapter titled "Selling Buy-and-Hold " helps solve the problem of when to sell long-term holdings.

Position Trading   The second part of *Fundamental Analysis and Position Trading* explores position trading. It introduces market timing to help remove the risk of buying and holding a stock for years.

Have you heard the phrase *Trade with the trend*? How often does a stock follow the market higher or lower? The section in Chapter 19 titled, "What Is Market Influence on Stocks?" provides the answer.

This part of the book looks at how chart patterns can help with position trading. It discloses the 10 most important factors that make chart patterns work and then blends them into a scoring system. That system can help you become a more profitable position trader when using chart patterns.

Six actual trades are discussed to show how position trading works and when it does not. Consider them as roadmaps that warn when the road is bumpy and when the market police are patrolling.

Swing and Day Trading

The last book of the series covers swing and day trading. The first portion of the book highlights swing trading techniques, explains how to use chart patterns to swing trade, and explores swing selling, event patterns (common stock offerings, trading Dutch auction tender offers, earnings releases, rating changes, and so on), and other trading setups.

It tears apart a new tool called the chart pattern indicator. The indicator is not a timing tool, but a sentiment indicator that is great at calling major market turns.

Day Trading   Day trading reviews the basics including home office setup, cost of day trading, day trading chart patterns, and the opening range breakout. It discusses research into the major reversal times each day and what time of the day is most likely to set the day's high and low—valuable information to a day trader.

An entire chapter discusses the opening gap setup and why fading the gap is the best way to trade it. Another chapter discusses the opening range breakout setup and questions whether it works.

Ten horror stories from actual traders complete the series. They have been included to give you lasting nightmares.

INTENDED AUDIENCE

The three books in this series were written for people unfamiliar with the inner workings of the stock market, but will curl the toes of professionals, too.

Research is used to prove the ideas discussed, but is presented in an easy to understand and light-hearted manner. You will find the books to be as entertaining as they are informative and packed with moneymaking tips and ideas. Use the ideas presented here to hone your trading style and improve your success.

Whether you are a novice who has never purchased a stock but wants to, or a professional money manager who trades daily, these books are a necessary addition to any market enthusiast's bookshelf.

Acknowledgments

So many people are involved in bringing a manuscript to life, and I play a small role. To all of those workers at John Wiley & Sons, I say thanks for the help, especially to Evan Burton and Meg Freeborn. They ironed the wrinkles and made the trilogy presentable, even fashionable.

CHAPTER 1

Introduction to Swing Trading

S wing trading reminds me of standing on the shore of an ocean, watching the waves. Each wave has a crest and trough—a swing from high to low or low to high that mimics the up and down motion of stocks. Swing traders do not try to surf that wave by riding near the crest, but by sailing their boat from trough to crest like in scenes from *The Perfect Storm*.

WHAT IS SWING TRADING?

There are two types of swing trading styles. The first is to range trade, that is, buy and sell as price bounces between a low and high price. If you know what a rectangle chart pattern is or a channel, then you can buy near the bottom and sell near the top repeatedly. I find that the profit potential of range trading is not exciting enough for me.

- Range trading is buying and selling as price bounces between highs and lows.

I prefer to catch a swing as soon as it starts and hold it until it ends. It is the same idea as a range trade but the high–low range is often much larger (if you are lucky) and you only trade it once.

- A trend trade buys near the swing low and sells near the end of a short-term trend (or the reverse: sell high and buy low).

1

Swing trading is trying to catch price as it moves between peaks and valleys. Another way to say this is that swing trading is capturing the move between layers of support and resistance.

Why not just hold onto the stock and ride it? You can do that, of course, but swing traders believe that they can increase profits by participating as the stock oscillates up and down like waves on a pond.

Look at Figure 1.1. If investors bought the stock at A and sold it at E, they would have made almost nothing since price did not change between those two points. However, perfect swing traders would sell short at A, cover at B and buy long, sell at C and go short, and so on, profiting from each swing of the stock. They could have captured roughly $3 per share on each of the AB and BC moves, and $2 on each of the CD and DE moves for a total of $10 per share. That is not bad for a stock that ends where it begins.

WHO SHOULD SWING TRADE?

As the hold time for a trade shortens, there is less room for error. You can ignore a stock for years using a buy-and-hold strategy and still turn a profit. With swing trading, a trader's skills need to identify turning points with accuracy. One mistake can be costly, which is why stop placement is important.

Swing trading demands a different personality than the longer hold time brethren. While a buy-and-hold investor watches autumn leaves changing color on the back porch, a day trader is injecting caffeine and hanging onto the computer desk, knuckles white. A swing trader is not as nervous as a day trader, but you get my point. Swing traders have to pay closer attention to their trades than do those with a longer hold time horizon.

One novice swing trader I know waits for his favorite stocks to drop by 20 percent before he buys. Then he closes his eyes and waits for them to recover, hoping for a 30 percent move before he cashes out. He turned an investment of $25,000 into almost $100,000 in a year using this simple idea.

He has three keys to success. First, he chooses to ignore mistakes. If the stock continues to drop, it turns into a buy-and-wait-for-recovery trade, praying for breakeven. Second, the stocks were also cheap, in the $2 to $4 range (like Citigroup) with high volatility. In the days of the banking crisis (2009), he could peel off a 30 percent gain in about three days, but would become trapped in a loser for weeks. Fortunately for him, his picks recovered and allowed him to minimize losses. Third, the banking industry was in turmoil, making large swings every few days, catering to his trading setup.

He enjoys this fast-paced trading action. It is not day trading, so he can still monitor his stocks a few times each day from his day job without getting into trouble. Recently, though, the setup has not been working as well as in the past. He has moved from banking stocks to housing stocks, and those do not bounce around as much. Any recovery for a losing position now takes not weeks but months.

- Swing trading is best suited for people who are accustomed to using stops and like to follow the market daily.

A SWINGING EXAMPLE

Perfect trades are rare, but I have made a surprising number. I am not claiming to be a perfect trader—not by a long shot—but the timing on some of them is well done. A trade in Exxon Mobil Corp. (XOM) is a particularly good example of a nearly perfect swing trade. **Figure 1.1** shows the setup.

FIGURE 1.1 This trade shows a perfect entry and sale on the day the stock peaked. Trailing stops mark the way higher.

On one of the passes through the nearly 700 securities that I look at, I spotted a rare bird: an ascending triangle. Normally I dislike trading ascending triangles because price rises 5 to 10 percent before reversing.

I logged the ascending triangle into my database two days before the breakout and then started my research. After looking at other stocks in the industry, I concluded that the oils were boiling, and I wanted to participate. I placed a buy stop at 52.06, which is a penny above the top of the triangle.

I scored the chart pattern and this one had a –1 score, meaning it was unlikely to reach the 65.91 price target.

Using the height of the chart pattern projected a more conservative target of 55.20, a gain of about three points over the expected fill price. I will explain the measure rule for calculating price targets in Chapter 3 (under the heading "Measuring Swings").

The company released earnings the day before the breakout. The next day (E), the buy stop filled a penny higher because price blew the lid off the top of the ascending triangle.

I always assume a throwback will occur, but it did not. Price just kept on rising. After entering the trade, I placed a stop at 49.21 that same day. I positioned the stop below the bottom of the chart pattern using the minor low (D) at the start of January as the reference.

As price climbed, I raised the stop as the chart shows, to 51.07. On February 10, I raised the stop to 52.93, using a 62 percent Fibonacci retrace of the move up from January 28 low (51.11, two days before the breakout) to the current high of 56.62, minus about 25 cents.

On February 16, I raised the stop to 53.93, again using a 62 percent Fibonacci retrace to price the stop. Two days later, I wrote in my notebook: "Stop raised to 55.93. I am getting nervous about the straight-line run, so I am tightening up the stop. A quick decline often follows a quick rise, so...."

I continued to raise the trailing stop and ended with it at 61.15. However, in a late-day sell off, the stock blew through my stop and filled at 60.90.

On the day I sold, the stock reached a new high of 64.37, fulfilling the scoring system's prediction that it would *not* reach 65.91.

Selling was the right move since the stock tumbled back to a low of 52.78 in less than three months. I captured a dividend payment during the hold time, giving me a net gain of 17 percent.

Why do I consider this a perfect swing trade? Entry was within 2 cents of the optimum breakout price and the stock peaked on the day I sold. Yes, the stop cashed me out near the low for the day, but that happens sometimes. Seeing the stock tumble after I sold gave me a warm feeling inside, but it could have been the jalapeños I ate.

- The ExxonMobil trade started with the breakout from an ascending triangle and ended using a stop.

LOOKING AHEAD

The pages that follow discuss the techniques that I use to swing trade and some tips from others. Since I like chart patterns, I will discuss event patterns and how you can profit from them. Those can be quite important for swing traders because the patterns have an opportunity to repeat periodically (such as every quarter).

The inverted dead-cat bounce is one of my favorites. Not only do you cash out when price shoots up, but you cannot beat the feeling of price confirming it by tumbling after you exit.

The event pattern is an easy way to capture profits. Sometimes price continues rocketing skyward after you sell, but the probabilities suggest a return to earth. I have developed a fondness for parachutes instead of moon shots. Perhaps you will, too, after reading about the inverted dead-cat bounce.

I have discussed busted chart patterns but they deserve another look. They represent a low-risk, high-success setup, and in Chapter 3 I discuss how to profit when you see them.

CHAPTER CHECKLIST

☐ Range trading is buying and selling as price bounces between highs and lows. See "What Is Swing Trading?"

☐ A trend trade buys near the swing low and sells near the end of a short-term trend (or the reverse: sell high and buy low). See "What Is Swing Trading?"

☐ Swing trading is best suited for people who are accustomed to using stops and like to follow the markets daily. See "Who Should Swing Trade?"

☐ The Exxon Mobil Corp. trade started with the breakout from an ascending triangle and ended using a stop. See "A Swinging Example."

CHAPTER 2

Swinging Techniques

The key to swing trading is learning to identify when price is going to turn. If you can do that, then it is easier to profit from a move.

Figure 2.1 shows an example of how that key turning point works in action. In early November 2010, Boeing (BA) gapped down and made a straight-line run lower until it found support at 62. The speed of the decline and the support layer that it would slam into made me feel confident that the stock was due to bounce. But how high would it bounce?

My guess was that the bounce would carry the stock back to the bottom of the gap, stopping at 67.69 (the high the day before the gap). I considered taking a huge position in the stock to boost the profit potential, but decided not to. I paper traded it instead. Why I chose to step aside is hard to explain, but I just did not feel confident that the trade would work as I expected.

Entry would have been at about 63.35 (the open on the day shown), and I would have planned to exit a bit shy of the target, say 67.43 (below the round number 67.50), probably using a limit order.

Since the stock dropped like a stone through water on the way down, I expected (hoped, really) a *quick* bounce. Instead, the stock seesawed up and down, taking its time as it trended higher. Three weeks later, the stock peaked and reached a high of 67.39, just 4 cents shy of my exit price!

Although that sounds like a near perfect call, it is a lot like throwing horseshoes or hand grenades: closeness counts. Missing by a few pennies would have turned a winning trade into a less profitable one, certainly, and my guess is it would have been much worse.

FIGURE 2.1   A potential swing trade would have missed its exit price by just 4 cents.

Since I am an end-of-day trader, the best I could have hoped for would have been an exit at the open the next day, at 66.19. More likely, though, I would have postponed selling for another day, exiting near 65.50. A trade worth $4 per share had turned into one making only about $2. That is still a profit, but it hardly compensates for playing with hand grenades.

I made the right choice to watch this trade from the sidelines. The stock dropped back to 63 in short order and got stuck at 65.

This chapter will give you several tools to help identify those swings in a timely fashion. I will expand the tool count in the later chapters. My favorites are *support and resistance* and *trendlines*.

QUICK REVIEW: SUPPORT AND RESISTANCE

I dedicated Chapter 4 in *Trading Basics*, the first book of this series, to support and resistance, but the topic is worth a quick review. **Table 2.1** shows the percentage of how often the technical features work to stop price movement.

TABLE 2.1 Support and Resistance Summary

Description	Percentage
Horizontal consolidation regions showing support	55%
Horizontal consolidation regions showing resistance	41%
Corrective phase of a measured move up or down stopping power	35%
Peaks showing resistance	34%
Valleys showing support	33%
Gaps showing resistance	25%
Round number support and resistance	22%
Gaps showing support	20%

For example, a horizontal consolidation region (HCR)—which is when price travels horizontally and has either flat tops, flat bottoms, or both—acts as a support area and stops price 55 percent of the time. When it acts as overhead resistance, it is not as effective, stopping price 41 percent of the time.

HCRs top the list for effectiveness. At the bottom of the table are gaps. In candlestick-chart-speak, traders call them rising windows or falling windows, but whatever you call them, they do not work well, showing support or resistance just 20 to 25 percent of the time.

Determining where support and resistance will cause price to reverse is crucial to making money. Buy at support and sell at resistance is one way to swing trade (like the example in Figure 2.1 shows). Another way is to sell short at overhead resistance and cover at support. Since price tends to drop faster than it rises (I described this phenomenon in *Trading Basics*, Chapter 5; see tip 23), you can make more bucks by shorting than going long. I am not recommending that you short stocks, just making an observation.

For more about determining support and resistance areas (and how to trade using them), refer to discussions of the following points in *Trading Basics*, Chapter 4.

- Price drops faster than it rises.
- Making money is almost as easy as determining where support and resistance are.

TRENDLINE TRADING

I discussed trendlines in *Trading Basics*, Chapter 3 (in the section "The Truth about Trendlines"), and showed how they can come in handy for buy and hold trading (see also the second book of the series, *Fundamental Analysis and Position Trading*, Chapter 16, under the heading "Timely Trendline Exits"). They are useful for all types of trading, including swing trading.

Figure 2.2 shows an example of using trendlines to signal entries and exits, drawn on the monthly scale. It is a realistic case from the Ultralife Corp. (ULBI) that I pulled from my database, not an example showing ideal conditions. Let us discuss each trendline one at a time.

Trendline 1 connects the bottom of the first price bar with the next minor low. If you were to look at the historical price trend not shown on the left, you would see that the trendline should be steeper, allowing a swing trader to short at a higher price (9.00). For this example though, let us assume it is drawn correctly. When price *closes* below the trendline, sell short at the open the following month. That would get you into the trade at 6.62.

Trendline 2 connects the first few peaks, but it is clear that price drops faster than the trendline. Another trendline that runs closer to price would give timelier signals. I show that as **trendline 3.**

Trendline 3 skims along the peaks like a water bug, and it would slice through the price bar at A except for the way I drew it. Since A does not close above the trendline, I redrew trendline 3 so that it just touches the

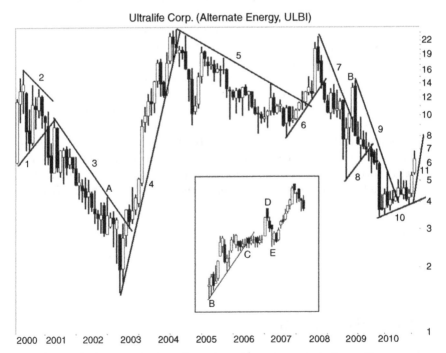

FIGURE 2.2 The stock moved nowhere over the period shown, but a swing trader could have made $20 per share. Note: monthly scale.

top at A. Either way, the trendline gives the same trading signal. When price closes above the trendline, cover the short position at the open the next month at 3.71.

Price trends higher, leading to **trendline 4**. This is an unusually steep trendline, and steep ones often do not last long. This case is an exception. It lasts over a year as the stock climbs into the clouds. This one trade represents the majority of the profits from swing trading this stock: over $16 per share. Price closes below the trendline, signaling an exit at the next price bar at the open.

Trendline 5 has many top touches, so it is well constructed. It follows price downward, and although the drop does not look like much, it is over 7 points due to the log scale I use on the chart.

Price rises and slices through trendline 5, closing out the short trade. **Trendline 6** begins by connecting the price bottoms, and here is where things go bad. Entry occurs at 12.74, the month after price closes above trendline 5. Where does the sale occur?

When price closes below trendline 6, sell the long position at the next bar. That occurs at 11.59 for a loss of $1.15 per share. You would go short at this point, and that would only compound the problem.

Trendline 7 leads the way lower, but the price bar at B signals an exit to the short and the next price bar does not offer much relief when it opens near the same price as the prior bar's close. This trade is another loser.

Since price has closed above the trendline, we assume a new uptrend has begun, so we go long…and price drops instead. This reversal hands us our biggest loss, nearly 7 points. **Trendline 8** saves us from disaster by closing out the trade and forcing a short sale.

Trendline 9 rides the stock lower, closing out the short at 4.52, for a gain. **Trendline 10** does nothing since price zips upward at a steep angle. **Trendline 11** hugs price and will capture more profit than trendline 10 will. Using the closing price on the last price bar gives a gain of 1.74 for that swing.

As I mentioned, the chart uses the monthly scale. Now imagine that it showed not months but minutes. Would the trades change any? In other words, the method of using trendlines as entry and exit signals works on all time scales.

- Trendlines work on all time scales.

Figure 2.2 shows one example of how traders can profit where investors cannot. By using a simple trendline to signal entry and exits, substantial profits accumulate.

Table 2.2 shows the profit and loss for each swing. If you traded only long positions, you would have made over $10 a share (not including

TABLE 2.2 Profit and Loss for Trendline Swings

Trendline	Trade	In	Out	Gross	$10,000
3	Short	6.62	3.71	2.91	$14,381
4	Long	3.71	20.00	16.29	$77,474
5	Short	20.00	12.74	7.26	$105,583
6	Long	12.74	11.59	−1.15	$96,043
7	Short	11.59	13.58	−1.99	$79,544
8	Long	13.58	6.76	−6.82	$39,592
9	Short	6.76	4.52	2.24	$52,697
10	Open	4.52	6.26	1.74	$72,970

commissions). Short positions would have done a bit better, making $10.42 per share, for a total of $20.48. For buy and hold, the stock opened at 6.13 and closed at 6.26 for a gain of just 13 cents over the nearly 11-year hold time.

Including commissions and a starting portfolio value of $10,000, the buy and hold value would have inched up to $10,201.86. However, using trendline trades, the investment would have grown to $72,970. This is an example of the power of swing trading over buy and hold.

Trendline Trading Tips

Here is additional help for swing trading using trendlines.

- Draw up-sloping trendlines along price valleys (minor lows).
- Draw down-sloping trendlines along price peaks (minor highs).
- If price moves too far above an up-sloping trendline (which shows increasing momentum), then draw a new trendline that better hugs price. This will help capture more profit. As a swing trader, learn to adjust your trendlines as necessary, even if they only touch two points.
- Similarly, if price drops too far below a down-sloping trendline, then redraw it.
- If price slices through a trendline, moving horizontally (or nearly so), then consider postponing the trade. Price is consolidating, so wait for the breakout. If the breakout is in a favorable direction (upward for up-sloping trendlines and downward for down-sloping trendlines), then do nothing. Redraw the trendline as necessary. An adverse breakout would require a trade to minimize losses.

The inset of Figure 2.2 shows this setup. Price climbs following trendline BC. At C, price slices through the trendline, moving horizontally. Selling when price closes to the right of the trendline would be a mistake since price resumes the uptrend.

- Price tends to move in a rise-retrace-rise fashion, with price then returning to the retrace area. For those versed in chart patterns, this is a measured move (up or down) pattern with price returning to the corrective phase 35 percent of the time (see Table 2.1). If price moves horizontal in the retrace phase, then expect a measured move.

    The inset of Figure 2.2 shows an example of this. Price trends upward from B to C and then moves horizontally before resuming the upward move to D. After peaking at D, price returns to the corrective phase C, at E.

- Steep trendlines tend to be shorter than shallower ones, so expect a quick exit signal.

- Practice drawing trendlines using historical data. My computer allows me to draw trendlines and scroll the chart to the left to see how well they play out. I can practice in a stock I am interested in trading using trendlines. If your chart does not have a horizontal scrollbar, then print the chart out and use a piece of paper to cover up the right side. Move the chart to the left, slowly uncovering new price action to see how well the trade progressed as you draw the trendlines. If you are serious about trading with trendlines, then you will do this exercise to practice and become familiar with how the stock behaves.

- If price *closes* below an up-sloping trendline or above a down-sloping one, it does not mean a trend change. However, for a swing trader, consider it a trading signal.

- The time scale you choose to trade should not change the trendline tactics.

- For the historical price behavior in the security you intend to trade, look for long moves up and down, not horizontal ones. You do not make money if the stock stays pegged near the same price for long.

    Figure 2.3 shows an example of this horizontal price movement on a weekly scale. Price moves up on the left of the chart in a series of straight-line runs, and then begins to move horizontally, bobbing up and down like a piece of wood riding the waves on a lake. This choppy up and down action is not long enough to make profitable trendline trades. A better strategy is to range trade the boxed area. Buy near the low about 22 and sell near the high, about 25. That is a $3 range, but you may be able to capture only half that.

    When price peaks or bottoms, the turn can be messy as in this case of a top. Price moves sideways, battling with the bulls and bears, trying to decide which way to trend. Until traders decide, look elsewhere for a better trading opportunity. Also notice that once price makes up its

Griffon Corp. (Building Materials, GFF)

Avoid Trendline Trades

FIGURE 2.3   Price moves horizontally in a trading range (boxed area), making profitable trendline trades difficult to achieve. Weekly scale.

mind to trend, it does so with force, shooting downward in a straight-line run that sees price tumble below 8.

- Combine trendlines with support and resistance areas, such as horizontal consolidation regions or prior peaks and valleys, for a better idea of what price will do. Expect price to reverse at support and resistance.
- Begin drawing a trendline at the bar *after* a tall or unusual price spike. Doing so often results in better alignment and better trading signals.
- If a substantial move occurs (like a one-week drop of 25 percent), then expect the move to continue after a pause, especially if it is a bear market.
- Draw a vertical line from a recent peak or valley and imagine price reflected around that peak or valley. These price mirrors may help you determine what price will do in the future.

As with any trading system, some trades will be profitable and some will not. Practice using trendlines before making any trades, especially when applying them to a security that you have not traded before. Try switching to other time scales to see what they show before making a trading decision.

For example, if price is closing in on a trendline using the weekly scale, switch to the daily chart for better timing of the exit. Look for nearby support or resistance areas where price might reverse.

Draw parallel trendlines (channels) to help gauge where price is going to change trend.

TRADING USING CHANNELS

Speaking of channels, let us discuss them. (In *Trading Basics*, Chapter 5, I include a section on how to draw three-point channels.) Let us take channels a bit further and trade using them.

Figure 2.4 shows a three-point channel, ABC, drawn on the daily price chart for United Parcel Service (UPS). Draw line CE parallel to line AF. I could lie and say I chose point C because long price spikes (point D) are often unreliable trendline starting points—which they are—but the real reason is that the trendline touches point E if I start it at C and not D.

FIGURE 2.4 A price channel highlights up and down price swings.

For a trend trader, the channel provides a unique timing mechanism. When price touches the trendline at E, it hits support, signaling a buy. At F, it is time to sell when price again bumps up against the top trendline.

Notice that the channel slopes upward. When that is the case, trade from the long side. Short the stocks that use a down-sloping channel. Never do the reverse—go long in a down-sloping channel or short an up-sloping one. The reason is that profits will be squeezed like garlic in a press even if you can call the turns properly.

Before trading a channel, measure the potential profit. It will be an approximation, of course, but it will give you some idea whether the reward is worth the risk. This is especially true of horizontal channels (rectangles). The height of the rectangle can mean the difference between retiring at 36, as I did, and working well into your senior years.

For an up-sloping channel, placing a 5 percent stop loss below the bottom channel line can help prevent a massive loss. It will not stop every loss (as in the case when price gaps lower), but it should limit them. Limiting losses in swing trading is paramount to keeping the risk-to-reward ratio high.

When price *nears* the top of the channel, be prepared to exit. If price approaches the channel line and then goes horizontal, consider exiting. This is different from a trendline trade where you wait for the breakout from the congestion region. With channel trading, the channel is a support or resistance area, and price is telling you that it has lost momentum. Frequently, that means it is going to reverse. Take the hint and close out the trade. Check the historical price record to verify that this is true for the stock you are trading.

A channel touch is also a timely trading signal. Be aware that price sometimes does not make it up to the channel before reversing.

Figure 2.4 shows an example of that at G (and notice how it appears rounded, signaling a loss of upward momentum). Price at G climbs toward the top channel line, but reaches only the price level of B. It forms a 2B chart pattern (see tip 1 in Chapter 5 of *Trading Basics*, Timing the Exit: The 2B Rule) and reverses, eventually digging its way to E before finally making a determined effort to reach the top channel line.

When I channel trade, I use any hesitation near the channel line as a clue to exit. Up-sloping channels are more forgiving in this manner because price has a tendency to rise over time (just look at the Dow Industrials from the 1920s until now).

If you miss selling near the channel line, you can wait for another attempt. That is not always the best choice, of course. Learning to sell and sell promptly can make the difference between a successful swing trader and someone who is, well, unsuccessful.

- Trade up-sloping channels from the long side.
- Trade down-sloping channels from the short side.

- Measure the height (risk versus reward) of the channel before taking a position.
- Do not expect price to touch the channel line before reversing. Exit the position if price hesitates (flattens or moves horizontally) near the channel line.
- Look for nearby support or resistance to help gauge where price is going to reverse.
- Eventually, price breaks out of all channels, so have stops ready to limit any adverse move.

THE THREE-BAR NET LINE SETUP

An interview with Joseph Stowell (July 1995) explained a chart pattern called the three-bar net line that he uses to uncover the intermediate-term trend in the bond market. I will explain it, test it, and then show how to use it to trade stocks.

Figure 2.5 shows an example of the three-bar net line for up and down trends (inset) and an example. Let us discuss the pattern in uptrends first. If price is trending upward, find the highest high, which I show as point 1. Follow four rules for each uptrend or downtrend.

1. Point 1 should be the highest recent high in a series of higher highs and higher lows (an uptrend). The low price on that day is point 1.

2. Look to the left and find the prior low that is equal to or lower than point 1. That is point 2.

3. Find a prior low that is equal to or lower than point 2. I show that as point 3.

4. If price closes below point 3, then the trend has changed from up to down. I show the line as the sell line.

For downtrends, reverse the setup.

1. Find the lowest recent low in a series of lower lows and lower highs (a downtrend). I show the high on that day in Figure 2.5 as point 4.

2. Look to the left of point 4 and find the prior high that is equal to or higher than point 4. The high on that day is point 5.

3. Look for the next price bar to the left of point 5 that is equal to or higher than point 5. I show that as point 6.

4. If price closes above the high at point 6, then the trend is said to have changed from down to up.

- The three-bar net line is a visual way to determine a trend change.

FIGURE 2.5   Shown is the three-bar net line for up and down trends (insets) along with a trading example.

Testing the Three-Bar Net Line

How well does it work as a trading system for exchange-traded funds (ETFs) or stocks? I programmed my computer to find the three-bar net line and used the following rules or parameters.

- $10,000 invested in each trade.
- 554 stocks, including AIG (which fell from the heavens and buried itself).
- 88 long-only ETFs.
- March 12, 2001, to October 1, 2010, but not all securities covered the entire period.
- Commissions: $10 per trade.
- Minimum price of $5 for each security at buy time.

The period chosen shows the Standard & Poor's S&P 500 index ending near where it began, having moved from bear market to bull market twice. I made no allowance for slippage or other fees.

Additionally, the table presents results using the following measurements.

- *Average gain/loss*. This is the per-trade average gain or loss, expressed as a percentage.
- *Average hold time*. This is the average trade duration.
- *Average max hold time loss*. The hold time loss is how far below the buy price the security drops during the trade. I find the maximum drop for each trade and average the results of all trades. If price did not drop below the buy price, zero is used. This is a measure of the average risk per trade.
- *Win/loss*. This is the ratio of winning trades to all trades, expressed as a percentage.
- *S&P 500 index*. This is how the index faired for the duration of each trade, averaged over all trades.

Table 2.3 shows the results for stocks and ETFs with and without a simple moving average (SMA). Your eye will probably drop to the ETF row where it loses 0.2 percent or $15.85 per trade. Adding in a 50-day simple moving average returns the system to profitability.

Why add a moving average? Doing so helps remove unprofitable trades in bear markets, so that is why I added it and that is why it improves results.

I also tested this using weekly data (see the 10-week SMA rows). For both stocks and ETFs, the average gain increases substantially, but so does the hold time loss. You make more money, but you stand to lose more, too.

To my knowledge, Stowell did not propose the three-bar net line as a trading system. In fact, he uses it to determine changes in trend on the monthly stock chart along with his cup and cap system. I did not test the three-bar net line using monthly data.

- The three-bar net line works well for longer time scales, but the hold time loss increases.

TABLE 2.3 Tests on the Three-Bar Net Line

Description	Average Gain/Loss	Average Max Hold Time Loss	Win/ Loss	Average Hold Time	S&P 500 Index
Stocks, daily data	0.2%	−6.0%	38%	26 days	−1.9%
Stocks with 50-day SMA	0.4%	−5.4%	40%	26 days	−1.9%
Stocks with 10-week SMA	3.7%	−11.6%	42%	122 days	−2.2%
ETFs, daily data	(0.2%)	−3.7%	39%	22 days	−2.0%
ETFs with 50-day SMA	0.3%	−3.0%	42%	23 days	−1.8%
ETFs with 10-week SMA	3.4%	−7.6%	49%	120 days	−1.5%

Three-Bar Net Line Example

Figure 2.5 shows an example of combining a trendline trade with the three-bar net line. I connected peaks D and E and extended the trendline lower until it intersected price at A. Looking back, point B is the lowest low in the recent downtrend, so that is where we will start looking for the three-bar net line in a downtrend.

Point C is the third bar with an equal or higher high to the left of B, including the high at B. A line drawn to the right of C becomes the buy line when price closes above it. That happens at A, right where the trendline also pierces the price bar. A confirmed trade signals and you would buy at the open the next day.

In this example, the trendline also signals a buy the next day.

Let us assume that you buy the stock and then price makes a substantial move up. You are looking to protect your profit so you draw another trendline connecting the lows at F and G. Price closes below the trendline at H, tentatively signaling a sale.

The three-bar net line should confirm the sale. Point I is the highest high in the recent up trend, so we use the low of that candle and find two equal or lower lows. That takes us back to candle G. A line drawn to the right of this low is the sell line. A *close* below this line would signal a sale. That does not happen, so you remain in the trade.

The Monsanto Trade

The Monsanto trade uses a modified three-bar net line exit that I will discuss in a moment. **Figure 2.6** shows the swing trade, based on an ugly double bottom chart pattern. The start of the ugly double bottom is not shown in the figure but it begins on July 7, 2010, and ends on October 5 (shown), the lowest low on the figure.

I bought the stock two days after the breakout, at A. Usually, I wait for price to close above the breakout price and buy at the open the next day. This trade has an additional day's wait that my notes do not explain.

I calculated a volatility stop at 57.93 but chose to place it above the round number of 58, at 58.07. That is below what I called a shelf or congestion zone, which I circled at E.

For the target, I was looking at 70 (bottom of a cloudbank) and then 88 (start of a Big W chart pattern) as locations of overhead resistance.

I scored the chart pattern using the generic scoring system (see Chapter 20, "Ten Factors Make Chart Patterns Work," in *Fundamental Analysis and Position Trading*) and found that it had a −1 score with a 78.27 target. The target is based on the median rise of chart patterns. The system said that it would be difficult for the stock to climb that

Monsanto Co (Chemical (Diversified), MON)

FIGURE 2.6 Two buys in this swing trade turn profitable when price advances.

high. That prediction turned out to be right since the stock dropped more than 20 percent (a trend change) before peaking at 78.71 about a year later.

I counted other stocks in the industry and found that 11 of 12 were trending higher, along with the overall market. The stock was in a stage 2 advance (see Chapter 16 in *Fundamental Analysis and Position Trading* under the heading "The Weinstein Setup"), and earnings were set for early January.

Finally, I noted that "70 should be easy."

It was not easy because the stock dropped after I bought. On November 17, I wrote in my notebook, "I removed the stop because world events are taking the market lower, potentially allowing the stock to be stopped out. I don't think this is going to fall far (not below 40), so I think I can hold until it recovers from any drop."

In fact, I doubled my position that same day, noting, "I am going to buy more because this has thrown back to (E) the tight congestion area (buy at support). With an ugly double bottom in place, I think this is a low risk, high probability win scenario. Sell at 70."

When price climbed above the 70 sell target, I placed a stop based on the three-bar net line, only I started counting at the day after D (which is the day I placed the stop). Counting back three candles gets me to C. I placed the stop a penny below the candle's low, at 71.68.

On January 19, I was cashed out a penny below the stop, at C. Using the correct placement of the three-bar net line would have meant a lower stop, costing me money in this trade.

On the swing trade, I made 15 percent on the first entry and 20 percent on the second, including a dividend payment, with a hold time of just over two months. After selling, the stock went horizontal for over a year, suggesting that selling when I did was the right move.

The Guppy Variation

Daryl Guppy (September 1999) has a variation of the three-bar net line that he shared with readers in a magazine article. When searching for the three price bars, he only allows higher highs or lower lows, and ignores price bars of equal value. **Figure 2.7** shows an example of this.

When price closes above the down-sloping trendline, it is a trading signal. The three-bar net line must confirm the entry before buying the stock.

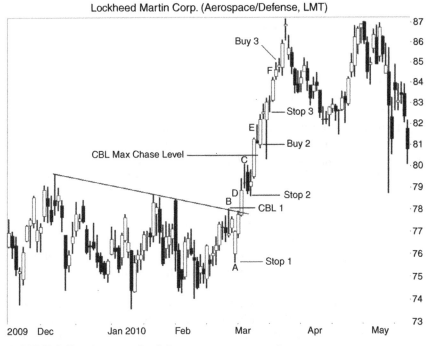

FIGURE 2.7   The count-back line acts as an entry trigger.

Begin with the lowest recent low, which is point A. The high of that candle is point 1. The prior candle has a higher high, which becomes point 2. The next higher high is at candle B, which ends the sequence. In the search for a higher high, Guppy does not allow ties like Stowell does. A line drawn from the right at B is called the count-back line, which I show as CBL 1.

When price closes above CBL 1, it is the buy signal. That occurs at candle D, so entry occurs the next day, at the open of candle C.

Set a stop loss using the same procedure for finding the three-bar net line, only in reverse. Begin with the day price signaled an entry, D. The low of this candle is point 1. The low of the prior candle is lower, so that becomes point 2, and point 3 is the lower prior low, which is candle A. The low at candle A is the stop loss price for this trade.

The next entry price will trigger when the stop loss price rises above the count-back line. The stop loss is three lower lows away from the current candle (including the current candle). If the current candle is to the right of E, the low of that candle is point 1 and the prior two candles show lower lows, giving points 2 and 3, which I show as Stop 2. The low at Stop 2 is the first candle above the count-back line, so you would buy at the open the day after E. I show that as Buy 2.

Guppy handles the next entry differently. Take the percentage difference between the high at B (the first count-back line) and the pivot low at A, and add it to the high at B to get the maximum chase level. I show that just above C. The next stop loss has to be above the maximum chase level. When price rises to the candle on the right of F, three lower lows bottom at Stop 3. Stop 3 is above the maximum chase level, so buy at the open the next day. I show that as Buy 3.

- The Guppy variation of the three-bar net line and his implementation of scaling in provides a methodical way of increasing the position size.

Step Summary

For all entries after the third buy, the stop loss has to rise above the high at the prior entry signal day. In this example, candle F is the entry signal day, so the next stop loss has to rise above the high at F before signaling a purchase. Here is a summary of the steps.

- Your trading setup signals a trade. In this case, I use a trendline pierce, but it could be a moving average crossover scheme or other trading setup.
- Find the three-bar net line beginning from the pivot low (most recent low). Find three higher highs, including the current candle's high. The highest high of those candles becomes the count-back line.

- Buy at the open the day after price closes above the count-back line.
- Set a stop loss at three lower lows, beginning with the current candle's low. All stop loss levels use this mechanism. I would also subtract a penny or two from the third candle's low because candles will often bottom at the same price before rising again. You do not want to be stopped out if that happens.
- Calculate a new stop loss (three lower lows minus a penny or two) as price makes a new high. When the stop price rises above the count-back line, buy another position.
- Calculate the maximum chase level by taking the *percentage* difference between the first count-back line and the swing low. Apply this to the maximum chase level to get the entry price. When the stop loss level rises above the maximum chase level, then buy at the opening price the next day.
- Set a stop loss as described.
- The next stop loss must rise above the high posted the day before you entered the trade to signal a new buy. When this occurs, buy at the open the next day. Set a new stop loss and repeat this step.

What Guppy is doing is buying at higher and higher levels—averaging up—but in a methodical way. He says that the most profit and lowest risk comes at the start of a trade. As price rises, the risk of the trend ending grows, so trim the position size. He writes, "We make the first entry because I *believe* the trend is changing. We make the second entry because I *know* the trend is changing. We make a third entry when I am *convinced* the trend has changed."

In this example, the third trade is stopped out for a loss, but the first two entries are sold for a profit. All three positions are sold at the same time, meaning you exit all open positions instead of scaling out.

Position Size

In a second article (May 1998), Guppy describes how he calculates position size. Suppose you have $100,000 in cash. Many money management texts will say not to risk more than 2 percent of this, or $2,000 for each trade, which Guppy agrees with. That will allow you to make 175 botched trades before you blow through the whole wad (meaning the value drops below $2,000, assuming $20 roundtrip commissions).

Place stop loss orders just below support levels and adjust the number of shares to keep the potential loss below $2,000. That is an important step to hold losses in check.

For the first trade shown in Figure 2.7, point A (stop loss) is at 75.62, so place a stop a penny below this, 75.61. The buy price is the open at 79.22 (point C). The position size for this trade would be $2000 ÷ (79.22 − 75.61), or 554 shares. Buying 554 shares at 79.22 would cost $43,887.88, and being stopped out at 75.61 would cost $41,887.94, for an approximate $2,000 loss. That is just as it should be.

However, in one trade, you have spent almost half your money. The second trade would require buying 830 shares, or $2000 ÷ (81.01 − 78.60), at $81.01, which would exhaust the portfolio's cash even though the value had climbed to about $101,000.

Would you risk most of your net worth on one stock? I have seen stocks drop by 70 percent—or more—in one session. If this happened, your $100,000 nest egg would be sliced to $30,000 overnight. You would have to triple your money and you would still fall $10,000 short of your original investment.

Remember Michaels Stores, the stock I wrote about in Chapter 1 of *Trading Basics*? I made almost 5,000 percent on that stock, but lost more than 15 percent on 18 separate occasions.

In other words, this money management approach places all of your golden eggs in one basket. That is fine, providing you watch the basket carefully and do not try to average up by more than two trades. It also helps if you are lucky.

Guppy acknowledges this type of risk. As the portfolio grows in size, many traders lower the risk they are willing to tolerate, from 2 percent to 1 percent and below. As Guppy adds open positions to a stock, he cuts the percentage.

For example, the first three trades share similar sizes (like $20k or $30k each), depending on the 2 percent stop loss calculation. After that, he cuts the available capital by 50 percent (or 30 percent for slower price trends and less volatile situations). Thus, he would spend $20k, $20k, $20k, followed by $10k, $5k, $2.5k, and $2k after that per trade (with $2k being a minimum investment).

His goal is to maximize the amount spent early in the trade and reduce the value of each trade as price climbs to its maximum.

- Decrease position size as price rises, scaling it to the risk of a trend reversal.

I take a different approach to money management as I mentioned in Chapter 2 of *Trading Basics* (under the heading "Position Sizing by Market Condition: Bull or Bear?"). I size my positions for the market conditions (cutting the amount traded by half as the S&P index moves into a bear market) then adjust the shares for market and stock volatility, coupled with a volatility based stop loss order.

FIRST THRUST PATTERN FOR SWING TRADING

Have you ever wondered how to get started swing trading? How do you know when to jump in? Here is a price pattern that answers that question.

Landry (December 2010) described a V-shaped chart pattern that can signal a trend reversal from down to up. Since the article had few details specific enough for computerized testing, I decided to tear it down and see if I could figure out how it worked.

Before I explain my statistical results, let us define the first thrust pattern. Look for a major low followed by a straight-line run up and then a pause. When the uptrend resumes, the first thrust pattern completes. Price should move higher.

Figure 2.8 shows an example. Price makes a major low at A, which is the lowest low of the past six months. I tested variations of that time and chose six months as the preferred minimum look back.

After reaching a new low, price makes higher highs and higher lows for at least two more days (a three-day run-up, minimum). After the run completes, it pauses at B. The retrace in this example is one price bar long and it has a lower high and lower low. When price rises above this bar, the first thrust pattern completes and a buy signals.

FIGURE 2.8   The first thrust pattern appears at the start of a straight-line run up.

Here are the identification rules for the first thrust pattern.

- Price makes the lowest low in at least six months.
- Price rises, posting higher highs and higher lows for at least two consecutive days (three days total, including the first day).
- Price makes a lower low and lower high. The downtrend retrace can continue, making lower lows and lower highs.
- When price rises at least a penny above the lowest low/lowest high price bar in the retrace, it confirms the pattern and triggers a buy.

To clarify the last point, I show the inset in Figure 2.8. Price moves up and then begins a retrace. Price bar D is the same configuration as that shown by point B in the price chart. In the inset, however, price makes another lower low and lower high, forming bar E. A buy stop placed a penny above E would trigger an entry. Bar F does not have a lower low (even though it *does* have a lower high), so the buy price remains as shown.

That is how I tested it on my computer, using a lower high and lower low combination for each price bar. You may want to use just a lower high to signal the entry. I did not test that scenario.

For some tests, I used the trend high as the exit. I show that at point C. Exit occurs at the open the next day. I define the trend high as the highest high from 5 days before to 5 days after a peak (11 days total). Think of it as the *perfect exit*, so you will not be able to duplicate the results in real time without potentially giving back profit.

First Thrust Testing

I used the same testing guidelines as described in the section "The Three-Bar Net Line Setup" in this chapter, but tested only stocks. **Table 2.4** shows the results, sorted by the average gain.

Test A looks for two consecutive higher highs and higher lows (using three days) and places a stop loss order a penny below the lowest of the three lows. There is no rule that says the first low must be the lowest low in *x* days or months.

Test B is the same as A except that it does not use a stop. Notice that when a stop loss order is used (test A), performance deteriorates. The hold time loss decreases, but the average gain drops significantly.

Test C uses three consecutive lows (four price bars) instead of two. This is the only test that uses 4 days. This test also requires that the first low be the lowest low in 1 month. Performance is not as good as other tests.

The remainder of **Tests D to H** vary by how significant the low is, whether it is the lowest low in 1 month, 2 months, and so on, up to a year.

TABLE 2.4 Tests on the First Thrust Pattern

Test Description	Average Gain/Loss	Average Max Hold Time Loss	Win/ Loss	Average Hold Time	S&P 500 Index
A. Stop penny below start of straight-line run up	2.2%	5.7%	56%	9 days	−1.3%
B. Two consecutive up days	3.8%	6.3%	71%	17 days	−1.0%
C. 1-month low, three consecutive up days	4.2%	6.4%	71%	17 days	−0.9%
D. 1-month low	4.6%	7.1%	74%	16 days	−0.9%
E. 2-month low	4.8%	7.8%	74%	16 days	−0.9%
F. 3-month low	5.0%	8.3%	74%	16 days	−0.9%
G. 6-month low	5.5%	9.1%	74%	16 days	−1.0%
H. 1-year low	5.6%	9.6%	73%	17 days	−1.2%

The more significant the low is, the better the performance (average gain) but hold time loss also increases.

Notice that the win/loss average remains in the low 70s except when a stop is used, in which case only 56 percent of the stocks show profits. The average hold time remains the same for most tests, about 16 or 17 days.

Of these tests, the 6-month line looks best. It has a decent average gain with reasonable hold time losses. Waiting another 6 months does not increase profit by much (from 5.5 to 5.6 percent), but the risk climbs.

Let me also remind you that the average gain includes an "optimum exit." That means I sold the day after price found the trend high. The gain represents an average of *perfect trades.*

Not shown in Table 2.4 are tests that used a time exit, such as sell 5 days after entry. I tested increments of 5 days starting from 5 and reaching 20, but none of the tests showed promise (average gain/loss ranged from −1.3 to +0.8 percent using the lowest 6-month low for entry). The first thrust pattern can get you into a trade, but you will have to find a way to get out.

- Use the lowest 6-month low followed by a straight-line run up and a pause to complete the first thrust pattern.
- The first thrust pattern creates an entry signal, not an exit signal.

CHAPTER CHECKLIST

As I mentioned earlier, my favorite techniques in this chapter are support and resistance and trendlines, but you may find value in the short-term price patterns discussed here. Test them on the securities you follow and see if they add value. Perhaps they will be a welcome addition to your technical toolbox. If not, then the chart patterns in Chapter 3 may be useful.

Here is a checklist of ideas covered in this chapter:

☐ Price drops faster than it rises. See "Quick Review: Support and Resistance."

☐ Making money is almost as easy as determining where support and resistance are. See "Quick Review: Support and Resistance."

☐ Trendlines work on all time scales. See "Trendline Trading."

☐ For trendline trading, see "Trendline Trading Tips."

☐ For channel trading, see "Trading Using Channels."

☐ The three-bar net line is a visual way to determine a trend change. See "The Three-Bar Net Line Setup."

☐ The three-bar net line works well for longer time scales, but the hold time loss increases. See "Testing the Three-Bar Net Line."

☐ The Guppy variation of the three-bar net line and his implementation of scaling in provides a methodical way of increasing the position size. See "The Guppy Variation."

☐ Decrease position size as price rises, scaling it to the risk of a trend reversal. See "Position Size."

☐ To identify the first thrust pattern, see "First Thrust Pattern for Swing Trading."

☐ Use the lowest 6-month low followed by a straight-line run up and a pause to complete the first thrust pattern. See "First Thrust Testing."

☐ The first thrust pattern creates an entry signal, not a sell signal. See "First Thrust Testing."

CHAPTER 3

Swinging Chart Patterns

In the Chapter 2, we looked at short patterns to see how they could help us time the market. In this chapter, we are going to look at the adult versions—the classic chart patterns to see how they can help us swing trade.

Before I get to the best chart patterns for swing trading, let me share this discovery. Knowing that a stock has a tendency to return to the breakout price (a throwback or pullback) is very important to swing traders. I found that stocks with low noise *after the breakout* (the definition of noise is complex, but it measures how much overlap a price bar has with adjacent bars; low noise means little overlap) tend to have more throwbacks and pullbacks than do their more-noisy counterparts.

Here is my interpretation of this: *stocks that form straight-line runs after the breakout tend to throwback or pullback more often than do those not forming straight-line runs.* If you are not paying attention, then take another sip of coffee because that is an important finding.

I checked my chart pattern database and found that 152 of 196 cases of a straight-line run during or after an upward breakout lead to a throwback. That is a 78 percent success rate. (The ascending triangle in Figure 3.6 shows an example as do Figures 3.9 and 3.11.)

Pullbacks show the same tendency to occur after a straight-line run down from a breakout. I found 104 instances out of 150 where it was true, for a 69 percent success rate. In other words, if price is making a straight-line run down after the breakout, then expect a pullback. (The busted descending triangle in Figure 3.8, later in the chapter, shows an example. Figure 3.5 shows the exception, a straight-line run breakout that did not pull back within a month.)

- Price throws back after a straight-line run from a breakout 78 percent of the time.
- Pullbacks occur 69 percent of the time after a straight-line run down from the breakout.

WHICH CHART PATTERNS WORK BEST FOR SWINGERS?

I found the breakout in each bull market chart pattern and then looked at the price performance from one to six months into the future.

Table 3.1 shows the top 20 chart patterns for upward breakouts (out of 32 possible patterns), sorted by the two-month performance. I list the top 20 patterns for downward breakouts in Chapter 4.

TABLE 3.1 Chart Patterns Ranked by Performance over Time, Upward Breakouts, Bull Market

Pattern	1 Month	2 Months	3 Months	6 Months
High and tight flag	22%	21%	21%	33%
Scallop, inverted and ascending	11%	12%	13%	16%
Eve & Eve double bottom	9%	12%	14%	17%
Rectangle bottom	8%	11%	14%	13%
Adam & Adam double bottom	8%	10%	12%	15%
Falling wedge	8%	10%	9%	13%
Rounded top	7%	10%	14%	19%
Adam & Eve double bottom	7%	10%	10%	14%
Pennant	8%	9%	9%	11%
Triangle, descending	8%	9%	9%	13%
Flags	8%	9%	7%	5%
Eve & Adam double bottom	7%	9%	14%	19%
Head-and-shoulders bottom	7%	9%	12%	13%
Broadening wedge descending	6%	8%	10%	14%
Cup with handle	6%	8%	9%	9%
Rectangle top	7%	7%	9%	15%
Complex head-and-shoulders bottom	7%	7%	8%	10%
Rounded bottom	7%	7%	8%	12%
Diamond bottom	6%	7%	9%	15%
Ugly double bottom	6%	7%	8%	7%
Total of all 32 patterns	221%	255%	291%	391%

The high and tight flag is a known performer, so its placing first is no shocker. However, the inverted and ascending scallop is a surprise. I never would have guessed that its performance would place so high on the chart. Eve & Eve double bottoms, which are the classic double bottom pattern (when you ignore the Adam and Eve variations), make a claim on third place, and they also tend to perform well historically.

Notice that cup with handle patterns are far down the list (15th out of 20). I have not found cup with handles to be worth trading because price tends to rise by 10 to 15 percent after the breakout and then die. The table shows my estimates to be generous, with rises starting at 6 percent and reaching just 9 percent six months later.

All of the numbers are averages, and the sample counts range from 186 (diamond bottom) to 616 (Eve & Eve double bottom). Keep in mind that anything can happen between the four sample periods. A stock could receive a buyout, sending the stock shooting skyward only to return to earth when the deal falls through. However, using hundreds of samples reduces the effects of those types of events.

The bottom of the table shows a total of each column, for all 32 chart-pattern types, not just those listed in the table. Notice that as time lengthens from one to six months, the percentages climb. On *average*, the longer you hold onto a stock, the more likely it is that time will correct a mistake. Of course, there is also a greater opportunity for taking a major hit, too, like a dead-cat bounce. But the market tends to climb over time.

To put it another way, it is easier to make money as an investor (buy and hold) than as a position trader. It is easier for a position trader to make money than it is for a swing trader, and so on.

Before I delve into individual chart patterns, look at the four measurement periods in Table 3.1. If your swing trades tend to last shorter or longer than two months, then you will want to sort the list accordingly.

What follows is a detailed look at the three top-performing patterns, the high and tight flag, the inverted and ascending scallop, and the Eve & Eve double bottom.

TRADING THE HIGH AND TIGHT FLAG

The high and tight flag (HTF) is one of the patterns I studied extensively. I wanted to understand how it worked so I could maximize profit and minimize situations where it would bust my bucks. The performance numbers cited below use updated data compared to the numbers listed in my books published before 2012.

Identifying an HTF is as easy as picking out a zebra from a herd of elephants. Here are two scenarios to look for.

1. Price doubles (or nearly so) in two months or less. This move becomes the flagpole.
2. After doubling, price retraces. This retrace is known as the "flag" portion of the HTF, but the congestion region often does not resemble a traditional flag pattern.

HTF Trading

If identification is easy, swing trading the HTF is not. First, you have to find the courage to buy a stock after price has doubled. It reminds me of standing on the edge of a cliff. There is a little voice inside that says, "Jump!" Buying a stock showing an HTF is like listening to that voice and jumping. It is scary since the stock is probably trading at prices it has never seen before.

The HTF is a momentum play: buy high and sell higher. How do you know price will rise? You do not, but here are seven tips that may help separate the Scuds from the duds.

1. Look for overhead resistance that occurred in the past. If a horizontal congestion region appears at a price level above where the stock is trading, then that could act as a ceiling.
2. Avoid loose-looking flags. A tight flag has price that overlaps from bar to bar. A loose flag meanders; there is marginal overlap and price seems to climb for a day or two and then drops back for a few days only to repeat the sequence. The pennant (BC) in Figure 3.1 and the flag in Figure 3.3 are tight ones with lots of overlap from day to day, and price not meandering up and down much. HTFs with loose flags show gains averaging 40 percent but those with tight flags gain 53 percent.
3. The most powerful HTFs have flags that retrace 10 to 25 percent below the top of the HTF, according to a study I conducted.
4. Flags 5 to 19 days long tended to see price outperform. Generally, the longer the flag, the worse the performance.
5. A receding volume trend in the flag portion of the HTF sees better post-breakout performance when price climbs an average of 50 percent versus 35 percent for those with rising volume.
6. HTFs with light breakout day volume tend to outperform, but not dramatically so: 52 percent versus 46 percent. I define the breakout as the day price *closes* above the highest peak in the HTF.
7. HTFs that do *not* throwback climb further after the breakout than those that do: 53 percent to 42 percent.

The study mentioned in number 3 above used 2,897 HTFs in 589 stocks from January 1995 to January 2011, but not all stocks covered the entire period. I programmed my computer to find stocks that climbed at least 90 percent in 2 months or less with a price of at least $1. If price continued to make higher highs, then the height of the flagpole grew. Once price stopped climbing then the flag began and continued until either price dropped below the start of the HTF or rose above the flagpole's top. The HTF trades were nonoverlapping, meaning that once an HTF completed the search for the next one began.

Thirty-eight percent of HTFs in the study occurred in bear markets. What does that mean? Answer: Not all stocks drop in a bear market. However, buying stocks showing HTFs in a bear market can be as risky as swimming with piranhas, depending on when they ate last. Bull market HTFs showed gains averaging 31 percent, but bear market ones gained only 22 percent after the breakout.

How did I measure that performance? I calculated the climb from the breakout to the ultimate high. The ultimate high is the highest peak before price drops at least 20 percent. It represents a perfect trade.

In the search for the ultimate high after the HTF breakout (a rise above the flagpole top), 19 percent dropped below the bottom of the flag, ending the ultimate high search. Price found the ultimate high 65 percent of the time. Two percent of the samples ran out of data and the remaining 14 percent are those that dropped below the start of the HTF (below the bottom of the flagpole).

In other words, if you place a stop a penny below the low in the flag, then 33 percent of the HTFs in the study failed (causing a loss of 27 percent) and 65 percent worked. Waiting for price to close above the top of the flagpole reduces the failure rate to 19 percent.

- Cut the failure rate of high and tight flags to 19 percent by waiting for price to close above the top of the flagpole. Otherwise, the failure rate is 33 percent.
- *Always* wait for price to close above the top of the HTF before buying.

The number one rule for trading HTFs is to wait for price to close above the top of the pattern. My first three losing HTF trades were caused by not knowing that I should wait for price to close above the top of the HTF. I bought on the breakout from the flag, or earlier, and price stopped me out. Do not let that happen to you. Never buy a stock showing an HTF until price *closes* above the top of the chart pattern.

Returning to the numbers, I found that half the HTFs failed to rise more than 19 percent after the breakout, and 18 percent failed to rise at least 5 percent. Sixty-two percent of the HTFs failed to cover the stop loss (meaning they climbed less than 27 percent). In other words, you can make a lot of money trading HTFs, but the road to riches is a bumpy one.

I also looked at the slope of prices before the start of the HTF. I thought that steep downtrends like those we saw during the 2007 to 2009 bear market would lead to unusually high HTF failure rates. **Table 3.2** shows what I found.

I used linear regression on the closing price a month or two months before the start of the HTF (to the left of point A in Figure 3.1) to determine the slope of the trend. For reference, Table 3.2 shows the median values for up and down sloping trends at the bottom of the table.

I found that steep sloping inbound trends, either up or down, resulted in worse performance by the stock after an HTF breakout. For example, price that trends down steeply (more than the "median slope down" value) for one month leading to the start of the HTF showed post-breakout gains averaging 25 percent. Those with shallow trends (less than the "median slope down" value) gained 34 percent. That is an increase in performance of 36 percent over those with steep trends.

I also show the performance of the HTF after price trends up or down in the month and two months leading to the start of the HTF. If price trends upward during the two months before the start of the HTF, price tends to do better (average gain 30 percent) than do those with a down-sloping trend (25 percent gain). Using one month as the look back for linear regression shows no performance difference.

I narrowed the parameters and those slopes within ±0.10 (including the end points) showed gains of 33 percent versus those with higher slopes averaging 25 percent performance, using 1-month linear regression look back. Using a 2-month look back shows the results narrow: 30 percent to 26 percent, respectively.

- Shallow sloping price trends leading to the start of the HTF result in better post-breakout performance.

TABLE 3.2   Post-Breakout Performance versus Slope before HTF Start

Price Slope	1 Month before HTF	2 Months before HTF
Steep up	27%	30%
Shallow up	30%	33%
Steep down	25%	24%
Shallow down	34%	27%
Up	28%	30%
Down	28%	25%
Flat (slope: ±0.10)	33%	30%
Not flat	25%	26%
Median slope up	0.08	0.05
Median slope down	−0.10	−0.08

HTF Trading Tips: What I Use

I looked at hundreds of HTFs to determine the shape of the inbound and outbound price trends. In one picture, a steep inbound trend led to a wonderful move and in another, the post-breakout move was a dud. So, I resorted to statistics to help determine the price trends that lead to the best performance. Mixed in with those results are some tips that I use when swing trading HTFs.

- If price drops below the flag low before the breakout, then look elsewhere. **Figure 3.1** shows an example of this. The HTF begins at A and climbs to B, which is the top of the flagpole. Then it forms a tight flag, to C (in the shape of a pennant chart pattern). Price drops out of the pennant and drops to D, below the low price posted in the flag portion of the HTF. Price moves horizontally before finally making a drive higher, rising just 17 percent above the top at B and then declining almost 35 percent to F.
- If price forms congestion regions and pauses during formation of the flagpole, there is a good change it will wobble after the breakout. Avoid the stock if the flagpole is not a straight-line run.

FIGURE 3.1 Price drops below the flag low, suggesting underperformance.

- Avoid HTFs in which price is trending lower for the long term, as in a bear market. **Figure 3.2** shows an example of this situation. Price bottoms at A and rises to the flagpole high at B. Then price makes its way higher to C, rising 25 percent above B.
- Avoid situations where the HTF looks as if it is a retrace in a downward price trend. Figure 3.2 gives an overview of the setup in the left inset. Price trends downward then retraces (moves higher) and forms an HTF before resuming the downward plunge. The HTF in the price chart is an example of the pattern shown in the inset.
- Avoid dead-cat bounces (an event pattern that I discuss in Chapter 5) where price may double in the bounce phase after a substantial decline. The dead-cat drops price between 15 and 70 percent (or more) in one session and then the stock bounces, forming an HTF before pooping out and sinking. Do not be caught expecting an extended upward run after the HTF completes in a dead-cat bounce scenario. Price might do that, but the probabilities suggest otherwise.
- In a similar manner, avoid inverted dead-cat bounces (another event pattern). The stock may double on good news, forming an HTF. Those

FIGURE 3.2 High and tight flag AB appears in a bear market and acts as a retrace of the downward price trend.

owning the stock will sell it, and traders will short it, putting more downward pressure on price.

- Avoid HTFs that appear as the second leg in a measured move up chart pattern. I show that scenario in the measured-move inset (right) in Figure 3.2. Price moves up in leg 1 (perhaps forming an HTF), retraces its gain in the corrective phase, and then forms the HTF as it zips higher in leg 2. The leg 2 HTF tends to underperform, especially if leg 1 also shows an HTF.

  Figure 3.1 shows an example of this. An HTF forms at G to H and tops out at I. The G-to-I move is the leg 1 HTF. The corrective phase is the drop from I to A. Leg 2 begins at A where the second HTF forms.

- If price moves horizontally and then drops down to form the HTF, it could fall short of the post-HTF target. Imagine a pothole in the road. The bottom of the pothole is where the HTF begins life. Price may double just to return to the surface of the road, but more often, it rises above the surface to complete the HTF. Then price gets run over by a semi and dies (meaning it does not climb much after the HTF completes). It is like a tire bouncing out of the pothole. The bounce is not very large.

- Avoid buying an HTF if price two months before the beginning of the HTF is above the starting price. For example, if the bottom of the flagpole is at 10, and two months before that price was at 11, avoid that setup.

- I tested combinations of price 1, 2, 3, 6, and 12 months before the start of the HTF versus the closing price at the bottom of the flagpole. The results say that if price is below the flagpole two months before, then the HTF stands to outperform (average gains of 33 percent versus 25 percent).

- Throwbacks to HTFs happen 57 percent of the time in a bull market. When they occur, performance suffers (54 percent average gain for those HTFs without throwbacks versus 43 percent for those with throwbacks). The median drop after a throwback is below the top of the HTF by 10 percent. Those with throwbacks having price drop less than 10 percent gain an average of 52 percent post breakout. Those with throwback drops equal to or larger than 10 percent gain 34 percent post-breakout.

That information is a lot to swallow in one reading, especially if you are not a coffee drinker (I prefer decaf green tea). However, if you are serious about making money by trading HTFs, then go shopping for some and see for yourself how they behave. Explore my findings and mold them to your own swing trading setups.

HTF TRADE IN INSTEEL INDUSTRIES

I have made money trading high and tight flags (HTFs) just 56 percent of the time, but on a dollar basis, they can be quite profitable. In Chapter 18 of *Fundamental Analysis and Position Trading* (under the heading "Example Position Trade"), I discussed an HTF trade in Ann Taylor. **Figure 3.3** shows another HTF trade, Insteel Industries (IIIN).

The split-adjusted price hit a low in December (point A) at 7.82 and then climbed up to 15 in early February, qualifying the chart pattern as a valid high and tight flag. The stock did not quite double in two months, but it was close enough.

When the flag formed, I considered my options. I show the flag circled on the chart, but it is not a "flag" pattern at all. Rather, it is just a region where price moved sideways for a few days, forming an irregular congestion area. That is typical behavior. In fact, it is rare that a true flag pattern will appear in an HTF.

I computed the upside target by taking the high on February 10 (15.10) and subtracting the trend low at 8.07 (on December 28) for a

Insteel Industries Inc. (Building Materials, IIIN)

FIGURE 3.3 A high and tight flag trade sees price double.

height of 7.03. The measure rule recommends using half the height and projecting that from the flag low, but I used the flag high instead, giving me an 18.62 target.

I scored the chart pattern and found that it had a +2 value, suggesting there was a good chance the stock would climb to or exceed the median rise target of $19.59.

The industry was mid-range for relative strength (18th out of 46 industries), but the stock ranked first out of 10 stocks that I follow in the building materials industry.

Overhead resistance came in the form of round numbers, specifically, 17.50 (35 pre-split). Below, support was at 14 to 15—the site of the flag.

The day after price closed above the top of the flag, I bought the stock at the open and received a fill at 15.52. I calculated a volatility stop and placed the stop slightly above the recommended level (which was 13 percent), at 13.91, for a potential 10 percent drop.

As price climbed, I computed the volatility stop and trailed it upward, avoiding numbers that ended in zero. For example, on February 19, the recommended volatility stop was 29.00, but I put it at 29.07 instead (split unadjusted prices).

Notes for the trade say this: "The market has been up, but the stock really has not followed. With intraday price range narrowing, I am thinking the stock will tumble, taking me out for a loss. Why not tighten the stop more? Because I want to give it every opportunity to climb, but my guess is it won't."

I raised the stop 10 times, or just about every trading day as price entered the clouds. To finish out the trade, here was my thinking about the stops on March 6, 2006: "Stop raised to 19.11. This is well above the 18.88 volatility stop setting, but the wide-ranging day two days ago caused the CCI (commodity channel index) to issue a sell. With today's small range, it suggests a topping out of the stock. So, I tightened the stop."

On March 7, 2006, I noted, "The stock closed lower, and I figure everyone else will sell at tomorrow's open. In the past, the stock has tumbled on the open then recovered throughout the day. Except for today. It closed lower. With CCI signaling a sell three days ago, I think it is time to cut the giveback to 0 and exit."

I sold the next day, receiving a fill at 19.95, above the scoring system's target of 19.59. The stock peaked at B, 21.17, so I gave up some profit.

If the stock continued lower as I expected, it would have been a near perfect exit. However, the stock had other ideas. The day I sold was the short-term low, and the mass exodus I expected never materialized. Instead, the uptrend resumed, peaking at 30, almost doubling the price at which I sold.

After the early April peak, the stock tumbled, retraced some to form a 2B top and then the decline became a snowball gathering speed and mass as the stock rolled downhill. It bottomed at D, 15.44.

I made 28 percent on the trade.

FISHING FOR INVERTED AND ASCENDING SCALLOPS

When I worked as a dishwasher at the Gould Hotel to save money for college, the chef often put scallops on the menu. Of course, scallop chart patterns can be just as delicious, so maybe you should add them to your technical menu. In fact, the four varieties of scallops are patterns that many people do not know about, judging by their emails when I have discussed them on my website.

The four varieties are ascending and descending scallops and their inverted counterparts. This section deals with just one of those varieties: the inverted and ascending scallop.

Figure 3.4 shows a wonderful example of an inverted and ascending scallop (which I will just refer to as a scallop). It begins at point A in a rising

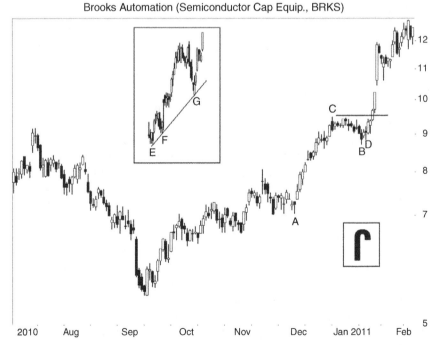

Brooks Automation (Semiconductor Cap Equip., BRKS)

FIGURE 3.4 An inverted and ascending scallop looks like the letter J, flipped horizontally and vertically.

price trend over the intermediate term, but the inbound up or down trend is irrelevant to selection.

Price peaks at C and then retraces to B. The scallop does not become valid until price closes above the top of the pattern. I show that as a horizontal line extending to the right of C.

Think of the scallop as the letter J inverted and then flipped horizontally. I show an example of that in the lower right inset. Price should begin the climb from A to C following a straight-line run or nearly so. That is not a deal breaker if there is a bend and price can hesitate (consolidate) along the way.

The top of the pattern should have a rounded turn that appears smooth, especially for smaller patterns, but larger ones often have an irregular shape.

The retrace to B can vary in size (that is, the retrace of the A to C move), but often measures about 53 percent. Be flexible with the retrace. The one shown in Figure 3.4 is 31 percent.

Here is a list of guidelines for scallop fishing.

- Price should rise in a nearly straight-line run, but sometimes it bends to the right. Allow minor consolidations to interrupt the run.
- Price should round over at the top. In small patterns, this should be a smooth-looking turn but for larger patterns, when joining minor highs, the turn often looks jagged.
- The average retrace of the 653 scallops I looked at is 53 percent of the prior move up.
- Discard those that retrace more than 62 percent.
- Price must *close* above the top of the pattern before it becomes valid.

SCALLOP TRADING TIPS

The following are trading tips and techniques designed for swing traders, but can apply to other styles as well.

- Figure 3.4 shows a higher downward spike at D (the low price at D is above the spike's low at B). That is a buy signal. Measure the distance between the current close and the top of the pattern. If it is worth swing trading, then buy the day after D and ride price higher. Place a stop a few pennies below B to keep losses small. If you are lucky, price will breakout upward from the pattern, confirming it as a valid scallop, and you can ride price higher.
- The inset of Figure 3.4 shows a scenario that sometimes occurs. The retrace at G rests on a trendline drawn beneath the lows at E and F.

Thus, turning point G represents a buy signal. Place a stop below the trendline at G with a short-term target of the scallop high.

- For the traditional entry, buy the day after price closes above the top of the scallop.
- Sell if price turns upward at B but then reverses, closing below the low at B. Most likely, price is going to continue down.
- Measure the height of the scallop from the low at A to the high at C. Multiply the height by 60 percent because that is how often the full height works to predict a target. The result is a price target that the stock should reach 75 percent of the time in confirmed patterns (a confirmed pattern occurs when price closes above the top of the scallop). Look for nearby support or resistance areas and watch for price to stall or reverse there. If it does, then take profits.
- Multiple scallops often appear in a single price trend. When price retraces *too far* on the right side of the scallop (that is, point B approaches the low at A), it signals the end of the trend. "Too far" means price drops below point A in Figure 3.4.

  A check of the numbers shows a V-shaped pattern of performance versus retrace depth. Performance is higher if the retrace is shallow but deteriorates as the retrace grows to 60 percent. After that, the right side of the V brings performance back up. It may sound weird, but shallow or deep retraces are good. Retraces in the 40 to 60 percent range hurt performance. The right side of the V is higher than the left and that means deeper retraces are better than shallower ones.
- The median time between the end of the scallop and the breakout is 17 days. Those patterns that take equal to or less time to breakout show gains averaging 44 percent. If they take longer, the gains drop to 34 percent. Trade scallops that make a quick drive to the breakout and avoid those that take their time.

TWICE IS NICE: EVE & EVE DOUBLE BOTTOMS

I already discussed the various combinations of Adam and Eve in Chapter 20 of *Fundamental Analysis and Position Trading* (under the heading "What Is a Double Bottom?"). Third on the list of best performing bottoms is the Eve & Eve double bottom pattern.

Figure 3.5 shows an Eve & Eve double bottom, but it is not a classic one. In the classic version, each bottom would be wider. By contrast, I show an Adam & Adam double bottom at C and D with twin downward price spikes. The Eve & Eve bottoms have more price bars gathered near the same price.

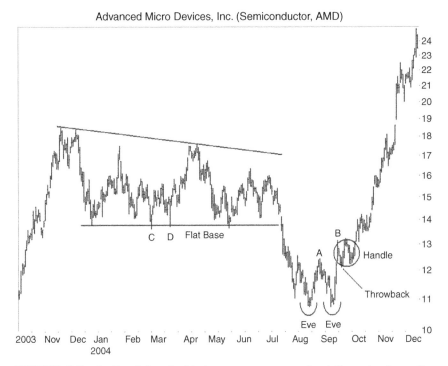

FIGURE 3.5 An Eve & Eve double bottom appears on the daily scale after a flat base, suggesting a more powerful setup.

When price *closes* above the high at A, it confirms the twin bottom as a valid double bottom. That happens at B. Just a few days later, price throws back to the breakout and does so again about two weeks after that before finally gathering strength for a push to higher ground. The stock doubles in about three months.

Although this double bottom is somewhat old, vintage 2004, I show it because of the flat base that precedes the chart pattern. I found that when the double bottom acts as a pothole in the road (a flat base followed by a double bottom), good gains occur. The combination is rare, but it is a setup worth remembering.

In this example, price forms a horizontal base starting in December 2003 and extending to July 2004. Then Price sinks into the pothole and jumps right back out again. A trader might worry about overhead resistance at 14, where the flat base resides, but as you can see, the stock pushed through that on its way upward.

The identification guidelines for Eve & Eve double bottoms are easy to understand. Here is the list.

- Price trends downward into the double bottom. The double bottom acts as a reversal of the prevailing trend, so if there is nothing to reverse, do not expect a large gain.
- The two bottoms are of the Eve variety, wide and rounded looking. If they have downward price spikes, they tend to be short and numerous.
- The rise between the two bottoms averages 26 percent (the median is 19 percent). I often set a minimum of 10 percent, but exceptions are numerous.
- The two valleys should bottom near the same price. How close? Use common sense. Ask yourself if others will agree that it looks like the two bottoms are near the same price. If the right bottom is higher by 5 percent or more, then it is an ugly double bottom. The average difference for double bottoms is 2 percent.
- The time between the two bottoms can vary widely, but the average is two months.
- When price *closes* above the peak between the two bottoms, it confirms the double bottom as a valid chart pattern. If price does not close above that peak, then the twin bottoms are just squiggles on a price chart.

TRADING EVE & EVE

Trading an Eve & Eve double bottom is like trading most other chart patterns. It helps if the market or industry trends after you buy. Be sure to check those two trends before you buy. Knowing that the other stocks in the same industry are hot air balloons soaring aloft can bolster your confidence to make a timely purchase. Here are some tips I noticed that might help you select better performing double bottoms.

- Since the right bottom in an Eve & Eve is a known support area, you can buy the stock and ride it up to confirmation. Place a stop a few pennies below the right bottom in case the stock reverses. This can be a risky play since 44 percent of twin bottoms do not make it up to the confirmation point (the highest peak between the two bottoms). Try it on paper to see if you can get it to work for your swing trades.
- Determine where the trend starts (see Chapter 20 of *Fundamental Analysis and Position Trading*, under the heading "Trend Start"). Price will tend to stall when it returns to the start of the trend. In other words, map where overhead resistance is strongest and expect price to stall or reverse there.
- Eve & Eve double bottoms in a bull market that do not suffer a throwback tend to outperform with gains averaging 48 percent versus

37 percent for those with throwbacks. How can you tell if a stock will throwback? The throwback rate is 55 percent, so you can guess and be right nearly half the time. Look for nearby overhead resistance, between 5 and 10 percent above the breakout price.

- If you wait for a throwback to complete before buying a double bottom, look at how far below confirmation price drops. The further it drops below confirmation, the worse post-breakout performance tends to be. The throwback in Figure 3.5 drops less than 3 percent below point A and the stock doubles. If the stock throws back, but remains above the confirmation price, then that is even better.

When the stock remains above the breakout price during a throwback, the 46 double bottoms gained an average of 57 percent. The 307 with throwback lows at or below the breakout price gained 33 percent.

- If price forms a handle near the confirmation price (consolidates just below to just above the confirmation price), then that can lead to powerful, bullish moves. Figure 3.5 shows a loose-looking handle on the double bottom. If price breaks out downward from the handle (closes below the handle low), then look elsewhere. A close above the consolidation region is a buy signal.
- Use the linear price scale and look for a flat base with the double bottom forming as sort of a pothole at the end of the flat base. These types of setups tend to lead to extended runs higher.

TOP SEVEN FREQUENTLY TRADED CHART PATTERNS

Which of the chart patterns have I swing traded most? Here is the list.

1. Symmetrical triangles
2. Ascending triangles
3. Head-and-shoulders bottom
4. Support or congestion
5. Flags, flat base, rounding bottom

Those names round out my top five, with number 5 showing a tie between three chart-pattern types. These patterns appeal to me, or at least they used to. I experimented with them and learned that if you want to lose money, ascending triangles with upward breakouts are the way to go. I will discuss more about that in a bit, but first, let us take a brief look at each one. Refer to **Figure 3.6.**

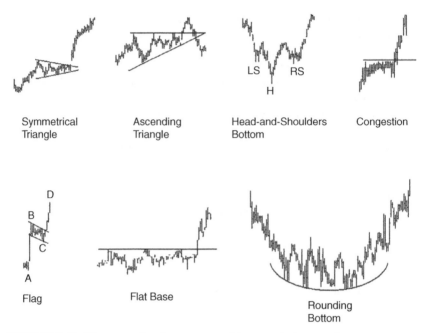

Symmetrical Triangle Ascending Triangle Head-and-Shoulders Bottom Congestion

Flag Flat Base Rounding Bottom

FIGURE 3.6 These are the chart patterns I have traded most often.

Symmetrical Triangle

A symmetrical triangle forms between two converging price trends. On the top, the trendline drawn along the peaks slopes downward. On the bottom, the trendline slopes upward, and the two trendlines join like a soon-to-be-married couple at the apex. Price should bounce between the two trendlines plenty of times, filling the area with price action. If I expanded Table 3.1, this pattern would rank 24th.

A symmetrical triangle can be a vicious bloodsucker of a chart pattern. Why? Because it tends to breakout in one direction, reverse, and breakout in the other direction only to reverse again. This double busting gives new meaning to the word whiplash.

Once the pattern figures out the trend it wants to take (after a double bust), the move can be worthwhile. If I have not lost interest in the pattern waiting for it to settle on a breakout direction, I may buy it and ride price higher. There is always a chance that price will reverse again, so the price action bears watching. I will discuss busted symmetrical triangles later.

- Symmetrical triangles have a tendency to double bust—breakout in one direction, reverse, and reverse again to resume the original breakout direction.

Ascending Triangle

I once thought that the ascending triangle chart pattern was the Holy Grail. Instead, it is the devil's triangle.

Price forms a flat top and up-sloping bottom, with the two trendlines merging at the triangle's apex. Statistics gathered in 2012 show that price breaks out upward 67 percent of the time in a bull market, but 14 percent of ascending triangles will fail to see price rise 5 percent before plunging. Over a quarter (28 percent) will see price climb 10 percent or less. In other words, this pattern busts (once) just like a symmetrical triangle, except that double busting is rare. This pattern ranks 28th for performance, almost at the bottom of the 32-pattern list.

I still trade ascending triangles, but do so with caution. If the market trend is up, and the industry trend is up, and all the other signs are pointing up, then up it is. Lacking any of those scenarios, then this pattern could do a better job of destroying your bank account statement than a paper shredder.

- Ascending triangles often see price rise by small amounts before reversing.

Just because I cannot get ascending triangles to perform with any regularity does not mean the pattern is a bad one. However, I tested almost two-dozen variations (setups) using ascending triangles. The best one requires the following three-point setup.

1. Place a buy stop a penny above the top of the ascending triangle.
2. Exit at the close three trading days after entry.
3. No stop is used.

This setup wins 63 percent of the time and makes an average of 1.8 percent ($183 on a $10,000 investment) in 4 trading days. The maximum hold time loss (the largest drop below the purchase price) is 23 percent. I used 1,293 trades for the test and it spans from July 1991 to February 2011. That test period includes two bear markets.

The other setups use moving averages, time exits, stop loss orders, profit targets, and so on. You can find the results on my website at http://thepatternsite.com/AscTriangleSetup.html. Please note that capitalization is important in the link. If you do not want to type all of that in, you can find the page by going to my website and clicking on the Trading Setups link. The page is listed as "Ascending triangle trading setup," unless I change the name, of course.

Head-and-Shoulders Bottom

The head-and-shoulders bottom is a chart pattern that resembles an inverted human's head and shoulders, hence the name. It sports a left shoulder (LS), head (H), and right shoulder (RS). The pattern should look like a human body, not have one shoulder higher than the other or unsymmetrical about the head. Allow exceptions, of course. This ranks 13th for performance, which is respectable.

I do not trade this one as often as I used to. I find that the head-and-shoulders bottoms that look best are death traps. The statistics show just the opposite with more symmetrical-looking patterns outperforming their hunchback counterparts. That does not change my opinion, though.

The largest loss I have ever taken in a trade started with a perfect-looking head-and-shoulders bottom, hence my caution. Price did not rise much for a few months, and as soon as the stock found I had dozed off, it started easing lower. And lower. And, well, you can guess the rest when the bear market of 2007 to 2009 kicked in.

Of course, it was not the chart pattern that was the problem, but money management. I was holding the stock for the long term, without a stop loss order in place. There is a joke that seems appropriate: In the stock market, if you want to make a small fortune, start with a large one.

Support or Congestion

You might not think of a support area (also called a congestion region) as a chart pattern, but it is. Congestion is a pattern that I find myself trading more often recently. I call it a congestion breakout. Price moves horizontally in a tight pattern and then breaks out. The details vary from pattern to pattern and stock to stock, and I use it only as an entry signal. I will check the fundamentals and other technical details (like industry and market trends) to qualify the stock before I go near it. When price closes above the region, I pounce. Congestion is not ranked for performance.

As a swing trader, I use a congestion breakout frequently. My job is to catch the breakout, ride the emerging trend until it stops, and then jump off before price reverses.

Figure 3.7 shows a congestion breakout circled in the middle of the figure. Notice how tight the congestion area is. By tight, I mean there is a lot of price overlap from price bar to bar as the stock moves horizontally. Volume at H drops to a low level. Two days later, the breakout occurs which sends price soaring.

The volume drop is something seen in many chart patterns a day or two before the breakout. This is especially true with ascending, descending, and

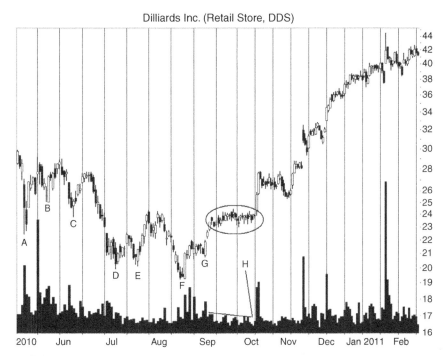

FIGURE 3.7 Price bottoms in the middle of the grid lines, helping swing traders determine when a new trend will begin or end.

symmetrical triangles, but it also occurs in congestion breakouts like this one.

Notice that volume trends downward as denoted by the diagonal line drawn along the volume peaks. You may see that trend as well in the chart patterns or setups you like to trade. My feeling, and I have not actually tested this, is that receding volume leading to a breakout from a congestion region helps performance.

After the congestion region, price breaks out upward. A buy stop placed a penny above the top of the circled region would give an entry price of 24.44. Selling three days later after a black candle showed price stalling would exit at the open, at 27.05. That is over $2.50 a share in three days, or 10 percent.

The vertical grid lines in Figure 3.7 make it look like you are peering out the window of a jail cell. Notice anything unusual about points A through G? The answer is that price tends to bottom in the middle of the grid, at least for a while.

This type of cyclical behavior can help you decide when to enter or exit a trade. Before swing trading, check to see if price tends to bottom or peak at the same, or nearly the same, intervals. I will warn you that I have not found cycles to be reliable. As soon as you find a cycle, it stops working.

For example, price seems to bottom between *every* grid line except for the channels between CD and EF. If you made a trade projection based on those two intervals, you would be scratching your head, wondering what happened only to see the pattern return a grid later. Nevertheless, it is worth checking because it may give you an edge over the competition.

- Look for a tight congestion area, one with a lot of price overlap. Those types of congestion areas can lead to powerful breakouts.
- Volume tends to subside dramatically a day or two before some breakouts.
- Look for cyclic tendencies—price bottoms or tops at the same or nearly the same intervals.
- Select stocks that show many long, straight-line runs instead of horizontal consolidation regions.

Flag

The flag pattern ranks 11th on Table 3.1 for performance, so it is a respected performer. I used to trade an event pattern called an earnings flag, but that one can be as treacherous as riding a bicycle on ice (which sometimes happened on my way home from washing dishes at the Gould Hotel as a teenager). A company announces earnings and the stock zips up, forms a flag, and then an upward breakout sends price higher. A regular flag follows the same pattern, like that shown in Figure 3.6.

Swing traders like flags, but I am appalled at some of the selections that others call flags. Just because price pauses is not an excuse to call the pause a flag. A flag should have defined boundaries sandwiched between two parallel or nearly parallel trendlines.

The appealing draw to trading flags is that they sometimes appear midway through a price move. Measure the move from the trend start (A in Figure 3.6) to the top of the flag (B) and project the height upward using the *bottom* of the flag (C to D). Price will reach the target 56 percent of the time, but it will take slightly longer (13 days from trend start to flag versus 16 days after the flag). The percentages of the two moves are similar, though, 17 percent versus 16 percent, respectively, based on a study of 248 flags in bull markets with upward breakouts.

- Flags can be half-staff patterns. The move before the flag mirrors the one after.

Flat Base

I have mentioned the flat base several times in this series, so I will not devote a lot of time to that pattern here. When prospecting for flat bases, use the linear or arithmetic scale instead of the semi-log one. Price should move horizontally for weeks or months and then break out upward from the trading range. I did not rank the flat base pattern.

The flat base remains a chart pattern for which I search. It allows a trader to find a stock, often at a low price, which is gathering strength for an elevator ride upward. Unfortunately, the stock may go nowhere for a year or more. When it moves, the launch can be like a moon shot, but I have seen other flat bases where price bobbles up and down like a piece of wood floating on water.

- Use the linear scale when searching for flat bases.
- The breakout from a flat base can take months before it occurs.

Rounding Bottom

Rounding bottoms rank 18th for performance, which is respectable. Determining when to buy the chart pattern is a difficult call. Often midway through the pattern, price will make a sharp move higher only to drift back down, giving back much of the gains. The decline will end above where it began, but not by much.

There is a tendency for some turns to form a descending scallop pattern instead of a complete rounding turn. In other words, price rounds downward, moves up, and then quits. The turn does not complete, leaving the right side of the rounding bottom missing.

- Midway through a rounding turn, price tends to jump upward only to ease back down to near the launch price.
- Watch for a descending scallop to develop instead of completing a rounding bottom.

MY FAVORITE CHART PATTERNS

You might think that the most traded chart patterns are my favorites, but that is not the case. After 30 years of terrorizing the markets, I learned that ascending triangles fail more often than I expected, so I filter them more closely before taking a position. It is a lot like deciding what flavor of potato chips to buy. The onion ones are good and so are the barbeque, but the rippled plain ones go better with salsa (I am getting hungry!). Over time, your taste may change, and so it is with chart patterns. They are a work-in-progress with some chart patterns gaining favor and others fading.

What are my current favorites? Here is the list, but they are not oriented specifically toward swing trading.

- Flat base
- Congestion breakout
- Busted descending triangle
- Busted symmetrical triangle
- Ugly double bottom

I already discussed the flat base and the congestion breakout. What I find myself doing now is ignoring the traditional patterns and just looking at what the entire stock landscape says.

As an example, the market turmoil in late February 2011 sent price dropping for the better part of a week, stopping me out of some big winners: Teradyne (up 194 percent), Frontier Oil (up 64 percent), and Pride International (up 21 percent, but I wanted to cash out after an Ensco takeover bid). The market zipped up and I was 12 percent in cash. That may not sound like much, but when it earns only 0.25 percent interest, and the market is climbing away, I want to be fully invested.

I spent Saturday morning paging through the 550 stocks I follow (which is a subset of the securities I look at). I was not looking for anything specific, but I found myself drawn to stocks that formed those congestion regions I wrote about earlier.

Flipping to the weekly scale showed how far price might climb in a year or two. I love seeing cloudbank patterns and found some in two stocks with prices well below the cloud base (that is, if price doubled, they would reach the cloudbank and be high enough to see my smile).

Both are semiconductor companies, which brings a measure of risk since that industry tends to be volatile and cyclical. The third stock caters to the homebuilding industry, a segment that had a near-death experience over the last few years. It shows an ascending triangle of three years' duration. I prefer to think of it as a flat top with a breakout waiting to send price 50 percent higher where it will join overhead resistance.

When I finished my chart search, I took my three candidates and checked the backstory. That included analyzing fundamentals, industry trends, outlook, insider trading, recent events, and anything else I could think of. I filled out my notebook, which also serves as a buying checklist.

Then I waited for the daily chart to signal an entry. I was in no rush. None of the three stocks were especially appealing for various reasons (lots of insider selling in one, weak growth potential in the other two, and price that moved higher for a few days and needed to drop back before I pounced).

My lack of enthusiasm suggested these three picks were duds. If you know a stock has a flaw, then why trade it? Why not wait for something better to come along? Maybe that explains why I am still single. Anyway, here are the patterns that interest me now.

Busted Descending Triangle

A descending triangle is another congestion region variant that I show in **Figure 3.8**. A classic descending triangle has price trending lower, following a down-sloping trendline along the top, but underlying support builds a floor that seems impenetrable.

Price digs its way through, but does not drop far before pulling back to the breakout price. So far, everything is normal. A downward breakout occurs in a descending triangle most often. However, price busts the triangle when it closes above the top of the pattern. When that happens, it screams, "BUY!" Buying then can lead to a powerful rally.

- If price breaks out downward from a descending triangle, reverses, and then closes above the top of the triangle, it busts the pattern and can lead to a powerful upward move.

Busted Symmetrical Triangle

A (single) busted symmetrical triangle is a classic symmetrical triangle except that price breaks out downward, turns around, and closes above the top of the triangle (or the reverse: upward breakout followed by a plunge). Traders anticipating one breakout direction panic when price reverses, and their exiting forces price further in the new direction. For example, a trader short a stock that moves higher will cover his position by buying it back, putting more upward pressure on the stock.

As I mentioned earlier, symmetrical triangles tend to double bust. It is rare that price will oscillate beyond two busts, but I have seen it happen.

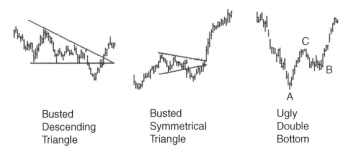

Busted
Descending
Triangle

Busted
Symmetrical
Triangle

Ugly
Double
Bottom

FIGURE 3.8 These unusual chart patterns can lead to profitable trading opportunities.

If I am going to trade a busted chart pattern, I prefer it to be a descending triangle, but symmetrical triangles are more common. Thus, I will hold my nose, buy the first bust, and then pray. Or just skip the trade altogether. No one is holding a gun to my head saying I have to trade. In fact, sometimes I look back at the stocks I decided *not* to trade and discover that they dropped like stones through water.

- A busted symmetrical triangle can lead to a powerful move providing it does not double bust.

Ugly Double Bottom

I discussed ugly double bottoms in Chapter 5 of *Trading Basics* (under tip 15, "Ugly Double Bottom: A Higher Bottom"), but they deserve mention again. I show an example of one in Figure 3.8. Bottom B should be at least 5 percent higher than A, but try to select patterns with a 5 percent to 13 percent differential. Those perform best. When price closes above the high between the two bottoms (C is the high, and to the right of it is a higher close), it signals a trend change from down to up and a buying opportunity.

Ugly double bottoms rank 20th for performance. Ranking so low suggests that the pattern has its share of problems, but that could be due to my research. I have not cataloged that many of them (566). Those that I have looked at were taken from a database that spans from 1991 to 1996. Their behavior could have improved since then, or not.

I do not trade this chart pattern often enough. When I have traded it, I have made money 80 percent of the time and decent-sized bucks, too.

- An ugly double bottom highlights a trend reversal from down to up.

SWINGING THROWBACKS AND PULLBACKS

I discussed throwbacks and pullbacks in Chapter 5 of *Trading Basics* (see tip 43, "Beware Throwbacks and Pullbacks"), but I wanted to discuss them in the context of swing trading. In that chapter, I provided averages for how throwbacks and pullbacks behaved. Here, I am going to discuss them by providing more color than I did earlier.

As you will recall, throwbacks occur after an upward breakout when price moves higher, rounds over, and returns to the breakout price or trendline boundary within a month, often leaving white space on the chart in this looping action. Refer to *Trading Basics*, Figure 5.16, for reference.

Pullbacks are similar, but apply to downward breakouts. Price drops out of a chart pattern, curls back up to the breakout price or trendline boundary before turning back down. Figure 5.17 in *Trading Basics* shows an example.

Swing traders can take advantage of this looping action since it occurs between 56 percent (throwbacks, all years) and 58 percent (pullbacks, all years) of the time, traveling a distance that averages 8 to 9 percent in the process. That is a best-case scenario—a perfect trade—one that measures to the highest high at the top of the throwback process, or the lowest low before price pulls back.

Let us go through the numbers shown in **Table 3.3**. I conducted a study of 19 types of chart patterns and found 19,070 samples. The duration of the two measurement periods (1988–2000 and 2000–2011) shown in the table are within two months of each other, so they are comparable. The first sample begins in May 1998 and the last in September 2011. The 2000 to 2011 period contains two bear markets, but the 1990s did not have any. Few stocks covered the entire range, too.

The numbers shown in the table differ to a small degree from those of the larger study reported in Chapter 5 of *Trading Basics*.

The throwback rate varies from 54 to 58 percent, depending on the years examined. After a breakout from a chart pattern, price rises and peaks 8 percent above the breakout, and it does so in an average of 5 days. Then price turns down and takes another 6 days before it returns to the breakout price or trendline boundary, for a total of 11 days to make the

TABLE 3.3 Performance Numbers for Throwbacks and Pullbacks

Measure	1988–2000	2000–2011	All Years
Throwback rate	54%	58%	56%
Average gain from breakout to throwback high	8%	8%	8%
Average time to throwback high	5 days	6 days	5 days
Average time for price to return to breakout/trendline	11 days	10 days	11 days
Percentage continuing higher	71%	65%	67%
Pullback rate	58%	58%	58%
Average loss from breakout to pullback low	8%	9%	9%
Average time to pullback low	5 days	6 days	6 days
Average time for price to return to breakout/trendline	11 days	11 days	11 days
Percentage continuing lower	58%	47%	51%

round-trip. After that, between 65 and 71 percent of the patterns see price resume moving upward. Notice that fewer patterns after year 2000 continue higher than in the 1990s.

The average *pullback* rate remained constant at 58 percent. From the breakout to the lowest low before price pulls back, the drop measures an average of 9 percent and takes 6 days. Then price returns to the breakout or trendline boundary, taking an average of 11 days between the breakout and return. After that, between 47 percent and 58 percent continue lower.

- Throwbacks see price gain an average of 8 percent in 5 days.
- Pullbacks lose 9 percent in 6 days.

Table 3.4 shows a frequency distribution of the time (top half) and gain or loss (bottom half) from the breakout to the day price peaks (throwbacks) or bottoms (pullbacks) for the period after 2000.

Why is this important? Because a swing trader placing a buy stop a penny above the breakout price can get in as soon as price breaks out and can then ride it upward and sell a few days later. The table shows how long and how far price moves in the coming days. Using the table, you can get a sense of how long it will take price to peak or bottom and decide whether you can build a trading strategy around that behavior.

For example, 21 percent of the chart patterns with throwbacks show price reaching the highest high in just 1 day. Another 10 percent take an extra day to complete the journey. The median time is 4 days, meaning that half the samples take 4 days and half take longer.

The columns are additive, so we know 31 percent peak in 2 days (21 percent + 10 percent) for throwbacks and 31 percent (22 percent + 9 percent) bottom in 2 days (pullbacks).

The bottom half of the table works in a similar manner except that it shows the percentage gain (throwbacks) or loss (pullbacks) to the highest high or lowest low, respectively. It gives you an idea of how *far* price moves after a breakout.

TABLE 3.4   Time and Gain/Loss of Throwbacks and Pullbacks

Days	1	2	3	4	5	6	7	8	9	>9
Throws	21%	10%	10%	10%	7%	8%	8%	5%	3%	17%
Pulls	22%	9%	9%	9%	9%	8%	8%	5%	3%	19%
Time Scale (Above) Gain/Loss (Below)										
Move	**2%**	**4%**	**6%**	**8%**	**10%**	**12%**	**14%**	**16%**	**18%**	**20%**
Throws	3%	14%	17%	16%	12%	8%	7%	5%	4%	13%
Pulls	−3%	−12%	−17%	−16%	−13%	−10%	−8%	−6%	−4%	−11%

For example, 3 percent of the chart patterns with upward breakouts gain 2 percent before beginning their return to the breakout. The pullback rate is the same, meaning 3 percent of the samples lose an average of 2 percent before beginning to return to the breakout.

Adding the columns, 34 percent (3 percent + 14 percent + 17 percent) gain up to 6 percent after an upward breakout and 32 percent (3 percent + 12 percent + 17 percent) lose up to 6 percent after a downward breakout.

* Half of throwbacks and pullbacks occur within 4 to 5 days of the breakout (respectively) with moves of 4 percent to 10 percent being common.

TRADING EXAMPLE

Figure 3.9 shows an unusual and perhaps extreme example of how trading a throwback could work. A high and tight flag appears when price skyrockets from A to B, more than doubling in just a few days, from a low of

Sealy Corp. (Furn/Home Furnishings, ZZ)

FIGURE 3.9 A high and tight flag leads to a trade that makes 40 percent in about two weeks.

1.38 to a peak of 3.65, respectively. A buy stop placed a penny above the peak at B gets you into the trade at C.

For most trades, I like to wait for a close above the breakout price, but with throwbacks, time and price are factors too important to waste (meaning use a buy stop for entry). In this example, price closes lower, but remains above the exit line, which is a trendline drawn along the bottoms, following trendline D.

Eventually, price begins moving up. As it does so, a stop loss order placed a penny below the prior candle's low would work well in this situation. That follows price as it powers higher, taking you out of the trade at E. From an entry price of 3.66 to an exit price of 5.15, the trade made 40 percent.

The throwback completes when price returns to F. Almost two calendar weeks (13 days) passed from the day price closed above the top of the chart pattern until it returned.

The large gain (40 percent) combined with the way this trade worked is unusual, as I mentioned. However, the trade shows that it is possible to make money by trading throwbacks. If you like to short stocks, then pullbacks might work well, too. However, swing traders have to be both skilled and lucky to profit from such short-term behavior.

You will not know how far price is going to rise, and the exit probably will not be as clean as trailing the stop upward beneath the prior candle, as in this example. Since the average gain from throwbacks is 8 percent, which measures to the day's high from the breakout price, that does not leave much room for error. The 8 percent rise represents a perfect trade: buying at the breakout and selling at the exact high before price collapses.

Perhaps a better way to trade is to wait for price to complete a throwback or pullback and then enter the trade. For throwbacks, wait for price to signal that the throwback is complete and price resumes moving higher. Then buy as it leaves a congestion area.

Pullbacks are more difficult to trade since almost half of the patterns result in a continuation of the downward move. Nevertheless, wait for the stock or security to signal a resumption of weakness and short the stock as appropriate.

- Consider waiting for a throwback or pullback to complete and for price to resume the breakout direction before trading.

CNO THROWBACK ENTRY

Figure 3.10 shows an example of how I bought a position after a throwback completed. Consideration of the entry begins with a rectangle top chart pattern.

CNO Financial Group, Inc. (Insurance (Diversified), CNO)

FIGURE 3.10 This trade begins with a throwback to a rectangle top chart pattern.

Rectangles have price that bounces between two horizontal or nearly horizontal boundaries. One trendline connecting the peaks and the other connecting the valleys shows where support and resistance occur. When price leaves those boundaries, a breakout happens and either buying demand has outstripped selling pressure (upward breakout) or the reverse for a downward breakout. Price breaks out at point A.

Like all chart patterns, the breakout can be premature, such as a quick jab upward followed by a return to the rectangle, or it can begin a straight-line run. Swing traders hope for an extended straight-line run, but those are rare.

In this case, the stock had a good reason for breaking out upward: the release of quarterly earnings. Price made like a bullet and shot out of the top of the rectangle, but then stalled at B. Then price threw back to the breakout. The pattern of an upward breakout after an earnings release followed by a throwback a week or two later is typical of an event pattern that I call a good earnings surprise.

Other factors I considered before buying were the strength of the market indices. They bottomed in September and made a nice move higher, without pausing until November 5, which matches the peak in the throwback (point B). Then the index moved downward until December. After that, it resumed its uphill run into the holidays.

With the general market moving higher and knowing that insurance companies invest in stocks, a rising market is good for them. Examining others in the same industry showed them to be a mixed bag. Some stocks were trending higher and some were suffering.

I waited until price returned to the breakout at C. Then it made a higher low a day later. Since price was resting on support setup by the top of the rectangle, I felt that it was a low risk, high reward entry. I bought at the location shown on the chart and received a fill at 5.69. The stock hovered around the rectangle for about two weeks and then started its straight-line run up.

- Waiting for a throwback or pullback to complete can setup a low risk, high reward trade.

MEASURING SWINGS

It is easy enough to find a chart pattern, set a buy stop a penny above the top of the pattern, but then what? How far is price likely to move after the breakout?

In my swing trading, one of the things that I found useful is knowing where price is likely to stop. To be fair, one cannot know for certain that a stock will stop or even pause at a given price, but if you like using risk/reward ratios (I do not), then planning the reward side is critical.

The reason I do not like using risk/reward ratios is because the reward side is often much higher than I estimate. Thus, I would be ignoring low ratio trades (like 2:1 or 1:1) that turn into big winners.

How do I predict the move? By using the height of the chart pattern as a guide.

Figure 3.11 shows an Eve & Adam double bottom on the daily scale. The pattern bottoms on the Eve leg, at 42.00, and rises to 50.55 during the peak between the two bottoms. The height of the pattern is 50.55 – 42, or 8.55. That suggests a target of 50.55 + 8.55, or 59.10.

When I studied chart patterns, I found that the full height worked for Eve & Adam double bottoms 66 percent of the time in a bull market, but only 47 percent of the time in a bear market (you can find those percentages for all chart patterns in my *Encyclopedia of Chart Patterns* book). The 2001 period shown is in a bear market that started in March 2000 and did not finish until October 2002. Thus, I would multiply the

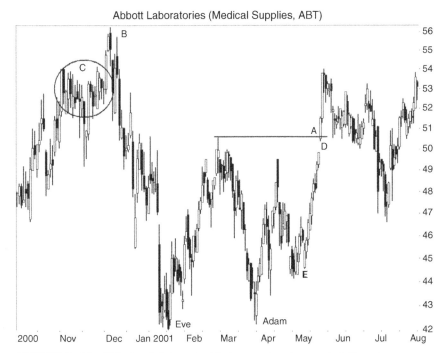

FIGURE 3.11 This Eve & Adam double bottom is a low probability winner.

height by 47 percent to get a closer target: 8.55 × 47 percent + 50.55, or 54.57. If the stock reached the target, it would mean a gain of almost 8 percent.

- Use the measure rule to predict how far price is going to move. Add the chart pattern's height to the top of the pattern for a far target. For a nearer target, reduce the height by how often the full height works for the chart pattern before adding it to the top.

Before I would trade this stock, I would look at the surrounding landscape to be sure there was not a tank hiding behind some bush, ready to blow me away. For example, starting in May at point E, look at the straight-line run up to D, the day before the breakout. How many more days could I expect such a run to continue?

As a swing trader, I want to buy at E and sell when it forms a congestion region at 53 to 54, not the reverse. As I discussed earlier, a straight-line run is more prone to a throwback than one that meanders higher. Thus, I would be suspicious that this rise would end, just after I bought in.

Another example: Price forms overhead resistance, which I show circled at C, where price might stop rising. It might not, but that is a good bet.

Point B is a prior peak. That is a known resistance area where price might top out, too.

Finally, if I looked at the bid/ask prices before the stock opened in the morning, I would wonder about the price gap at D being an exhaustion gap. That type of gap would scare any swing trader. Why? Because exhaustion gaps precede congestion areas. The scoring system for this pattern (see Chapter 20 in *Fundamental Analysis and Position Trading*) showed a −1 score, meaning a diminished chance of reaching the median 63.96 target.

All of this technical information suggested that this stock had a low probability of making a good run upward. I would avoid the trade, especially since the stock appears to have wild intraday swings (that is, it is too volatile). In fact, the stock climbed to 54, just short of the 54.57 measure rule target for double bottoms found above.

The point I am making here is to use the measure rule for chart patterns to give a clue how far price might go. If you do not have the probabilities of how often the full height works (so that you can adjust the height accordingly, as I did above), then use just the full height of the chart pattern added to the highest price in the pattern. Look for overhead resistance that could block the way to the target. If the measure rule target and overhead resistance coincide, then price stands a good chance of stopping there.

- Combine the measure rule for chart patterns with overhead resistance to determine how far price is going to move *before* taking a trade.

Let me also say that the measure rule does not work the same way for all chart patterns. The head-and-shoulders chart pattern is one notable exception. Measure the height from the head to the neckline vertically and add (for bottoms) or subtract (for tops) that height from the breakout price. Flags and pennants are another exception, but see my *Encyclopedia of Chart Patterns* book for details.

FTO TRADE

Let me give you an example of a swing trade I made in Frontier Oil, shown in **Figure 3.12**.

In late November 2010, I had a bunch of cash collecting almost zero interest, so I went shopping for stocks to buy. I found one in Frontier Oil. I checked its competitors and felt that this one showed the most promise at a good price. Mostly, though, the setup swayed me. I like to see a technical reason for buying the stock. The stock has to whisper, "Come buy me because I'm going to move up. Now!" Many times that whispering is just

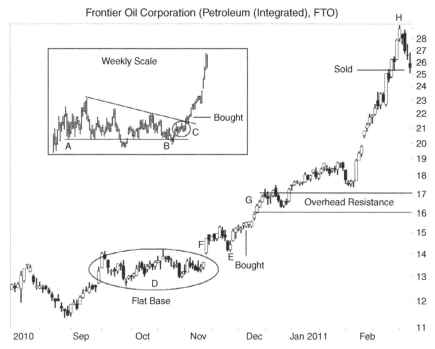

FIGURE 3.12 The weekly scale shows price rising above a down-sloping trendline, signaling a buying opportunity.

voices in my head trying to seduce me into believing that everything will turn out peachy.

On the weekly scale (inset), I saw a large descending triangle starting in June 2009. Price along the tops followed a down-sloping trendline. Along the bottom from A to B, price created a flat base (extending back to January 2009), but it was not that flat. Price poked through it like a car hitting potholes. The flat base suggested a good support area that might hold the stock in the future, should it drop back that far. Apparently, the smart money knew that the bottom of the descending triangle meant the stock was cheap and sold when it became too dear near the top of the triangle.

The shorter flat base shown at C and D, each circled, looked like another support area in case the trade went wrong. On the daily chart (D), the stock meandered up and down somewhat, but remained range bound for almost two months.

Price exploded out of the congestion region at F on better than expected earnings. This was a good-earnings-surprise event pattern, and you can see how price climbed. However, it soon approached the breakout price in a throwback, bottoming at E.

Before buying, I checked the industry and general market. In this case, the industry was in fine shape with stocks moving higher, but the market was dropping over the prior month. Nevertheless, I felt that the market setback was temporary.

Upside targets were 17 and 25. The 17 area showed a knot of resistance from July to September 2008 and back into 2005 (not shown on the chart). You can see on the daily chart where price struggles in the 16 to 17 area, which I show as area G, a reflection of that anticipated resistance.

The 25 region had numerous valleys poking down from the clouds in 2006 and 2008. The top of that cloud was 33.

In my trading notebook, I wrote, "Buy reason: Upward breakout from down trendline on weekly scale since June 2009. Overhead resistance at 17 is going to be a problem, and who knows about environmental regulations going into 2012. I do not see this doing much, but it could begin trending based on the monthly scale and past rises followed by 1–2 years of flat movement."

I bought the stock and received a fill at 15.47. The stock hit overhead resistance at 17 and had trouble pushing through. Then in late January, it dropped and found support near the same area. After that, it began shooting higher like an oil well having a blowout.

Such straight-line runs at steep angles make me nervous. When do you sell? I used the three-bar exit approach, placing a stop three lower lows below price, and trailing it upward. From the peak at H, the first low is on that price bar and the lowest one is shown. Following a market swoon down, price hit the stop and sold at 25.35, 2 cents below the low. I made 64 percent on the trade in about three months.

This is the type of swing trade that I like to see. A large gain in a short time. Yum!

- Check the longer-term chart for tradable patterns.

CHAPTER CHECKLIST

This chapter covered many ideas for swing trading using chart patterns. Here is a checklist.

☐ Price throws back after a straight-line run 78 percent of the time. See the introduction.

☐ Pullbacks occur 69 percent of the time after a straight-line run down from the breakout. See the introduction.

☐ Cut the failure rate of high and tight flags (HTFs) to 19 percent by waiting for price to close above the top of the flagpole. Otherwise, the failure rate is 33 percent. See "HTF Trading."

☐ *Always* wait for price to close above the top of the HTF before buying. See "HTF Trading."

☐ Shallow sloping price trends leading to the start of the HTF result in better post-breakout performance. See Table 3.2.

☐ See "HTF Trading Tips: What I Use" for high and tight flag trading tips.

☐ "Fishing for Inverted and Ascending Scallops" discusses identification guidelines.

☐ See "Scallop Trading Tips" for details on how to profit by trading scallops.

☐ See "Twice is Nice: Eve & Eve Double Bottoms" for identification tips.

☐ See "Trading Eve & Eve" for trading tips.

☐ Symmetrical triangles have a tendency to double bust—breakout in one direction, reverse, and reverse again to resume the original breakout direction. See "Symmetrical Triangle."

☐ Ascending triangles often see price rise by small amounts before reversing. See "Ascending Triangle."

☐ See "Support or Congestion" for tips on how to trade those areas.

☐ Flags can be half-staff patterns. The move before the flag mirrors the one after. See "Flag."

☐ Use the linear scale when searching for flat bases. See "Flat Base."

☐ The breakout from a flat base can take months before it occurs. See "Flat Base."

☐ Midway through a rounding turn, price tends to jump upward only to ease back down to near the launch price. See Rounding Bottom.

☐ Watch for a descending scallop to develop instead of completing a rounding bottom. See "Rounding Bottom."

☐ If price breaks out downward from a descending triangle, reverses, and then closes above the top trendline, it busts the pattern and can lead to a powerful upward move. See "Busted Descending Triangle."

☐ A busted symmetrical triangle can lead to a powerful move providing it does not double bust. See "Busted Symmetrical Triangle."

☐ An ugly double bottom highlights a trend reversal from down to up. See "Ugly Double Bottom."

☐ Throwbacks see price gain an average of 8 percent in 5 days. See "Swinging Throwbacks and Pullbacks."

☐ Pullbacks lose 9 percent in 6 days. See Table 3.3.

☐ Table 3.4 shows a frequency distribution of time and gain/loss for throwbacks and pullbacks.

☐ Half of throwbacks and pullbacks occur within 4 to 5 days of the break-out (respectively) with moves of 4 to 10 percent being common. See "Swinging Throwbacks and Pullbacks."

☐ Consider waiting for a throwback or pullback to complete and for price to resume the breakout direction before trading. See "Trading Example."

☐ Waiting for a throwback or pullback to complete can setup a low risk, high reward trade. See "CNO Throwback Entry."

☐ Use the measure rule to predict how far price is going to move. See "Measuring Swings."

☐ Combine the measure rule for chart patterns with overhead resistance to determine how far price is going to move *before* taking a trade. See "Measuring Swings."

☐ Check the longer-term chart for tradable patterns. See "FTO Trade."

CHAPTER 4

Swing Selling

So much time is spent determining *what* to buy and then *when* to buy that selling seems like an afterthought. Chapter 5 in *Trading Basics* (under the heading "Fourteen Selling Tips You Need to Know") discussed the selling basics, but this chapter is going to drill down into swing selling techniques, most of them based on chart patterns.

You might think that a complex head-and-shoulders top, for example, would be a signal to short a stock and that is certainly true, but what if you own the stock? Should you sell it? Not necessarily. Many factors come into play when determining when to sell, such as the holding time (short-term versus long-term for tax reasons), trading style (an investment versus a trade), and anticipated extent of the decline. If price drops by only a nickel and then pretends it is a rocket reaching for the stars, selling would be a mistake.

Tax treatment of trading is beyond the scope of this book, and it changes so frequently that it is best left for discussion elsewhere. However, I once delayed selling to push a profit into the next year. That happened with a trend channel trade in Varco, now National Oilwell Varco (NOV). The first magazine article I had published (April 1996) discussed that trade. Delaying the sale by *one* day changed a potential 40 percent gain into a 27 percent one.

- Sometimes selling for tax reasons can be a mistake.

Let us move away from me complaining about taxes and look at chart patterns that tell when to sell.

SELLING IDEAS

When is a stock worth selling? When is a stock worth shorting? Let us answer those questions with a hypothetical trade.

Figure 4.1 shows a descending triangle at E. Prices along the top form lower highs, bumping up against a down-sloping trendline connecting the peaks. Along the bottom, price finds support, resting on a horizontal trendline. Price crosses the pattern from side to side plenty of times, covering the white space with traffic sparked by fear and greed.

Notice that at F price pokes its head out the top of the triangle, but closes within the chart pattern. Thus, it is not a valid breakout. We are looking for a *close* outside of the triangle boundary to signal a breakout. That is an important distinction, but I confess that I have often traded by placing a buy stop at the top of a triangle to get me into a trade as soon as possible. The bottom of the triangle represents support. If price *closes* below the bottom trendline, then that is the sell signal.

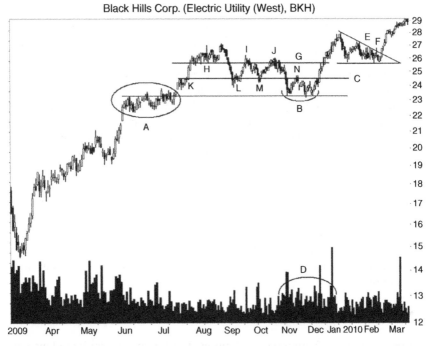

FIGURE 4.1 A descending triangle breaks out upward, but what if it broke out downward? Would it be worth trading?

I have extended the bottom of the triangle using line G to show support. The valley at H along with peaks at I and J are the features where support or overhead resistance appears in this example.

Let us assume that the triangle will break out downward. How far will price drop? Answering that question will tell us if we need to sell a long holding or if the stock represents a good short sale candidate.

The first support comes at C, set up by a small knot of support at K, valleys L and M, and peak N. Below that is the longer support region stretching from A to B.

With a straight-line run higher starting at B, my guess is that price would drop to between B and C. When retracing a straight-line run, often price remains above the launch price, but not by much (meaning it would probably bottom above 23).

Let us say that price drops to B and then bounces higher. How much of a drop does that represent? The bottom of the triangle is at 25.65 and B is at 23.16. Thus the drop is (25.65 − 23.16) ÷ 25.65, or 10 percent. If price drops only to C, the decline would be (25.65 − 24.50) ÷ 25.65, or 4 percent.

Is a potential decline between 4 and 10 percent worth shorting? If you own the stock, can you ride out a 4 percent drop? How about a 10 percent drop? Shorting an electric utility is probably not a good idea since it may be hard to find the shares to borrow and the stock pays a dividend that you must pass along.

For an investor or position trader, a drop of 10 percent is nothing to worry about. As a swing trader, I would probably place a stop loss order a penny below the bottom of the triangle and hope that if price staged a downward breakout that it would not gap lower, triggering my stop at a significantly lower price.

Always remember that the stock could continue lower, that just because support appears below the pattern, it does not mean that price will reverse there.

- Determine how far price is likely to move before selling a holding or shorting a stock.
- If support is closer than 5 percent, a downward breakout may push through it.

TOP 20 CHART PATTERN PERFORMERS

I looked at 30,085 chart patterns and sorted them by breakout direction. Table 3.1 in the previous chapter showed the performance of chart patterns for upward breakouts. **Table 4.1** shows them for downward breakouts, but

TABLE 4.1   Chart Patterns Ranked by Performance over Time, Downward
Breakouts, Bull Market

Pattern	1 Month	2 Months	3 Months	6 Months
Diamond bottom	−10%	−5%	−4%	−2%
Complex head-and-shoulders top	−8%	−10%	−10%	−9%
Diamond top	−8%	−7%	−6%	−3%
Head-and-shoulders top	−7%	−8%	−7%	−4%
Scallop, descending	−6%	−5%	−4%	0%
Rounded top	−6%	−4%	−4%	1%
Adam & Adam double top	−6%	−4%	−3%	0%
Triangle, ascending	−6%	−3%	−2%	4%
Triangle, descending	−5%	−4%	−3%	2%
Right-angled and descending broadening formation	−5%	−4%	0%	−3%
Adam & Eve double top	−5%	−3%	−2%	1%
Eve & Eve double top	−5%	−3%	−1%	4%
Flag	−5%	−2%	−1%	−1%
Scallop, descending and inverted	−4%	−4%	−4%	−2%
Pennant	−4%	−3%	−2%	2%
Triple top	−4%	−3%	−2%	0%
Broadening bottom	−4%	1%	2%	5%
Broadening wedge descending	−3%	−3%	−2%	−1%
Rising wedge	−3%	−3%	−1%	−1%
Right-angled and ascending broadening formation	−3%	−2%	−1%	3%
Total of all 28 patterns	−121%	−76%	−42%	30%

this time sorted by their 1-month performance. I chose the 1-month period since the most violent drops often come quickly. The declines emphasize how much money you can lose if you do not exit in a timely manner.

Diamonds and head-and-shoulders populate the first four slots in the table. I understand why the two head-and-shoulders are there, but I would not have guessed that diamonds would place so high.

Notice that the diamond bottom is in first place. By definition, price drops into the pattern and being a bottom, I would expect an upward breakout when price reversed. In fact, 69 percent of diamond bottoms break out upward. When the breakout is downward and you own the stock, the numbers say that things go bad quickly.

Complex head-and-shoulders tops do not throw their knockout punches until two to three months after the breakout. That is when the decline reaches 10 percent.

At the bottom of the table, I sum the performance numbers, just to emphasize the trend over time. The 28 chart-pattern varieties declined a total of 121 percent during the first month, but the decline registered only 76 percent after two months, and posted a 30 percent gain after six months. Each period measures from the closing price the day before the breakout. Thus, if price drops 10 percent in the first month, but registers a drop of 5 percent in the second month, then the stock climbed between those two periods.

Before I explore the top three performing patterns, notice that a few chart patterns show price *gaining* over time. That is especially true for the 6-month column, but broadening bottoms show a pronounced weakness in this regard. They post gains after one month.

- The decline one month after a breakout is often small and tends to lessen because price rises over time.

DIAMOND TOPS AND BOTTOMS

Diamonds may or may not be a girl's best friend, but they are miserable for traders. Why? Because they are hard to identify. Here are the rules for finding diamonds.

- The price swings widen in the first part of the diamond, forming a broadening top or broadening bottom pattern. Look for higher highs and lower lows.
- In the second part of the pattern, the price swings diminish such that they make lower highs and higher lows. This portion of the pattern takes on the shape of a symmetrical triangle.
- For diamond tops, the price trend leading to the pattern enters the diamond from the bottom. Ignore overshoot.
- For diamond bottoms, price trends downward into the pattern. Ignore undershoot.

Let us talk about overshoot and undershoot.

Overshoot, Undershoot, and Identifying Diamonds

Overshoot, as a trading behavior, can be likened to driving down the street, talking on your cell phone, and driving past your turn. You drive a bit past, back up, and make the turn. If a semi does not rear-end you, then you might survive. With price, it shoots past a trendline boundary but then returns to begin forming a pattern.

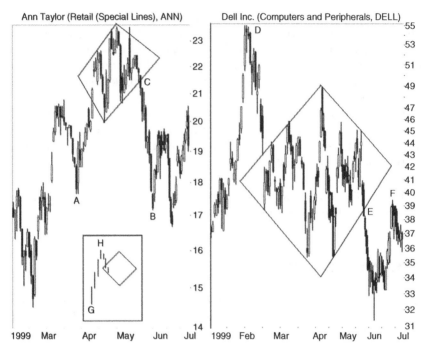

FIGURE 4.2   A diamond top and bottom appear on the daily chart, both with downward breakouts.

The inset in **Figure 4.2** shows an example of overshoot. Price trends higher from G to H, overshooting the start of the pattern and then dropping back inside. Undershoot is the same behavior only the GH move is downward (so flip the image vertically). The diamond, as shown in the inset, is a top and not a bottom even though price enters the pattern from the top.

Undershoot and overshoot occur not only with diamonds, but other chart patterns as well. What appears as overshoot at point D in the chart of Dell is not overshoot because price travels too far and lasts too long. Overshoot lasts less than a week, and often just a few days pass before price enters the chart pattern.

The point of overshoot and undershoot is not to be fooled by price behavior just before a chart pattern begins. Correctly identify a top or bottom by the primary trend, not the squiggles of a very near-term move.

Diamonds are hard to identify because they can vary far from the perfect shape. Often the diamond is pushed to the right or made to look as if a giant stomped on it, flattening it out. The variations are so numerous that it can take a vivid imagination to connect the four trendlines into a diamond shape.

Often diamonds can be confused with other chart patterns. Is it a head-and-shoulders top? Is it a broadening top or bottom, or how about a symmetrical triangle?

Finding price that bounces from trendline to trendline reminds me of when children learn to color within the lines. The black lines are no impediment to coloring where they want. Diamonds are similar, with price peaks and troughs either falling short or zipping outside of the trendline borders with seeming ease.

- Price may overshoot or undershoot the entry to a chart pattern. Ignore it when determining whether the chart pattern is a top or bottom. Instead, use the primary price trend as the direction of entry.
- Many diamond patterns tilt to one side and can appear irregularly shaped.

Diamond Price Behavior

Having beaten identification to death, let us turn our attention to price behavior. The Ann Taylor chart in Figure 4.2 shows price launching from A in a straight-line run up to the diamond top. This diamond acts as a reversal of the upward trend. Price consolidates for over a month before breaking out downward at C and returning to near the launch price, at B.

This quick rise, quick decline behavior is rare, but one I associate with diamonds. However, it can happen with any chart pattern and it is something I am wary of when buying a stock. That is why it is so important to wait for a confirmed breakout. Confirmation usually means a close outside of the chart pattern boundaries. Points C and E are the confirmed breakout locations in Figure 4.2.

If you short a diamond on a downward breakout after a quick rise, keep in mind that price often falls short of its target. In this example, price at B bottomed below A, but that is rare. Price usually finds support at a slightly higher level.

Also, the straight-line run heading down like the one shown in Figure 4.2 may not appear. Price may still drop, but the route will not be a quick descent. Price will meander lower. When I looked for the quick rise, quick decline scenario, I was surprised at how often a quick decline after a quick rise did *not* occur.

In many diamond patterns, I see a pullback ending the decline. That is, price breaks out downward and drops for less than a week before pulling back to the breakout price and then continuing higher. A check of the industry strength (verify that other stocks in the same industry are falling) and market weakness will go a long way to ensuring a successful short.

The Dell picture is an example of a diamond bottom with a downward breakout. It is a diamond bottom because price drops into the pattern from above (starting at D). This diamond is one of the better-shaped examples. The price swings widen in the first part of the diamond and then narrow, just as they should. Then price exits the pattern at E, drops, and pulls back at F. The spike low in June marked the end of the decline.

- Quick declines sometimes follow quick rises.
- A pullback may end the decline if the industry and/or market are trending higher.

Diamond Trading Tips

Diamonds do not have many specific trading tips, but some general rules can give you an edge. Here is a list.

- Reversals need something to reverse. If price is moving horizontally for a month and then jumps up a few dollars and forms a diamond, how far down would you expect the stock to drop after a downward breakout? Answer: back to the horizontal base. In other words, look for the nearest underlying support and assume price will reverse there. If it does, can you make money by playing the drop?
- Diamonds can act as half-staff patterns. That means the move leading to the diamond can equal the length of the move after a diamond, both in duration and percentage.
- The slope of the price trend frequently resumes after the breakout (mirroring the slope before the diamond).
- If price has a high velocity going into the diamond, it can exit with a similar velocity, providing the diamond acts as a continuation of the price trend.
- Stocks with higher inbound velocity (above the median 7 cents per day) outperform those with a lower velocity. Again, assume a continuation and not a reversal.
- Price recovers quickly after a diamond bottom with a downward breakout. That is what Table 4.1 shows. Price drops 10 percent after one month but then climbs.
- Measure rule: Measure the height of the diamond from highest peak to lowest valley and subtract it from the price where it pierces the pattern's boundary, heading down. The result is a target that price hits 69 percent of the time for diamond tops and 63 percent of the time for diamond bottoms. If you multiply the height by the associated percentage and then subtract it from the breakout price, you will get a closer, more reliable target.

- After projecting how far price may drop, look for nearby support. If both support and the measure rule target are near the same price, then it is more likely that price will stop there.

COMPLEX HEAD-AND-SHOULDERS TOP

Finding a complex head-and-shoulders top (CHST) is as easy as finding a simple head-and-shoulders pattern, except that it has more shoulders, more heads, or both. You might not believe how often that works, but try it. Look for additional shoulders surrounding a single head.

Sometimes finding a double top and looking for a shoulder to the left of the first peak and another to the right of the second will identify a CHST. Many rounded tops are composed of multiple peaks that seem to climb like stairs leading up, topping out, and then descending on the other side. That configuration might be a CHST, too.

Judging by the numbers in Table 4.1, the decline peaks in months 2 and 3, and remains strong 6 months later with declines hovering around 10 percent. That suggests the reversal has staying power, meaning if you own a stock and it confirms a complex head-and-shoulders top, then consider selling (but check for underlying support, first).

What is involved in identifying a CHST? Here is the list.

- Price must climb into a CHST. Continuation patterns, where price drops into the CHST, do happen, but too rarely to worry about. Look for patterns that act as reversals of the upward trend.
- Price forms a head-and-shoulders pattern with multiple shoulders, multiple heads, or both. The head should be above the shoulders. The shoulders should be symmetrical about the head (distance) and priced near the same value. In other words, the mirror image of each shoulder about the head should top out near the same price.
- Often the head-to-shoulder distance is less than in a regular head-and-shoulders top.
- Shoulders tend to be the same shape as their mirror opposite: both thin or both wide.
- The neckline, which is a line connecting the lowest valleys on each side of the head, tends to be more horizontal than do those in regular head-and-shoulders tops.

Figure 4.3 shows an example of a CHST. This stock has two heads and it is a more rare combination than those with multiple shoulders.

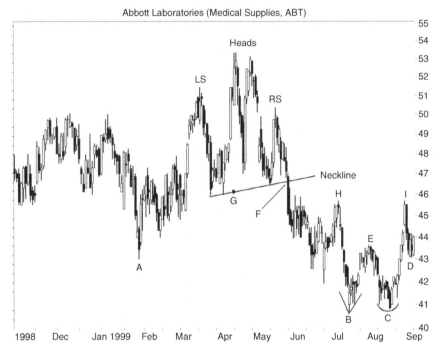

FIGURE 4.3   A complex head-and-shoulders top reverses the upward price trend.

The left shoulder (LS) mirrors the shoulder on the right (RS). Each shoulder tops with a short spike and just below that, the shoulder widens out. In other words, the two shoulders *look* similar. They both top out near the same price (I think my head is tilted).

The two heads tower above the shoulders, but not by a huge degree. Even the two heads look like duplicates. The neckline joins the armpits and this one slopes upward. The slope of the line will vary depending on the aspect ratio of your chart, and it will appear different than that shown on this page. Thus, be flexible. Do not discard a CHST just because the neckline has a steep slope.

In this example, the short-term upward price trend appears to begin at A, but the wider view shows the uptrend really starting in January 1996 at 13.69. When price closes below the neckline at F, it stages a breakout. This CHST marks a major reversal that sends price down to a low of 29.50 in March 2000.

Points B and C mark an Adam & Eve double bottom. Price makes a straight-line run up and then throws back (D) to the confirmation price (E, the peak between the two bottoms). Price made another attempt at a new high (not shown), but failed, peaking at 45.88 before collapsing.

Trading a Complex Head-and-Shoulders Top

Use the measure rule to help gauge how far price is going to drop. In Figure 4.3, measure vertically from the highest peak to the neckline directly below. I show that as a dot at G. The height measures 51.31 – 46, or 5.31. Subtract this from where price pierces the neckline to get a target: 46.69 – 5.31, or 41.38. Price reaches the target 53 percent of the time.

For a closer target, multiply the height by 53 percent and complete the math as discussed above: 46.69 – (5.31 × 53 percent), or 43.88. Price reaches that in early June and it hits the more distant target in July.

It might be helpful to think of the two targets as a minimum and maximum, but that is not how they are supposed to work. Both are minimum targets with the closer one being a more conservative guess. Either way, look for underlying support that might cause falling prices to reverse.

- Before shorting a stock, make sure there is a reason the stock is weak. Wishful thinking will not cause price to drop.
- Check other stocks in the same industry. If they show topping patterns or show price already falling, that bolsters the case for a good decline and a profitable swing trade.
- Are the indices also falling? If you are considering shorting a tech stock, then use the Nasdaq composite since that is a tech heavy index. Otherwise, use an index that is appropriate for your stock (I prefer the S&P 500 index). If the index is also headed lower, then that improves your chances for a profitable trade.
- Avoid shorting a stock unless both the industry and market are weak or showing signs of heading lower. If the industry is strong or the market is strong, then you increase your chance of a losing trade. Look elsewhere or wait for a more promising setup.
- Do not short stocks making new yearly highs just because they seem overbought. Pricey stocks tend to get even more expensive. Those moon shots are where 10-baggers come from.
- Weak stocks tend to remain weak. I proved that with statistics. Buy my *Encyclopedia of Chart Patterns* book that details which third of the yearly price range the chart pattern does best, and see for yourself.
- Pullbacks occur 67 percent of the time. Consider waiting for a pullback to complete and price to start back down before shorting. If you are nimble, you can short on the breakout and cover just as the pullback begins. That is tough to do, so try it on paper first to hone your skills. In CHSTs, price takes an average of nine days to return to the breakout price. That suggests price often bottoms in about three days (just short of halfway since price drops faster than it rises). Thus, if you see strength three days after the breakout, then cover the short.

THE EIGHT BEST EXIT SIGNS

I discussed the top three chart patterns that are best for short sales based only on their performance after a month. Let us say that you are like me and do not like to short stocks. What are the best exit signals for stocks you own? What price behavior says "Sell NOW!" for swing traders?

2B

For short-term swing trading, before I buy after a congestion breakout or throwback, I gauge how far price is going to rise. That distance is determined by overhead resistance, especially if price is below a major peak. Using Figure 4.3 as an example, say I believe that the stock has found support at C. It bottomed at B and now is showing a white candle as it begins to move higher.

How far will price rise? The confirmation price, which is the highest peak between the two bottoms, marks overhead resistance. I would expect price to stall there. If it can push through that, then another resistance area is at H. To the right of H, price dropped into the double bottom in a straight-line run, tunneling through any prior support until bottoming at B. Would it also make a straight-line run higher, from C to I? That is rare, but as you can see, it does happen and when it does, it sure looks pretty. The move (HBCI) forms a Big W chart pattern.

When price climbs to the old level at H and stalls, there is a danger that it will reverse, forming a 2B top. That is what happens here. If I expect that price might stall, I would use a limit order to sell just below the old peak. H is at 45.69, so I would use something like 45.43. That is below the round number 45.50 and perhaps low enough to catch price if it falls short, which it sometimes does.

For more details on trading with the 2B pattern, see tip 1, Timing the Exit: The 2B Rule, in Chapter 5 of *Trading Basics*. If you trade using 2B often enough, you will discover that it usually marks a short-term turning point. That is, price will drop but then attempt to move higher and often succeed. As a swing trader, we do not care about that. All we are trying to do is ride the straight-line runs higher, and when they stop running, we head for the restrooms, too.

- If price forms a 2B top in a swing trade, then sell.

Hit Target

Swing trading is about timing, getting in at the right time and making sure not to overstay the welcome by holding on to a trade too long and seeing profits dwindle. That is where a profit target comes in.

For example, I used limit orders to sell CH Energy (in mid-June 2012 shareholders voted to approve its acquisition by Fortis) when it reached 52. Why? Because when it climbed into the low 50s, it tended to reverse. I wanted to sell high and buy back when it dropped into the low to mid-40s. When it was that cheap, the dividend rate was about 5 percent.

When I am swing trading a stock, I will sometimes use a target exit. The target is placed where I think overhead resistance will either stall or reverse the trend. I do not use the target exit much because I try to let the stock tell me when it is tired and time to sell.

How do I do that? When a straight-line run ends, meaning that prices start overlapping, and instead of shooting higher each day, the stock goes sideways, then it could be time to look elsewhere for a more promising situation.

The danger with targets is that price can blow right through a resistance zone and continue higher. Using a target exit means you will be taken out at a price below where the stock finishes its run. However, how many times have you looked at a stock and said, "I should have sold right there!" Those are the days when price barely climbs to the target and then fades back down.

I have seen that scenario unfold often enough. I remember one trade where I thought seriously of using a limit order to exit when price hit my target but did not. It hit the target and then reversed, leaving me holding a stock with less profit.

What I find surprising is that with experience, you can determine with a good degree of accuracy how far price is going to move. You will not know for sure, but with practice, you can get good at it.

- Sometimes using a profit target exit makes sense.

The Scrolling Method

Try this. Either print out some price charts or use your computer's charts with scroll bars. Remove the date scale, if you can, since that is a dead-giveaway as to how price will trend in the future. If you have a significant other, have them pull up a stock at random for you and use that.

Scroll price to the left and try to guess where it is going to stall or reverse as each new price bar appears on the right. Where would you put a limit order to sell? If you are a day trader, you get this practice every time you trade. For swingers, you can do the same by spending a morning following a stock intraday or after hours using the scrolling method. This is especially important to do if you are contemplating trading a stock. Become familiar with how it moves and the scrolling method will help you learn that behavior.

I have used the scrolling method to practice many times. And the best thing about the method is it did not cost me anything except time.

Overhead Resistance

Overhead resistance comes in many forms, but it is a general category that is a must-have on the best exit signals list. If you can determine where overhead resistance is going to force price lower, then the keys to the money vault are yours.

In *Trading Basics*, Chapter 4 covered support and resistance, so I do not have much to add here. Remember these tips:

- Price rises in a series of waves. If you are an Elliott wave lover, then look for a stepladder climb of five waves (a rise-retrace sequence of three waves higher interspersed with two retraces). Try counting the waves. If you are about to buy on wave five, then you could be walking into a trap.
- Straight-line runs follow the rise-retrace pattern, too. If price makes a strong move up after breaking out of a congestion area and then pauses, another run up could follow, mirroring the duration and percentage change of the first move. I am describing a measured-move chart pattern (covered in Chapter 4 in *Trading Basics* (under the heading "Measured Move Support and Resistance").
- Flip to a higher time scale and look for overhead resistance. Find peaks or valleys that line up near the same price. Look for *unusual* price overlap in a straight-line run especially if it is on high volume. That may be a source of support or resistance in the future. By *unusual*, I mean that price is moving higher each day with little overlap and then for three days it moves sideways, forming a small knot in the string of prices. That knot might be where price pauses/reverses in the future.

Inverted Dead-Cat Bounce

In Chapter 5, I will cover event patterns, of which the inverted dead-cat bounce (iDCB) is one. However, I would be remiss if I did not include it as one of the best exit signals, too. The iDCB occurs when price makes an unexpected move higher, such as after the announcement of better than expected earnings or the success of a drug during clinical trials. Price can move from 5 to 20 percent (or more) with the first price bar (a gap higher) and then continue rising throughout the day.

Holding on after an iDCB completes may mean seeing profit diminish each day. It does not always happen that way, but I have learned that when Mr. (or Mrs.) Market gives you a gift, have a garage sale and cash out.

I *love* selling after price zips higher in one session. It is a quick swing trade that is almost painless. The pain comes when deciding if I should take profits today or tomorrow, that is, which day will see a higher high? I will explore that behavior in the Chapter 5.

- If price rises by 5 to 20 percent or more in one session, consider selling.

Double Your Money

Arrowhead Research (ARWR) is a stock I own now. I only own a small position since it is a risky biotech play. It is a long-term holding, hoping that the company can translate its work into a major success.

What is the problem? I bought the stock at 84 cents a share about a week after ARWR announced a medical breakthrough. Price retraced after the quick move up (an inverted dead-cat bounce, by the way), and I bought on the very day price bottomed. Two months later, the stock had doubled, peaking at 1.85 (all prices have *not* been adjusted for a reverse stock split).

Did I sell? No. Why not? Because this was going to be a *big* winner. Huge! I was not going for a double; I was shooting for a 10-bagger. After the double, the stock started trending lower and continued moving down. The double turned into a loss.

What I learned is this: If a risky stock doubles in price, then sell it. You can still hold a portion of it, but use zero-cost averaging. That is where you sell enough shares to cover the original cost so that if the stock drops to zero, you will at least break even.

- If a risky stock doubles in price, then sell it or sell a portion of it.

Chart Pattern Trend Change

Another top selling technique is to realize that some chart patterns act as reversals of the existing price trend. If a reversal appears on a price chart and you own the stock, then that is potentially bad news. Price may not drop much, but if it does, you are toast unless you cash out in time.

I remember seeing a head-and-shoulders top form in a stock I owned. Underlying support was not far beneath the chart pattern, and I felt that if the pattern confirmed, price would not drop much. That is exactly what happened. The stock hit support and bounced like a basketball filled with helium. It just kept rising and rising, and I had to call air traffic control so they could warn airplanes.

In other words, I made a calculated guess and got lucky. I play it smarter now. I check the market trend first to see if it is about to reverse or showing signs of weakness. Then I check the industry. If stocks are turning there, then that is a danger signal.

Yes, a company can screw up all by themselves, but if jet fuel prices are rising and you see a diamond top forming in JetBlue Airways, then there is a chance that American Airlines and Southwest are suffering, too, and probably showing a diamond in their stocks as well. They might hedge their fuel costs to limit the damage, but industry stocks run like a herd of cattle spooked by a gunshot. The industry test can save you a bundle.

- Look at how other stocks in the same industry behave. They may show the same chart pattern.

Weinstein's Approach

Recall that in Chapter 16 of *Fundamental Analysis and Position Trading* (under the heading "The Weinstein Setup"), I explored and tested Stan Weinstein's approach to trading. It is worth mentioning again here because it works.

According to Weinstein, price cycles in four stages. The 30-week moving average is climbing during stage 2 and it tangles with price like teenage lovers making out in the back seat of a car, forming stage 3. When stage 3 turns into stage 4, price drops, leaving the moving average behind. The drop may seem reluctant at first, but it soon gathers speed and plunges, taking the moving average down with it.

Holding a stock during stage 4 is never fun, but I have done it. I have also bought stage 4 stocks, and that is another no-no, according to Weinstein. Those are some of the problems with position trading or investing where you try to weather the minor retraces while holding on for bigger gains. Detecting a trend change is a lot like driving down the freeway and saying, "I should have taken that exit," as you drive past it.

Learn the signs of price topping out. If you need an indicator like a moving average or maybe something else, then use it. Just do not overdo it by piling on indicator atop indicator. I am content with using price. That is all I need.

- Avoid buying and consider selling stocks in stages 3 or 4.

TEN FAVORITE SELL SIGNALS

What techniques have I used most to time my selling? To answer that, I consulted a spreadsheet that holds the details of all of my trades since birth. It contains surprises, such as the absence of chart pattern names. Some are there, but mostly it's touchy-feely stuff. Here is my Top 10 list, sorted by the most frequently used technique first.

Hit Stop

This should not surprise anyone since a stop loss order for a trader or even an investor can be a worthwhile tool. About two-thirds of the time when it is used, I will be stopped out for a loss. The other third is when price has climbed far enough that the trade is profitable and I am trying to maximize my gain by trailing the stop as price rises. I discuss this in *Trading Basics*, Chapter 3 (titled "Do Stops Work?").

Weakness

What do I mean by weakness? Imagine buying a stock like Dow Chemical in late July 2005, shown in **Figure 4.4**. The stock confirmed a head-and-shoulders bottom (in June) and completed a throwback. The throwback dropped price down far enough so that the head-and-shoulders disappeared and an Adam & Adam double bottom took its place. Price climbed and confirmed the pattern, threw back again, and looked as if it was ready to move higher.

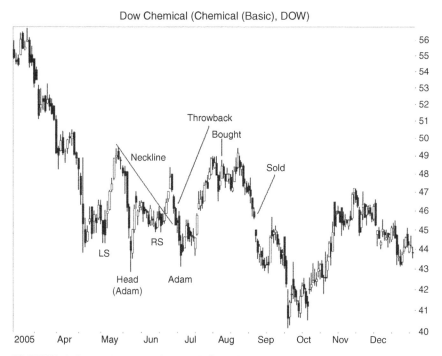

FIGURE 4.4   Weakness in this stock forced a sale.

That is when I became interested. The company released earnings the day before I bought and that sent the stock rising. I put a 10 percent stop in place and raised it (to 6 percent loss) because I got the feeling that I would be stopped out and did not like to take such a big hit.

Less than a month later, the stock turned down and what is worse, others in the industry were looking to tumble. Since price seemed destined to hit my stop, I just threw in my chips and sold before the stop could trigger. On the trade, I lost 5 percent.

Selling because price is heading down and *looks* to go lower is an example of weakness. Oddly, my gains using this technique outnumber losses by almost three to one. That ratio tells me that this is more of a mental issue: "I'm getting nervous making so much money. It must be time to sell to protect those profits." I had that issue in my early days when I focused on money instead of technique. When profits climbed into four figures, I began to feel that it was time to sell. I know better now. If you concentrate on trading well, the profits will come. Do not focus on the money, honey.

- Improve your trading skills instead of focusing on the money.

Fundamentals

Third in the list of sell reasons are fundamentals. For example, in May 2010 I owned an electric utility called Ameren (AEE), which I mentioned buying in *Fundamental Analysis and Position Trading*, Chapter 6 on dividends (see Figure 6.1). Days after the stock hit bottom in March 2009, I jumped in and bought the stock, collecting a tasty 7.5 percent dividend.

Just over a year later the company's request for a large rate increase had been denied, setting the stage for a more difficult future.

Looking at the price chart showed a large head-and-shoulders top chart pattern spanning from August 2009 to April 2010. Combining that bearish chart pattern with a hostile regulatory environment suggested that future gains in the stock would be hard to come by. I decided to sell and made 36 percent on the trade, including five dividend payments.

I lump into the fundamentals category almost anything that is not related to technical analysis. I do not usually sell because the price to earnings (P/E) ratio has exploded or the price to sales ratio is above 1.0 or anything like that. If same-store sales continue to be negative at my favorite retailer then I will look for additional evidence that confirms the bleak outlook and will make a trading decision accordingly.

Recently, I sold Pride International (PDE) because the corporation had just received a buyout offer. The offer was for part cash and part stock in a company that I was not interested in owning. I put a limit order on the stock to dump it should it reach 41. That was 60 cents below the value of the deal. I thought that was a fair exchange. The order triggered and I sold the stock for a 21 percent gain in just over a month. Unfortunately, with the price of oil zipping up, so did the value of the deal such that the stock reached 44 and change. Normally, stocks with buyout offers on the table flat line like a dead animal. It is safe to exit because price is not going to rise much, but it can sure drop in a hurry if the deal falls through.

- If the fundamentals change, then consider selling.

Diversification

After the 2007–2009 bear market ended, I was holding most of my portfolio in cash or utility stocks, collecting fat dividends (when they did not cut them, that is). With the stock market transitioning into a bull market, it was time to diversify. Utility stocks can rise and give you a capital gain, but they tend to be slow movers. Diversification allows you to jump out of slow movers, onto the fast track so you can beat the returns of the overall stock market.

Sometimes, though, the utilities do well, too. In 2007, the Dow utility index gained over 16 percent while the Dow, S&P, and Nasdaq remained in single digits. In the bear market of 2008, the utilities beat most of the market averages. Only the transports lost less.

- Diversify your holdings so any one position does not dominate your portfolio.

Support Pierced

Underlying support, by definition, is below price. Thus, when price punches through a support area, it means price is going to drop more. Selling when price pierces support does not necessarily mean a loss, but 70 percent of the time in my trades, it does.

Looking at some of my trades, especially those in the housing sector, shows that cutting losses short by selling on an adverse breakout from support is a capital-saving decision. When faced with such a sell decision, I keep hoping that support will do its job and allow price to rise.

That is true in some cases, but most times, it is not. Hope will not save a falling stock and neither will a support region. Price burrows through like my neighbor's dog (he is a digger) and it is time to sell and sell quickly. The drop after a congestion breakout is often a swift one, so taking quick action can save money.

- If price pierces support, expect a swift decline.

Inverted Dead-Cat Bounce

As you might imagine, the inverted dead-cat bounce is one of my favorite patterns. I already mentioned it as one of the best exit signals, but any time I can make a big gain in one session, I am thrilled.

My spreadsheet shows that I have never taken a loss when selling after an inverted dead-cat bounce. That is not a coincidence; rather, it is just the nature of the event pattern. Price springs up like bouncing off a diving board, and many times the stock eases lower over the coming weeks. Taking profits when price is high is the best way to play this event pattern.

Symmetrical Triangle

Symmetrical triangles are the first classic chart pattern to appear on this list. That is probably because they are so prevalent on the charts that it is natural to use them as sell signals. When price pierces the lower trendline boundary, then it is time to sell.

A check of the numbers shows that I sold for a loss 77 percent of the time. I am not sure why that is so high. It could be that I was unlucky enough to see it form a symmetrical triangle with a downward breakout soon after buying.

One of the difficulties of trading a pattern with a slanting trendline is stop placement. Each day the stop price changes, and the chart pattern may be in the formative stages where it is difficult to recognize anyway. That combination suggests that price will break out of the chart pattern, and as an end-of-day trader I will decide to sell it the next day, at the market open.

That is what happened in Vivus. Price formed a symmetrical triangle and broke out downward. The drop was swift even though I exited a day later with a 37 percent gain. The stock bottomed and pulled back to the triangle pattern and pushed toward the top of it.

Then the unexpected occurred. The company announced that the FDA disapproved their weight loss drug. The stock pretended it was a skydiver without a parachute. It dropped 55 percent in one session, creating another event pattern called a dead-cat bounce. Fortunately, I had already sold the stock.

- Symmetrical triangles can make for good exit signals.

Dead-Cat Bounce

The dead-cat bounce is one of those chart patterns I hate. Why? Because if you trade or invest in stocks long enough, then you will probably get hit by one. Like Vivus, the stock gaps open lower between 15 to 70 percent or more. Price often bounces up and then continues down.

In the Vivus case, I was lucky to have sold the stock a month before the event, but the stock bounced, eased back down to a higher low, and then began a slow recovery. It took six months for the stock to recover before falling out of the plane again. The stock went down over 40 percent from the January 2011 high and then began another recovery. In early 2012, the FDA committee backed approval of their weight loss drug, sending the stock shooting up.

Like the other event patterns I mentioned, I will discuss the dead-cat bounce in the Chapter 5.

- Either sell immediately or sell at the top of the dead-cat bounce.

Resistance

When price bumps up against overhead resistance, sometimes I sell. When I sell, it is for a profit 82 percent of the time. Since resistance is ranked 9th out of the top 10, I frequently do not exit using this technique. Why not? Because price can act like termites chewing through wood and eventually pierce overhead resistance if it keeps trying. When it does, it tends to shoot higher, starting a straight-line run up.

If the resistance area looks formidable enough (and that means a wide band of resistance, perhaps scattered through time), I will use it as a way to capture profits. I will place a limit order to sell just below the resistance area and hope that price can rise far enough to trigger the exit.

- Sell if overhead resistance looks like it will reverse a trend.

Head-and-Shoulders Top

Table 4.1 shows the head-and-shoulders top as the 4th best performing bearish pattern when ranked over the move from the breakout to the close a month later. When I see one forming in a stock I own, the grin on my face disappears.

I do not automatically sell because I want to wait for the pattern to confirm. Sometimes I get lucky and price never confirms the head-and-shoulders top. The stock just rises away from the neckline. For the other times, it is bad news. How bad? I have lost money 30 percent of the time when it appears.

I remember exiting a trade in Graco (GGG). I bought the stock after an earnings flag (an event pattern). Even before I could pay for the trade, the head-and-shoulders top started to appear. The day after it confirmed the pattern, I sold the stock.

The good news is I limited my loss to $46 (that is total, not per share). The bad news is that the stock bottomed a day later. From there, a straight-line run took it back up to the price level of the head in the head-and-shoulders top. With more time, a head-and-shoulders *bottom* appeared which sent price rising from 25 where I bought to 41. Unfortunately, I watched that rise from the sidelines.

- Wait for bearish chart patterns to confirm before selling a stock.

That completes my top 10 favorite sell signals based on my historical record of trades. The following takes a detailed look at a few trades, focusing on the sell side.

TRADING EXAMPLE: THE TERADYNE EXIT

After a bear market, if you can determine when the price trend changes from bear to bull, buying almost anything can be a lucrative endeavor. The bear market ended on March 6, 2009, when the S&P 500 index bottomed. On that date, Teradyne completed the right bottom of a double bottom.

I did not buy the stock until price climbed above confirmation, the high between the two bottoms. The day after it confirmed, May 1, 2009, I bought and received a fill at 5.94.

For this chapter, the entry is not as important as the exit. I will show a picture of the sale in a moment. Based on the weekly chart, I placed a target for the stock at 17. That price was the top of a cloudbank that extended from late 2004 to 2007.

For investment purposes, I was content to wait for price to reach the target, believing that the recovery from the bear market would take price that high. That is what a cloudbank pattern says, that the *normal* price of the stock used to be within the cloudbank. All you had to do was wait for price to return to normal. Think *regression to the mean*, if you are familiar with that phrase.

Fast forward to April 2010, about a year after buying the stock. Price had peaked three days earlier at 13.37. I had doubled my money. That made me nervous, so I put a conditional order to sell the stock if it closed below 9.93. That is below a round number (10).

Why so far away? I used the Weinstein approach to stop placement, meaning that I found the nearest minor low (which bottomed at 10.05 on March 15, 2010), below the 30-week simple moving average. I tucked the order below that minor low.

In the weeks that followed, the order must have expired because price closed below 9.93 on June 9, 2010, and yet I continued to own the stock.

During May 2010, the S&P closed below the 30-week simple moving average, warning of an approaching bear market. That made me

FIGURE 4.5 After gaining almost 200 percent, the stock reached its target and was sold.

nervous, so I started selling off my portfolio when the market turned lower in July.

On July 5 (C in **Figure 4.5**), I placed a limit order to sell the stock at 10.43. The stock had closed below a long-term trendline (support), a portion of it I show as the slanting line. The limit order price matches a 38 percent retrace of the drop from E to C and is just below the gap pointed to by D. Clearly, I was expecting a bounce and hoping for a higher exit price.

On July 8, I changed the limit order to a stop order at 9.78. If price dropped, I would be stopped out. I raised the stop to 10.05 four days later. The following day, Intel reported the best quarter in a decade, according to news reports, so I cancelled the stop, thinking that Teradyne would also do well.

On January 6, 2011 (F), I thought that the stock would drop back to 13 then 12 and 11, with each level showing support where it might stop. I also noticed that insiders dumped the stock in April, when it peaked near 13, so that seemed like a good selling price.

Instead of dropping, the stock recovered and resumed its up move.

On February 16, I placed a stop below the minor low at 17.55 (B). A week later, the market started getting nervous about oil prices and it sent the Dow down 280 points in 2 days. The market undertow was enough to force Teradyne down as well, and it hit my stop for a gain of 194 percent.

I knew that the wild market swings were temporary and that they could cash me out prematurely, but if I was wrong and the market started going down with gusto, that would mean less profit. My only regret with the trade is that I wished I could have raised the stop price to an even triple.

- Try to predict how far price will move, set a target, and use a stop to protect profits.

TRADING EXAMPLE: EXITING FOREST

The Forest Oil trade shown in **Figure 4.6** is an example of selling at a 2B top. The stock peaked in July 2008 at over 83, but I got interested when I saw a flat base forming near 13 in November 2008. That is quite a drop (84 percent), but that is what a bear market can do to some stocks.

I do not show the flat base in Figure 4.6, but it was an irregular one with many peaks and valleys. Calling it "flat" is like saying the moon does not have craters.

FIGURE 4.6   The stock sold after reaching the price level of a prior high.

I analyzed the stock in May 2009, and made note of three targets: 29, 40, and 50, but the chart shows an additional sell target at 28. I had hoped to sell at 52, a good gain from the $20 where it was currently trading.

The relative strength index (RSI) was approaching overbought and that turned out to be true. I bought the stock when it broke out of the flat base, filled at 20.90, the opening price. If you look at the chart for that day, shown in the inset, you will see that price ran to a new high, but closed well below that. After the day I bought, the stock would not make a new high for almost six months.

Here is a reminder to turn off all of your bells and whistles and look at a naked chart before buying a stock. I do not do that often enough and if I had, I would not have bought the stock on the day that I did. Now, I have my program calculate the probability of price continuing to trend and have that as a bullet item in my checklist.

Price eventually dug itself out of its hole and began to climb to my first sell target. I wrote in my notebook, "Sell reason: 2B top. This has reached my 28 target, but more importantly, if you look on the weekly chart, the 'normal' price for this from 2001 to 2005 was between 20 and 28. With this now at 28, it is at the top end of that trading range. Time to sell. This has also shown 2B weakness, a potential double top that could see price drop back to 17, worst case."

Figure 4.6 shows how price peaked at A and then formed the second top at B. If price then closed below 23, it would have confirmed the pattern as a double top, but that did not happen. After B, price made a strong one-day move lower, to C. I decided to sell and the stock filled the next day at the open, 27.95. I made 33 percent on the trade with a hold time of about 10 months.

This trade is an example of exiting at a 2B top. It is not a wonderful example since price climbed for two weeks after I sold but then it dropped—not much, but it hit 25 in March.

If you look at the price chart after June 2010 and before the price adjustment for the spin off of a subsidiary in October 2011, you will see that the stock made large price swings, forming a broadening top, before making a strong push up to 40. Then its world ended and the stock took a toboggan ride down to 8 and change. That is quite a drop (78 percent) from 40.

The 2B top is often a temporary peak, especially in a bull market, when the market current is pulling everything higher. Selling prematurely is the chance you take when trading a 2B. However, if you are a swing trader, the 2B can get you out near a short-term peak. Then you can take your money and invest it elsewhere in another swing trade.

- A 2B top is often a temporary peak but sometimes it indicates a lasting reversal.

TRADING EXAMPLE: SWINGING CNO

Sometimes traders get lucky, and the CNO swing trade pictured in **Figure 4.7** is one example of that.

My notes to the trade say that I bought the stock on May 5, 2009, because of a flat base. As I look at the chart, I do not really see a flat base. Flat bases are often long features, say, several months to a year or more in duration.

The only flat base I see is better categorized as a roof chart pattern, and the figure shows a wonderful example of it. Price rests on a flat base but peaks in the middle of the pattern with an up-sloping start and a down-sloping finish. It *looks* like the roof of a house.

The risk associated with trading this stock was of a rumor circulating that the company could file for bankruptcy. However, the company straightened out the auditor's concerns and insiders were buying huge amounts of stock.

When price started moving up, I bought and received a fill at 1.64.

FIGURE 4.7 This swing trade, coupled with an inverted dead-cat bounce, led to a 111 percent gain in a week.

Six days later, May 11, the company released earnings before the market open. The stock gapped higher and I sold, receiving a fill at 3.47 and making 111 percent in a week.

One of the rules I obey is not to buy a stock within three weeks of an earnings announcement. My notes show a date of April 5 when I first started looking at the stock, with a May 4 earnings announcement date. At that time, the announcement was far enough away that it did not concern me. Apparently, I forget to check for an updated earnings date and got lucky when the stock cooperated. Had I known earnings were going to be released, I would not have made the trade.

This trade is also an example of exiting after doubling your money, something I suggest doing with risky positions, such as biotech stocks. Notice how the stock behaved after the sale: The price dropped.

- An inverted dead-cat bounce presents a selling opportunity.

CHAPTER CHECKLIST

The following checklist summarizes the selling techniques outlined in this chapter.

☐ Sometimes selling for tax reasons can be a mistake. See the introduction.

☐ Determine how far price is likely to move before selling a holding or shorting a stock. See "Selling Ideas."

☐ If support is closer than 5 percent, a downward breakout may push through it. See "Selling Ideas."

☐ The decline one month after a breakout is often small and tends to lessen because price rises over time. See Table 4.1.

☐ Identify diamond tops and bottoms: see "Diamond Tops and Bottoms."

☐ Price may overshoot or undershoot the entry to a chart pattern. Ignore it when determining whether the chart pattern is a top or bottom. Instead, use the primary price trend as the direction of entry. See "Overshoot, Undershoot, and Identifying Diamonds."

☐ Many diamond patterns tilt to one side and can appear irregularly shaped. See "Overshoot, Undershoot, and Identifying Diamonds."

☐ Quick declines sometimes follow quick rises. See "Diamond Price Behavior."

☐ A pullback may end the decline if the industry and/or market are trending higher. See "Diamond Price Behavior."

☐ See "Diamond Trading Tips" for, well, trading tips.

☐ See "Complex Head-and-Shoulders Top" for identification guidelines.

☐ See "Trading a Complex Head-and-Shoulders Top" for trading tips.

☐ If price forms a 2B top in a swing trade, then sell. See "2B."

☐ Sometimes using a profit target exit makes sense. See "Hit Target."

☐ See "Overhead Resistance" for selling tips.

☐ If price rises by 5 to 20 percent or more in one session, consider selling. See "Inverted Dead-Cat Bounce."

☐ If a risky stock doubles in price, then sell it or sell a portion of it. See "Double Your Money."

☐ Look at how other stocks in the same industry behave. They may show the same chart pattern. See "Chart Pattern Trend Change."

☐ Avoid buying and consider selling stocks in stages 3 or 4. See "Weinstein's Approach."

☐ Improve your trading skills instead of focusing on the money. See "Weakness."

☐ If the fundamentals change, then consider selling. See "Fundamentals."

☐ Diversify your holdings so that any one position does not dominate your portfolio. See "Diversification."

☐ If price pierces support, expect a swift decline. See "Support Pierced."

☐ Symmetrical triangles can make for good exit signals. See "Symmetrical Triangle."

☐ Try to sell at the top of the dead-cat bounce. See "Dead-Cat Bounce."

☐ Sell if overhead resistance looks like it will reverse a trend. See "Resistance."

☐ Wait for bearish chart patterns to confirm before selling a stock. See "Head-and-Shoulders Top."

☐ Try to predict how far price will move, set a target, and use a stop to protect profits. See "Trading Example: The Teradyne Exit."

☐ A 2B top is often a temporary peak, but sometimes it indicates a lasting reversal. See "Trading Example: Exiting Forest."

☐ An inverted dead-cat bounce presents a selling opportunity. See "Trading Example: Swinging CNO."

CHAPTER 5

Event Pattern Setups

Have you ever felt like telling an analyst to keep quiet (to be polite), because what he or she said just sliced big bucks off your net worth? Whether it is a downgrade or new guidance on a company's prospects, analysts' words can send a stock tumbling. However, each move provides the nimble swing trader with an opportunity to profit.

When stocks make similar patterns because of repeatable events, I call them event patterns. For swing traders, these events might be as delicious as peanut butter and jelly. However, event patterns are a treacherous bunch because the move after them often does not last long and there is a wide variation in how each stock behaves. This chapter takes a closer look at several of the more common event patterns.

Let the trading setups discussed in this chapter serve as kindling for a fire of ideas. Use those ideas to build and shape a robust and effective trading plan that will make you big bucks. If that does not happen, then be sure to have children that can take care of you when you get older.

For a complete treatment of event patterns, refer to the latest edition of my *Encyclopedia of Chart Patterns* book.

COMMON STOCK OFFERINGS SETUP

In *Fundamental Analysis and Position Trading*, Chapter 11 reviewed some of the findings related to common stock offerings. If you are serious about swing trading this event pattern, then review the material under the heading "Event Pattern: Common Stock Offerings" in that chapter. This section puts those results to work for swing traders. First is a description of the pattern, followed by an example, and then test results.

During a common stock offering, a company announces the sale of stock to the public (not an initial public offering and not to private individuals or institutions) often at a discount to the current market price. That announcement sends the stock tumbling (92 percent of stocks drop when news of the announcement hits the market), but the severity of the decline varies from 0 to 12 percent about evenly, with some drops substantially more (almost 50 percent). It is what happens after the decline ends that is exciting, so get the popcorn ready.

Unless you are an insider, trying to anticipate the offering is ill advised and probably a waste of time anyway. Instead, view the offering as an opportunity to buy shares on sale like buying a snow blower in summer or a bikini in winter.

- The best performance comes when price trends down before the announcement, but the breakout is upward.

The performance difference, 24 percent versus 21 percent, is not much, but a trading edge is a trading edge.

Let me explain the measurement. It begins from the *trend start*, which is the highest high or lowest low *before* which price drops or rises, respectively, at least 20 percent (see Chapter 20 of *Fundamental Analysis and Position Trading*, under the heading "Trend Start"). The trend start determines the inbound trend direction, either up or down, leading to the common stock offering.

The event pattern lasts from the announcement of the offering to the day it is priced. Sometimes, those two announcements occur in the same press release, but a week or more can separate them. For an upward breakout, price has to close above the range made between those days. For a downward breakout, price has to close below the range.

I measured the move using the highest price (upward breakout) or lowest price (downward breakout) during the event to the *ultimate high* (or low), which is the highest high (or low) before a trend change—before price drops/rises at least 20 percent, respectively. The definitions for trend start and ultimate high/low are the same ones I used in my other books.

All of this is a complicated way of saying reversals of the inbound price trend outperform continuations when the breakout is upward. Downward breakouts show no tradable difference (11 percent drop for continuations and 12 percent for reversals—the effect is still there, it is just muted).

In short, look for a reversal of the downward price trend after the company announces the offering price.

- Price tends to make lower highs for a few days, so trail a buy stop a penny above the lowest high until buying the stock.

If there is a delay between the announcement and pricing of the offering (the average is 3.4 days, but the median is 1 day), then expect price to drop between those two dates. Do *not* take a long position until you know the price at which the company is offering the stock. Knowing the offering price gives you an idea of how far price might drop. Consider it a floor, but one that might not hold much weight.

After the company announces the offering price, the stock should drop. If you want to own the stock, place a buy stop a penny above the prior day's high, trailing it lower, until the order executes. This technique works well for this event pattern since price tends to drop, making lower highs, until price reverses.

The only time this technique is a danger is if the stock continues dropping. That is a real possibility, so be sure to qualify the stock by researching the company before buying. Since more shares will be outstanding, quarter-to-quarter and year-to-year comparisons of earnings per share, book value per share, and so on, will be weaker going forward.

Also, the company is issuing new stock for a reason. Find out what they intend to do with that money. If they are struggling to pay their bills, then consider looking elsewhere for a more promising situation. If they want to build a new factory, then that is a plus. They are investing and growing their business and need the capital to help. That will enhance future growth.

- Price bottoms or peaks quickly. In two weeks or less, 65 percent reach bottom after a downward breakout and 49 percent peak after an upward breakout.

For this event pattern, as I explained, a breakout occurs when price closes outside of the high-low range between the initial announcement and the day the company prices the offering.

Like most event patterns, the effect of the event is usually short-lived—a week or two. The stock drops after the company prices the offering and continues down for two weeks, but then the stock should begin to recover. When the downtrend ends, that is the time to buy, providing the quality of the company merits owning it.

How long does it take the stock to return to the price the day before the announcement (bull market, after a downward breakout)? The median recovery time is 29 calendar days, but the average is 77. A frequency distribution shows that 39 percent recover within 10 days, but 26 percent take over 100 days. Between those two extremes, the numbers are single digits. Thus, recovery can be quick or long.

* The median recovery time for the stock to return to the pre-announcement close is 29 calendar days.

Atlas Air Example

Figure 5.1 shows a common stock offering by Atlas Air Worldwide Holdings (AAWW). The stock made a short-term bottom in July 2009, but a wider view (not shown) reveals a major bottom in March 2009, along with the rest of the market. That is when the bear market turned bullish.

Thus, the stock was trending upward when the company announced a common stock offering at A, for 5.25 million shares. As the figure shows, price gapped lower on the news. However, on the same day, the company announced "a 181 percent increase in net earnings for the third quarter of 2009 compared to the third quarter of 2008," but revenue dropped from $460.7 million to $255.5 million. It is hard to say which event—or if both— were responsible for sending the stock lower.

FIGURE 5.1   This chart shows a common stock offering by Atlas Air Worldwide.

At B, the company priced the offering at 25.75, but reduced the number of shares offered to 4 million along with an option for 600,000 shares sold to the underwriters.

The AB span represents the event pattern. A close above A or a close below B would constitute a breakout. In this case, price broke out downward.

At C, the company announced completion of the offering, selling 4.6 million shares.

Using the buy-and-hold setup discussed in the introduction to this chapter, you would place a buy stop a penny above B initially. Each day, lower the buy stop to a penny above the prior day's high until the stock hits the stop. That would occur at the open at E.

Then, place a limit order to sell when price returns to the close before the company made the announcement. That date is shown by point D. The trade made 33 percent in just over a month.

Trading Offers

Based on the ideas discussed so far, I programmed my computer to find a trading setup by going long once the high price stopped dropping and exiting after either being triggered by a trailing stop or price reaching the close the day before announcement of the offering. On a $10,000 investment, each trade made an average of $53.35 with a 43 percent success rate.

If I required a 3 to 1 reward/risk ratio before trading, then the gain climbed to $167.68, but just 19 percent of trades win. On a $10,000 investment, that is a gain of 1.7 percent.

Excuse me while I yawn.

Since the stock drops, I thought I would try shorting the event. The numbers were worse! Each trade lost $62.57 but won 34 percent of the time.

The only setup I tried that made enough money to make things interesting is to buy and hold. Here are the rules/testing procedures I used.

- Each trade gets $10,000.
- Commissions were $10 per trade ($20 round trip).
- The 267 common stock offerings came from the period March 2004 to November 2009. The period included the 2007–2009 bear market.
- After the company prices the offering, set a buy stop a penny above the day's high and trail it lower.
- If the difference between the buy-in price and the close before the company announced (not priced) the offering is less than 10 percent, then skip the trade. I want at least a 10 percent profit margin.
- Once in the trade, set a limit order to exit when the stock reaches the closing price the day before the offering announcement.

TABLE 5.1 Testing Buy-and-Hold on Common Stock Offerings

Bull Market Only	Result
Average profit per trade	$2,500.35
Average gain on $10,000	25%
Average maximum hold time loss	−14%
Win/loss ratio	100%
Average hold time	116 days
Number of trades	65

Bull and Bear Markets	Result
Average profit per trade	$2,697.91
Average gain on $10,000	27%
Average maximum hold time loss	−17%
Win/loss ratio	100%
Average hold time	127 days
Number of trades	71

Table 5.1 shows the results for varying market conditions.

The setup requires that you hold until price returns to the pre-announcement close. Selling before that could mean a loss. That is why every trade became a winner, even during a bear market. The average maximum hold time loss per trade is the maximum drop while owning the stock, averaged for all trades. Since it is an average and is not an equity drawdown that most software packages report, consider doing your own testing.

SURVIVING A DEAD-CAT BOUNCE

I did not coin the term "dead-cat bounce" (DCB) to describe this event pattern, so do not blame me, even though I prefer dogs.

As the name suggests, this event pattern occurs when price makes a substantial drop, bounces, and then continues lower. **Figure 5.2** shows an example of a dead-cat bounce based on a study using 887 bull market samples from July 1991 to February 2011.

The dead-cat bounce, by definition, takes price down between 15 and 70 percent or more in one session, but that often does not complete the decline. Price continues dropping for an average of six days, sinking 32 percent below the close before the event started. That plunge is called the event decline.

- The event decline sees price drop an average of 32 percent in six days.

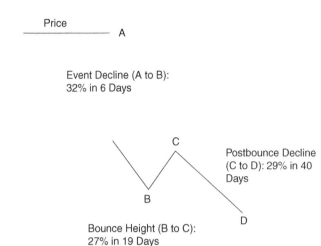

FIGURE 5.2   The average dead-cat bounce scenario.

Events, such as when a company says that quarterly earnings will fall short of expectations, can cause a massive drop. The event is such a surprise that investors need to change their underwear: Price gaps lower 77 percent of the time. The most likely drop ranges between 25 and 40 percent (70 percent of the samples fall within that range) and takes just two days (52 percent of samples) to hit bottom.

Once the drop completes, price bounces. The bounce averages 27 percent in 19 days. The most likely bounce ranges between 15 percent and 25 percent (53 percent of samples) and takes up to 15 days (63 percent of samples).

• The bounce sees price rise an average of 27 percent in 19 days.

Here is the big surprise. After the bounce finishes, price resumes dropping. The average drop is 29 percent and takes 40 days before it bottoms. It drops up to 30 percent most often (encompassing 62 percent of samples) and takes up to 50 days to finish dropping (68 percent of samples).

• The postbounce drop averages 29 percent in 40 days.

Large event declines lead to larger bounces. If the event decline is larger than the 29 percent median, the bounce averages 37 percent. Those stocks with event declines that are less than the median bounce only 21 percent.

• The larger the event decline, the larger the bounce.

One dead-cat bounce follows another 29 percent of the time within three months and 42 percent within six months, since problems that cause these types of events are not solved quickly. To put it another way, there is a 29 to 42 percent chance of a second dead-cat bounce within three to six months, respectively. That should send a chill down the spine of every investor and most swing traders.

- Another dead-cat bounce follows the first one between 29 percent and 42 percent of the time within three to six months.

I recall spitting expletives at management of Michaels Stores during each of the 18 times it dead-cat bounced while I held the stock. My neighbors may have moved away because of it.

If a dead-cat bounce occurred within six months of a stock that you want to buy, then consider looking elsewhere for a more promising situation. Stocks with DCBs tend to underperform more often than do those without DCBs.

- Avoid buying a stock showing a dead-cat bounce within the past six months.

DCB Example

Figure 5.3 shows an example of an actual dead-cat-bounce pattern. After the close on January 24 or before the open the next day, the company reported quarterly earnings that were worse than expected. How do I know that? Because price gapped open lower, 19 percent lower, in fact. The decline did not end there. Rather, price continued dropping until reaching the low at B, a decline of over 25 percent from the close at A.

Traders believed that the stock was on sale, like buying a fishing lure for 25 percent off because it is winter. That buying demand overwhelmed selling pressure and sent the stock moving up. The rise lasted 11 days and during that time, the stock recovered about 10 percent, peaking at C.

After that, a new reality set in and selling pressure forced the stock down to D, a drop of 13 percent. But the decline was not over. The stock continued lower, bottoming at 3.67 in mid August, for a decline of 49 percent from the close the day before the event (A).

- The belief that the event decline is oversold creates buying demand that pushes price higher for a time.

FIGURE 5.3 An example of a dead-cat bounce in Tellabs.

Trading the DCB

If you own stocks long enough, especially holding stocks in industries that are prone to dead-cat bounces, then a stock you own could be hit by a falling body. What do you do? Since the event will often force price to gap lower in one session, you will take a big hit. The easiest way out is to sell the stock during that first day. If Figure 5.3 is a typical example, then price wobbles higher and lower than the opening price (see point E), so maybe you can catch the stock as it rebounds.

If you decide to hold the stock for the long term, the numbers say that the gap closes 20 percent of the time during the bounce phase. In other words, there is a 20 percent chance that price will rise far enough to fill the gaping hole between A and E in Figure 5.3. Within three months, 37 percent of the stocks close the gap and within six months, 55 percent close the gap. Six months later, you will still be wondering what happened to your wallet or purse in almost half the cases.

If you add up the event decline (−32 percent), bounce rise (+27 percent), and postbounce drop (−29 percent), the numbers suggest a drop of 34 percent from top to bottom. The drop averages 18 percent from point B, the event decline low, to where price bottoms at D (assuming that it did in Figure 5.3).

In other words, if you decide to ride out the event decline with the hope that the worst is over, you might be right, but the numbers suggest more monetary potholes ahead.

- Price averages a drop of 18 percent below the event decline low.

Another way to trade the DCB is to sell when price bounces. That looks easy in Figure 5.3, but it is not because trying to determine when price bounces can be difficult. Sometimes the highest bounce the stock sees is the day after the major loss (that is, point C1, and price becomes quicksand thereafter).

I do not have room to show a dozen examples, but perhaps the best thing for you to do is to practice on charts like Figure 5.3 and scroll the figure to the left. See if you can polish your skills at selling during the bounce. The YRC trade discussed in the inverted dead-cat bounce section discusses a DCB (Figure 5.4).

From the short side, wait for the bounce to peak and then short the stock or buy a put. Ride price lower, perhaps following a trendline such that when price closes above the trendline, cover the short or sell the put.

For another example of a dead-cat bounce, flip back to Chapter 22 in *Fundamental Analysis and Position Trading* (under the heading Medivation: Selling Too Late), and read how I handled a dead-cat bounce in a stock I owned.

THE INVERTED DEAD-CAT BOUNCE SETUP

I have made a big to-do about the *inverted* dead-cat bounce (iDCB) throughout this trilogy, but there is not much to tell. The dead-cat bounce is to a nuclear meltdown as the inverted variety is to a winning lottery ticket. In one session, price jumps higher by 5 to 20 percent and sometimes more.

What causes price to jump? Most often, it is earnings related. A company announces earnings that are better than expected and people line up to buy the stock before the market opens. That causes price to gap open higher.

That is the good news, and a swing trader should take the opportunity to exit the stock immediately. After that, and here is the bad news, price often drops—not always—but I have had a number of them occur in stocks I have owned. The smart play is to sell. That is what I do now for stocks I *trade* (not buy-and-hold).

A study of 30,985 iDCBs using data from January 1988 to May 2004 in 253 stocks shows that the rise on the day price jumps upward averages 7.9 percent. The next day, price makes a higher high, showing a total gain of 8.7 percent. Both numbers measure from the close the day before the iDCB to the high of the day(s) after the iDCB. After that, the high price drops and remains below the 8.7 percent gain for three weeks, on average.

All of this means one thing: Either sell on the day price jumps higher or try to time a higher exit the next day. Most often, I just sell as soon as I learn about the iDCB. That means I sell at the open the next day. The next section discusses an actual iDCB trade.

* Price in an inverted dead-cat bounce jumps by 5 to 20 percent or more in one session.

The YRC Worldwide Tour

Sometimes you are in the right place at the right time and that certainly was the situation with YRC Worldwide, the trade shown in **Figure 5.4**.

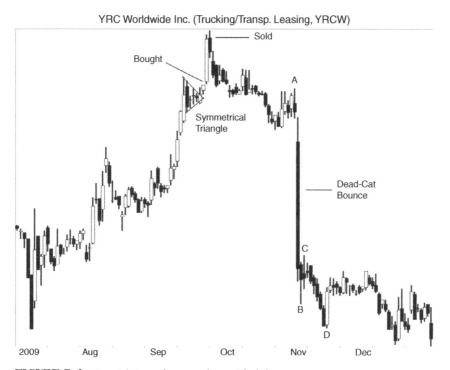

FIGURE 5.4 A quick in-and-out trade avoided disaster.

If you ignore the price action after I sold and look back from 2008 to the day I bought (not shown), the stock on the linear price scale looks like a long flat base, starting in October 2008.

I was worried about bondholders renegotiating terms the following April, so I decided not to buy twice the normal position size. I felt that if they could come to terms, the stock would skyrocket, and if not, then it would plummet. I also did not like the rating services being negative on the stock.

In September 2009, price broke out of a small consolidation region (a symmetrical triangle) formed during the prior week or so. I bought the stock on September 23, as shown on the chart, at the market open, receiving a fill at 4.40 (all prices are before a 1-for-25 reverse split).

By day's end, the stock had climbed to as high as 6.01 but closed lower, at 5.86. That means I made 33 percent, on paper.

In my trading notebook, I wrote, "I think it will make a new [higher] high but close lower. I am just going to sell at the open tomorrow." That is exactly what happened. In fact, the stock peaked the day I sold and started heading lower. It made a dead-cat bounce, which dropped price 64 percent in one session (see Figure 5.4) on news of a debt exchange offer. Then it split 1 for 25 a year later and continued dropping. I was lucky to escape when I did. I sold at the open and received a fill at 5.91, for a one-day gain of 34 percent.

Look again at Figure 5.4. The drop from A to B is the event decline, and it measures 71 percent (close to low). The bounce takes price up to C, a gain of 37 percent (low to high), followed by the postbounce drop, C to D, which measures 38 percent (high to low).

TRADING DUTCH AUCTION TENDER OFFERS

I covered Dutch auction tender offers in Chapter 11 of *Fundamental Analysis and Position Trading*, but here is a refresher. If a company is growing slowly (to boost earnings per share), has an abundance of cash, or views its stock as compelling as chocolate smothering ice cream, then it might choose to invest in itself. That is the idea behind a modified Dutch auction tender offer. The company offers to buy shares within a price range. Stockholders get to decide if they want to sell their shares and at what price.

As a swing trader, how could you profit from the auction process? **Figure 5.5** helps to answer that by showing the typical (median) price behavior based on a study of 107 cases.

The two horizontal lines, the top one at 22.50 and the bottom one at 19.50, represent the high and low range of the median tender offer. Point A

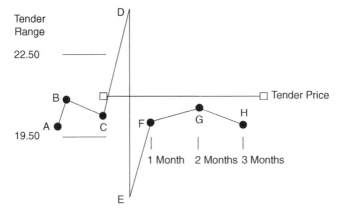

FIGURE 5.5 The median price profile of a stock involved in a Dutch auction tender offer.

is the median price the day before the offer is announced. Its price, 19.73, is slightly above the low range of the offering price of 19.50.

The next day, B, the company announces the tender offer and price shoots up to 20.79. The stock has moved 43 percent across the offering high-low range. Then price trends downward to C, the day the offer expires. The median price is 20.32.

The barbell shaped line above C and extending to the right represents the tender price. The tender price is the final price set by the company to buy the number of shares it wants. Notice that the box, at 21, is above C. If you bought the stock at less than the final tender price, you would make money.

After the auction completes, the price of the stock follows the trail of a balloon. Price skyrockets to D, peaking at a median of 24.30 sometime within three months (that is the range that I limited the measure to), but the rise occurs within the first month most often (48 percent of the time). Price then drops to E and reaches a low of 17.86 sometime with three months. Again, price hits the low within the first month 47 percent of the time, but it occurs after D. Point D is the median of the highest high prices found within three months of the end of the auction. Point E is the same, but it represents the median of all low prices.

Over the next three months, the median closing price does not change much, from 20.15 at F, to 20.50 at G, and ending the period at 20.14 at H.

The chart shows us the template of how the median stock would perform. It gives us an idea of how to trade the auction.

If we buy the stock at a price below the low of the offering range (19.50 in this case), then we can offer it to the company. If our offer is accepted, we make money. However, holding onto the stock gives us a chance of making a larger profit. That is especially true for investors with a buy-and-hold mentality. With fewer shares outstanding, the financial returns such as earnings per share will improve (all else being equal).

We can sell short at D and cover at E. If E comes first, then buy at E and sell at D. If we choose not to participate in the auction or if the company rejects our bid, then we still can make money. I mean that point A (19.73), the day before the announcement, is priced below the three points (F to H, the lowest is H at 20.14) after the auction ends.

- If you bought at the closing price the day before the auction's announcement and sold at the tender price, you would make money 85 percent of the time.
- After the auction ends, price often trades outside of the auction's high-low price range within the first month.

After the Auction

How do you apply the numbers to create a swing trading opportunity? Almost three-quarters of the time, price will be below the tender price at the end of the auction, so tender your shares at a price you think is appropriate.

If you still view the stock as worth owning, then buy it back after the auction ends. Recall (from Chapter 11 of *Fundamental Analysis and Position Trading*) that 95 percent of the time price drops below the tender price within three months of the auction, making a median decline of 13 percent, so try to time the drop. Almost half the time, the low will occur in the first month (16 percent bottom within the first week, 9 percent during week 2, and 11 percent in week 3 with single digit percentages thereafter), so if you tendered the stock for a loss, then watch out for the wash sale rule.

- Nearly all of the time (95 percent), price drops below the tender price within three months of the auction's end.

When the stock rises above the tender price, which happens 79 percent of the time within three months, then consider selling. In 47 percent of the cases, price bottoms first and then rises above the tender price with gains averaging 28 percent, low to high. Thus, there is money to be made by playing the rebound if you are lucky enough to see price bottom first. If you choose to short the stock, you can make money that way as well, but I do not recommend it. I think that fewer shares outstanding means a higher valued stock, one that will rise over time.

- Price rises above the tender price 79 percent of the time within three months of the auction's end.

I looked at the shape the stock makes up to two months after the auction ends. In 32 percent of the cases, price makes a V-shaped drop. In other words, the stock drops and then pulls back. In 36 percent of the cases, the shape is just the opposite: Price rises and then falls. In 14 percent of the cases, the stock just trends lower, and the remaining 18 percent show price rising.

Sorting the trends by buyback size (meaning above or below the 14.6 percent median of shares outstanding) finds that 67 percent of large buybacks have price making either a V-shape or a straight-line run down. For small buybacks, 67 percent have price making either an inverted V or rising.

This finding suggests a way to trade. Most auction news releases describe how many shares are being purchased as a percentage of shares outstanding (or you can do the math yourself). If the percentage is above 14.6 percent, then it is a large buyback. Sell during the auction and wait for price to bottom in a V-shaped or downward move after the auction ends.

For small buybacks, price tends to rise, so hold onto the shares, and sell when price peaks after the auction ends.

- Buybacks of more than 14.6 percent of shares outstanding tend to see price decline after the auction ends. Small buybacks tend to see price rise.

Of course, anything can happen to a stock, so you might want to do an Internet search, find a few Dutch auctions, and practice trading them on paper before committing real money.

EARNINGS SURPRISE SETUP

Earnings surprises come in three flavors: good, bad, and indifferent. I will not be discussing the indifferent flavor since price has as much reaction as does a child tasting tap water. However, let us take a closer look at good earnings announcements.

When a company announces earnings that are better than expected, the stock can take off like a jet fighter leaving the deck of an aircraft carrier. However, that is the exception covered by the inverted dead-cat bounce. Earnings surprises tend to be more relaxed. Here is a list of what to search for.

- Look for the earnings announcement to occur in a rising price trend.
- Price should either gap higher or make a large intraday price swing, creating a candle that is taller than the one-month average. In other

words, the height of the high-low swing on the announcement day (or when it trades next) should be unusually tall.

- Price must break out upward. That means a close above the announcement day's high.

Here are additional tips that may help separate the also-rans from the exceptions.

- Good earnings surprises tend to outperform in a bull market, so check to make sure that the market is also trending upward.
- The industry to which the company belongs should be trending higher, too.
- In a study of almost 400 events in a bull market, the best performers occurred when price was within a third of the yearly low. Second place went to those stocks trading within a third of the yearly high.
- The taller the price bar, the better the stock tends to perform, but the more rare they are.
- The median rise is 11 percent (average is 24 percent), measured from the high on the announcement day to the ultimate high. That means half the time price rises less than 11 percent before the trend reverses.
- For an idea of how far price might rise, calculate the height of the price bar on the announcement day and add it to the day's high. Price reaches the target 75 percent of the time. Alternatively, compute the height and multiply it by 75 percent for a closer, more reliable target.
- Throwbacks occurred 41 percent of the time, but when they did happen, performance suffered. Thus, look for nearby overhead resistance to an upward breakout.
- Expect price to top out quickly after an upward breakout (a close above the announcement day's high): 41 percent peak within the first week, gaining an average of 5 percent.

When swing trading the good earnings announcement, the setup is probably what matters most. Find a quality stock in an industry that is performing well and in a rising market. Look back at prior earnings announcements and see how the stock reacted. Check its competitors to see how the market accepted their earnings. If their stocks made big upward moves, perhaps yours will too.

Table 5.2 shows the percentage change over time, measured from the close the day before the earnings announcement to the close on the announcement day, then a day later, a week later, and so on to three months later. The 688 event patterns (385 in a bull market, 303 from a bear market) occurred from January 1995 to September 2003.

TABLE 5.2 Gains over Time as Measured from Close before Announcement

Sell Date	Day Announced	+1 Day	+1 Week	+2 Weeks	+3 Weeks	+1 Month	+2 Months	+3 Months
Bull market average change	0.4%	2.2%	3.0%	3.5%	4.8%	3.7%	4.0%	5.1%
Bear market average change	0.2%	2.8%	2.9%	4.1%	4.7%	4.2%	0.3%	−4.0%

For example, one week after the announcement, price moved up by 3 percent in a bull market and 2.9 percent in the 2000 to 2002 bear market. The big gain comes the day after the announcement in both bull and bear markets when price shows gains averaging 2.2 percent and 2.8 percent respectively. The strength continues into week 3 for both market conditions, but then weakens going into the next month in a bull market. For a bear market, the weakness continues after week 3 for the remainder of the period studied.

Since the table only shows upward breakouts, wait for price to close above the high posted on the announcement day before taking a position (unless you have a good reason for entering earlier). The breakout should happen quickly, in an average of five calendar days or a median of two (meaning half of all samples will take two days or less to break out). If it takes longer than a week or so, then look elsewhere for a more promising opportunity.

If you do buy into a stock, then look for price to peak beginning two weeks after the announcement. That will be the time to sell. This is especially true in a bear market where a downward current will tend to suck everything lower.

- Price peaks three weeks after the announcement of good earnings.

Good Earnings Example

Figure 5.6 shows an example of an earnings announcement. Price formed an Adam & Eve double bottom at A and B, confirmed when price closed above the peak, C, between the two valleys.

The tall left side at D suggested that this was also a Big-W pattern. If price on the right mirrored the move on the left, then the stock would rise back to the price of D, pause, and then continue higher. As the figure shows, price climbed to E before pausing, but it still fulfilled the Big-W pattern by climbing well above D.

Flir Systems Inc. (Aerospace/Defense, FLIR)

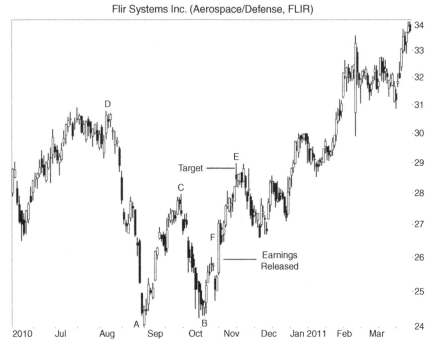

FIGURE 5.6   After an earnings announcement, price moves higher.

The company announced earnings at F. On that day, price made a tall swing, peaking at 27.14, bottoming at 25.48, for a height of 1.66. When added to the price bar's high, the target became 28.80.

After the announcement, price took a few days before finally breaking out upward (a close above the high at F). Then the stock moved up to E, just above the 28.80 target, before retracing. In this example, the target would have made for a wonderfully timed swing trade. Holding through the inevitable retrace meant additional gains, with the stock peaking at over 37 in May 2011, before diving for cover and bottoming at 21.86 in mid-August.

Bad Earnings

Imagine owning a stock that announces worse than expected earnings. What happens to price? It drops, but the numbers suggest that is only the beginning. The decline that follows is not like what happens to a flight attendant who is sucked out of an airliner after the plane's skin peels back. Rather, the decline is more sedate, like a river flowing toward the ocean. Before I discuss the numbers, let us talk more about the event pattern, beginning with identification.

- Look for a tall (high to low) intraday price swing the day the company announces earnings (or the next trading day if the market was closed) that is taller than the 30-day average. Sometimes (8 percent of the time) price gaps lower. The taller the intraday price swing, the better.
- Price must close below the announcement day's low, staging a downward breakout.

That is all there is to identifying a bad earnings announcement. The following may help you select stocks for swing trading that may decline more than usual. For those wishing to maintain their position, the numbers will give you some idea of what to expect.

- Price should be trending downward leading to the earnings announcement.
- Both the market and industry should also be trending lower, preferably in a bear market. If a rising tide lifts all boats, so does a receding tide lower all boats. Trade with the trend.
- If the height of price on the announcement day is two or three times (or more) the 30-day average height, expect a larger postbreakout move.
- Price may bottom in a week or two. If so, then cover your short. A pullback is an indication of this timing. Pullbacks occur 41 percent of the time and take a median of 14 calendar days (15-day average) to return to the announcement day's low price. That means price bottoms sometime before the two-week period.
- The average decline is 13 percent in a bull market and 17 percent in a bear market, but that measures from the high price posted on the breakout day to the ultimate low. The breakout day is when price closes below the announcement day's low. The ultimate low is the lowest low before price changes trend (before it rises at least 20 percent or closes above the announcement day's high).
- A frequency distribution of the time to reach the ultimate low shows that one week after the breakout, 47 percent hit bottom in a bull market and 48 percent bottom in a bear market.
- The decline is often shallow, with 31 percent dropping between 0 and 5 percent, 51 percent dropping less than 10 percent, and with almost half (47 percent) reaching the low in a week (bull market). The drop in a bear market is more severe with 26 percent hitting bottom between declines of 0 to 5 percent, and 57 percent finding the bottom before a decline of 15 percent.
- It takes a median of nine days (but average is 28) to reach the ultimate low.
- When price breaks out downward within a third of the yearly low, the decline tends to be more severe.

- For an idea of how far price might decline, measure the high-low price range on the announcement day and subtract it from the day's low. The result is a target price, which the stock reaches 69 percent of the time.

The numbers above describe how price drops, but not very far or for very long before a bounce begins. It may sound like the wise thing for an investor or position trader to do is to hold onto a long holding and ride out a decline. For a swing trader, the decline does not seem to provide enough oomph to get excited about. However, the numbers only tell part of the story. Here is the rest.

Table 5.3 looks at the how the trades faired over time, beginning with the close on the announcement day compared to the prior day's close. In a bull market, price drops 1.1 percent and in a bear market, it is twice as bad, 2.2 percent. The next day, the loss doubles again to 2.9 percent and 5.1 percent, respectively.

The bear market losses are about twice as large as are those posted in a bull market. Thus, if you want to swing trade this event, then you will have better luck in a bear market.

Sometime between the second and third weeks, we see the effect that pullbacks have on results. The drop shallows somewhat in both bull and bear markets. The reason you do not see a more dramatic improvement is that price may have peaked midweek only to drop back down by the time sampling occurred. Also, since you are dealing with averages of hundreds of samples, the timing will tend to smooth the numbers over time.

Table 5.3 gives a good snapshot of how the average stock behaves after a bad earnings report. What may appear to be a small price drop on the announcement day may only be the start of a growing loss.

- After a bad earnings announcement, price drops and continues lower for two to three weeks before rebounding somewhat and then continuing lower.

TABLE 5.3 Losses over Time as Measured from Close before Announcement

Sell Date	Day Announced	+1 Day	+1 Week	+2 Weeks	+3 Weeks	+1 Month	+2 Months	+3 Months
Bull market average change	−1.1%	−2.9%	−4.1%	−4.3%	−3.8%	−3.6%	−5.8%	−4.0%
Bear market average change	−2.2%	−5.1%	−6.9%	−7.1%	−5.8%	−7.1%	−9.8%	−10.9%

Bad Earnings Example

Figure 5.7 shows two consecutive earnings announcements. The first one begins the day after price peaked (A) at the highest high in about 1.5 years. It took the stock three trading days before price closed below the low on the announcement day, staging a downward breakout. Another three days passed and price pulled back to near the peak, at C.

Novice traders who did not recognize a pullback were in for a shock when price resumed heading downward.

Three months later, with price substantially below the peak near A, the company issued another earnings report. This time the stock gapped lower (B) and continued down for about a month. Price found support at valleys in 2008 and 2009 (not shown) when it bottomed in August below 43.

Shorting the stock or selling a long holding during the descent would have made for a profitable trade or retained more money than selling near the low. Also, notice that one bad quarter follows another. That is not always the case, but sometimes a company can be as difficult to turn as the Titanic.

Raytheon Co. (Aerospace/Defense, RTN)

FIGURE 5.7 Two earnings announcements help send the stock tumbling.

EARNINGS FLAG SETUP

When I first discovered the earnings flag event pattern, I fell in love with it, and traded it more than I should have. Like most event patterns, it is not as reliable as your typical chart pattern. Ten percent fail to have price rise more than 5 percent above the breakout. When judged against most event patterns (the ranking does not include the inverted dead-cat bounce), however, it ranks first for performance. Here is what to look for.

- A company announces surprisingly good earnings, sending the stock higher, creating the start of a flagpole.
- The stock must make an immediate move higher. If it takes longer than two days after the announcement to begin its run, then look elsewhere.
- The flagpole should be a near vertical run of several days' duration. The median flagpole lasts five days.
- After the flagpole, price consolidates, creating the flag. The "flag" need not look like a flag chart pattern at all (a flag has price bouncing between two parallel lines, often slanting against the trend). Any *tight* consolidation region will do, providing it is not too long in duration. The median flag duration is 18 days.
- When price closes above the higher of the flagpole or flag, then that is the buy signal.
- For the best performance, avoid earnings flags in the middle third of the yearly price range. Those near the yearly low or high perform best.
- Throwbacks occur 63 percent of the time, but performance suffers when they occur. Thus, look for nearby overhead resistance before taking a position.
- Eighteen percent top out in the first week, but 48 percent take longer than 70 days to reach the ultimate high, and the average is 114 days (about four months).

Earnings Flag Example

Figure 5.8 shows an example of an earnings flag. The company released earnings before the market opened at E, sending the stock gapping higher. Price continued moving up to B, reaching the top of the flagpole, which started at A. The AB height is 8.11 − 6.26 (high to low), or 1.85.

Price drifts downward to C, forming a brief consolidation region (the flag). Then the stock gaps up on a breakaway gap and powers higher to peak at D.

Using the height of the flagpole gives a target of 1.85 + 7.63, or 9.48, when added to the flag low at C. Price only reaches 8.98 (D).

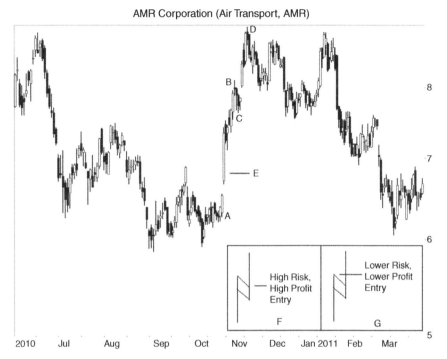

FIGURE 5.8 A good earnings announcement sends price higher, forming a flag and then continuing the move upward.

My study of earnings flags shows that price only reaches the target 86 percent of the time. Thus, for a closer and more reliable target, multiply the height by 86 percent and then add it to the flag low. That would give a target of 1.85 × 86 percent + 7.63, or 9.22 in this example.

As a wreck check, compute the percentage of height to price, namely 1.85 ÷ 7.63 gives 24 percent. That kind of move is certainly possible since the stock already proved that on the way from A to B with a 30 percent gain, but it is a stretch to believe that the stock could continue flying without running into turbulence.

Also, notice that if you wait for price to *close* above the top of the flagpole, you will be giving up precious profit (since you enter at the open a day later). Therefore, you might want to consider using a buy stop a penny above the flagpole (or flag, whichever is higher) as an automated entry mechanism. That will get you in on the same day, but the risk of a failed trade increases. I show this entry in inset G, using the top of the flag/flagpole as the entry price.

I would *not* use a trendline break in the flag as an entry signal. Why? Because price can and often does reverse as it approaches the flagpole top.

The trendline break I am referring to would be a down-sloping one drawn along the flag top. I show this setup in inset F when price pierces the top, down-sloping, flag trendline.

My final suggestion about earnings flags is to find a number of them and see if you can make money paper trading them. Since they happen quarterly in stocks, you will have many opportunities to find prospective candidates.

- Experiment with entering a trade when price rises above the higher of the flag-flagpole instead of a *close* above the pair.
- Divide the height of the event pattern from flagpole base to flagpole top by the lowest low in the flag. If the projected gain is unusually high, then it is probably unrealistic.
- Multiply the flagpole height by 86 percent (which is how often the full height works) to get a closer target.

STOCK UPGRADES AND DOWNGRADES

Before I buy a stock, I review several research reports to learn what I can about a company and its business. I consider their analysis useful because they can kick a company's tires easier than I can. They may turn up something of interest, and if other reports are saying the same thing, then that serves as a significant warning.

I remember looking at the buy/sell/hold rating for a stock and seeing only shades of sell (sell, strong sell). The bloody colors made me think I was watching a CSI episode, and they sent me running for a blanket to hide under. I decided to skip the trade. Another time, I saw only green in Gulfmark Offshore ("strong buy," they said), so I bought the stock and promptly lost money. The stock went nowhere for over 1.5 years. That is a long time to wait for a "strong buy" to perform.

Table 5.4 shows where in the yearly price range upgrades and downgrades occur. For example, 47 percent of the time a rating upgrade occurred in a bull market when the stock was priced within a third of the historical yearly high. Looking ahead a year, only 22 percent remained near the yearly high. As the stock climbed, the upgrade price slid to a lower bracket. That is the type of trend you want to see. In the year after an upgrade, the more upgrades that occur in the lowest third, the timelier was the upgrade. In this case, half of upgrades (50 percent) fell into the low category (bull market).

You might think of this idea as a house being flooded. Water is below the floor and the weatherperson says to expect a flood. If the floor

TABLE 5.4 Yearly Position for Upgrades and Downgrades

	Year Before			Year Ahead		
Upgrade	**High**	**Middle**	**Low**	**High**	**Middle**	**Low**
Bull	47%	30%	23%	22%	28%	50%
Bear	17%	25%	58%	51%	31%	18%
				Bad		**Good**
Downgrade	**High**	**Middle**	**Low**	**High**	**Middle**	**Low**
Bull	40%	26%	34%	26%	26%	48%
Bear	13%	17%	70%	48%	30%	22%
				Good		**Bad**

represents the price of the stock on the upgrade day, and the water represents price over time, the floor (upgrade price) is high in relation to the water level (the current price).

When the flood comes and water reaches the ceiling, the floor (upgrade price) is low compared to the water level (current price). The upgrade price migrated from a high bracket to a low one, and that is what we are looking for in Table 5.4. Yes, it is confusing, and you are probably telling me I am all wet, but the analogy is the best I could think of.

Let me try again with numbers. If a broker upgrades the stock when it is priced at $10, which also happens to be the yearly high, and a year later, the stock is trading at $20, the upgrade price ($10) is low compared to the current price ($20). The "high bracket" at upgrade time moved to a low bracket a year later after price climbed. That high-to-low move is the type of shift you want to see in the table.

Regardless of the market type (bull or bear), upgrades should see a high percentage in the low bracket a year after the announcement if the upgrade had merit.

Brokers issuing upgrades did well in a bull market. Even if they upgraded a stock making a new yearly high, the stock tended to climb the next year (sliding the 47 percent, high bracket number, into the low bracket and populating it with 50 percent of the samples).

In a bear market, stock upgrades were untimely. Yes, 58 percent of those stock upgrades were near the yearly low on the upgrade day, but the upgrade became near the yearly high as price tumbled. Just 18 percent were near the yearly low after the upgrade. In a bear market, buying stocks after a broker upgrade made you broker.

Using numbers, if our $10 stock was at the yearly low on the day a broker upgraded the stock in a bear market, the upgrade price would be considered high if the stock dropped a year later to $5. The bracket shifted from low to high. If the broker's upgrade was right, the stock should have moved higher during the coming year, not lower, thereby remaining in the low bracket.

- Ignore stock upgrades in a bear market.

Downgrades

For downgrades, you want to see the reverse. It is not important where in the historical yearly high-low range a downgrade occurs, it is what happens to the stock the following year. A perfect downgrade would see the price on the downgrade day within a third of the year-ahead high. That means the stock must have tumbled a year after the downgrade, regardless of whether it was a bull or bear market.

To put it another way, when the floodwaters (current stock price) are near the ceiling and the weatherperson says the water will recede in the coming year – and it does—that is a good call. The high water mark represents the price of the downgrade. It is near the ceiling (a high bracket) and the water (current price) recedes below the floorboards (to a low bracket). The price at which the downgrade occurred migrated from low to high as price dropped.

To use numbers, a $20 stock at the time of the downgrade became a $10 stock as price tumbled a year later. The $20 downgrade price is high compared to the $10 price. If the downgrade was a timely one, the high bracket a year later should have a high percentage.

Table 5.4 shows that just 26 percent of the stocks were within a third of the yearly high during the year after a downgrade compared to 40 percent on the day of downgrade. In other words, the stocks that they predicted would underperform actually improved. Price climbed, pushing the upgrade price into a lower bracket.

The bear market numbers show that 70 percent of stocks receiving a downgrade were within a third of the yearly low and price tended to drop during the next year—which is good for a downgrade. Just 22 percent remained near the yearly low, meaning price climbed, sending the downgrade price into a higher bracket.

To make interpretation of the statistics easier, I have added "good" and "bad" labels in the appropriate columns of Table 5.4. You want to see high percentages in the good column(s) and low percentages in the bad column(s).

- Downgrades in a bull market tend to be less effective than downgrades in a bear market.

An Example

Figure 5.9 shows upgrades and downgrades by various brokers. The first, at A, downgraded the stock from "market outperform" to "market perform." Based on the stock's swift rise after the event, the downgrade was a mistake.

Notice how price moved higher, rounded over, and bottomed at E. That hooking action is something that *upward* breakouts from both upgrades and downgrades share. The upward hook from A to E is unusual for downgrades (you see it more often with upgrades since an upgrade is interpreted as good news, sending the stock higher only to collapse in a week or two).

Point B is another upgrade that has the distinction of coming near the top of a straight-line run. It is as if they are yelling, "Buy now, suckers!"

The downgrade at C from "top pick" to "sector perform," while a good short-term call, is peculiar. The same firm upgraded the stock to "outperform" at D, the day before earnings came out at H.

At G, a firm initiated coverage of the stock with a "buy" rating, and the stock promptly dropped.

The real test of an upgrade or downgrade will not be short term in its effect as the chart suggests, but longer-term in its timeliness. For example, if the stock performs as well as the general market in the coming months,

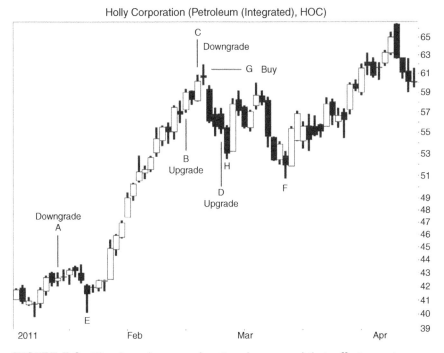

FIGURE 5.9 The chart shows stock rating changes and their effect on price.

then the downgrade at A would be the right call. However, a near 50 percent gain in two months is not what I consider "market perform."

Notice the looping action from B to D. Another example of this looping motion is the D to F move. D is another upgrade that occurs in a falling price trend. The stock moves up in a choppy manner and then rounds back over to bottom at F. After F, a recovery sets in that sees price moving up.

I mention the looping price action because it is a common occurrence. For upward breakouts, when price closes above the announcement day's high, price tends to move higher for one to three weeks before cresting.

For downward breakouts, where price closes below the low posted on the day of the upgrade or downgrade, price drops for two weeks or less before beginning to recover.

You might look for this looping price behavior to see if it is a pattern worth trading. You can enter using a conditional order to buy at the open if price closes above the high or below the low posted on the announcement day. Then, watch price and expect it to peak or trough in a few weeks.

Once price has finished looping, either up or down, then you might reenter the stock. Broker up- and downgrades tend to affect the stock for a week or two, and that is it. That is a generalization, of course, so check your stock to see how it behaves (look at past upgrades and downgrades).

If you are interested in owning the stock, then perhaps you can pick it up at a lower price once it finishes bouncing around after an upgrade or downgrade. In other words, do your homework before you go shopping.

Here are some trading tips.

- Upward breakouts tend to see price rise for one to three weeks before reversing.
- Downward breakouts after an *upgrade* see price drop for about two weeks before recovering, but 38 percent will see price drop less than 5 percent. Be careful trading downward breakouts.
- For downgrades, about 25 percent will not see price rise or fall more than 5 percent after an upward or downward breakout, respectively.
- Swing trade in the direction of the breakout, but expect price to reverse quickly.
- A safer way to swing trade upgrades and downgrades is to wait for price to reverse after the breakout and then take a position. In Figure 5.9, that means buying after E, H, or F.
- Compute the height of the announcement day's high-low price range and add it to the high price or subtract it from the low price for up and down price targets, respectively. This works at least 67 percent of the time (for up- or downgrades, up or down breakouts), but can be as high as 81 percent for upgrades with upward breakouts.

STOCK SPLITS

When a company splits its stock, it is not like breaking an arm or a leg. In fact, it is rather painless. It cuts the stock's price, but increases the number of shares outstanding. If a dividend is paid, it slices that, too.

For example, on June 14, 2010, Danaher split its stock 2 for 1. Price before the split was 78.66. After the split, the price on that day dropped to 39.33—exactly half what it was. The number of shares outstanding changed from 324,484,000 shares in the 10-Q filed on April 22, 2010, to 652,478,000 shares on July 22, 2010. The share count doubled (plus a bit extra) between the two periods.

If you owned 100 shares at 78.66 before the split, you would own 200 shares at 39.33 after the split. The total value of those shares did not change: $7,866.

If the stock paid an annual dividend of $1, it would pay $0.50 per share after the split. You would make $100 in dividend payments in the year before and after the split.

Years ago, I looked at the price history of a stock I owned and examined the behavior of it after two forward splits. In each case, the stock declined. Based on that research, I sold the stock just before the next split. What happened? The stock climbed. Go figure.

- Neither a forward nor a reverse stock split has any effect on the value of a holding.

Academic Research

Fama, Fisher, Jensen, and Roll (1969) wrote a paper that said, "expected returns cannot be increased by purchasing split securities after the splits have become effective. After the split, on the average the returns on split securities immediately resume their normal relationships to market returns." Their evidence suggests that any price increase surrounding a stock split is due to the anticipated rise in future dividends.

A paper by Grinblatt, Masulis, and Titman (1984) says, "there is a significant increase in a firm's stock price at the announcement and that, in general, this upward revision of the firm's value cannot be attributed to any other contemporaneous announcements. This increase may be partially due to forecasts of imminent increases in cash dividends, but a subsample of stocks that paid no dividends in the three years prior to the announcement displays similar price behavior."

Ikenberry, Rankine, and Stice (1996) discuss their study with results that are often cited. They found that the excess returns are 8 percent in the first year and 12 percent in the first three years after a stock split compared to stocks that do not split using 1,275 samples of 2 for 1 stock splits. Those percentages do not include a 3 percent announcement return, either.

Desai and Jain (1997) found nearly the same results, with gains averaging 7 percent and 12 percent over the 1- and 3-year periods, respectively, using 5,596 forward stock splits from 1976 to 1991. Seventy-six reverse stock splits over the same period showed abnormal returns of –11 percent and –34 percent (losses) over the 1- and 3-year periods.

Martell and Webb (2005) use data on Nasdaq stocks from 1982 to 2003, whittling down the number of reverse stock splits to 1,199. They write, "Reverse split stocks generally experience significant under-performance afterward." They found that the median excess return from stocks reverse splitting during the 1980s and 1990s was a drop of 27 percent six months after the split. However, for the 2000 to 2003 bear market years, they found that the median post-split excess return was a decline of 13 percent. They conclude that stocks with reverse splits tend to do better when the split occurred in a poor (bear) market.

The historical research seems to be contradictory, at least in part. I did not study the effect of dividends, but looked at performance over the near term.

My Results

I found 960 splits from 517 stocks stretching from June 1981 to July 2010. **Table 5.5** shows the close-to-close price change of the Standard & Poor's S&P 500 index and various stocks from one month before to three months after each split, dividends not included. All values measure using the closing price the day before the split took place.

For example, one week after a 2 for 1 stock split, the S&P was flat (0 percent), but the split stocks showed losses averaging 1 percent. Three months after a 3 for 1 split, the S&P was down 2 percent, but the split stocks had gains averaging 2 percent. Few samples were involved, so the numbers are likely to change.

The two "All" rows show average gains or losses for all ratios of stock splits, except for reverse splits. The two "Rev" rows show the *average* performance over time of stocks with reverse splits only, with the last row showing the median performance.

The "Min Samples" column shows the fewest number of samples involved in the test. Few samples can give unreliable results.

The "Max Value" column highlights the highest value in each row to help make comparisons easier, but it does not include the move before the split. The column shows that there is not a significant difference between the average performance of the S&P 500 index and various stocks involved in forward stock splits.

TABLE 5.5 Common Stock Split Ratios and Performance over Time

Ratio	1 Month Before*	1 Week After*	2 Weeks After*	3 Weeks After*	1 Month After*	2 Months After*	3 Months After*	Max Value	Min Samples
2:1 S&P	1%	0%	0%	0%	0%	1%	1%	1%	558
2:1 Stock	4%	-1%	0%	0%	0%	-1%	-1%	0%	558
3:1 S&P	0%	0%	0%	0%	1%	-1%	-2%	1%	35
3:1 Stock	-4%	3%	1%	1%	-1%	-4%	2%	3%	35
3:2 S&P	1%	0%	0%	0%	1%	1%	2%	2%	231
3:2 Stock	4%	0%	0%	-1%	-1%	0%	2%	2%	231
All S&P	1%	0%	0%	0%	0%	1%	1%	1%	905
All Stock	3%	0%	0%	0%	0%	-1%	1%	1%	905
Avg rev S&P	1%	0%	1%	1%	1%	3%	3%	3%	103
Avg rev Stock	-7%	2%	3%	-1%	-1%	9%	11%	11%	103
Rev Median	-10%	-3%	-3%	-4%	-7%	-4%	-6%	-3%	103

*The actual measures are 31 days before the split; and 7, 14, 21, 31, 62, and 93 days after the split—all measured starting from the day before the split.

127

Notice, however, that stocks tend to gain 4 percent leading to the day before a 2:1 or 3:2 stock split versus a 1 percent rise for the index. When you include all splits, the index gains 1 percent versus 3 percent for stocks.

How often do stocks rise above the index's 1 percent in the month preceding a stock split? Answer: 62 percent of the time. That is a bit shy of 2 out of 3. If your crystal ball works, then buy stocks that will split in the near future. According to my data, the performance results between stocks that split and the S&P index are not strong enough on which to base a trading strategy.

- Stocks gain 3 percent during the month before a stock split, climbing higher than the S&P 500 index 62 percent of the time.

Reverse Stock Splits

Reverse splits are just like forward splits except the ratio is reversed. If a company declares a 1-for-2 reverse stock split, your 200 shares become 100 shares at twice the price. The number of shares outstanding drops by half and any dividend payment doubles. The *value* of the shares remains the same. However, liquidity can become an issue since a smaller number of shares will be outstanding. Expect fewer shares to trade.

For example, American International Group (AIG) did a 1 for 20 reverse stock split in July 2009 for a closing price of 18.08 from a pre-split price of 18.08 ÷ 20, or 90 cents.

Stocks will reverse split their shares often when an exchange threatens them with delisting. The Nasdaq exchange requires a minimum of $1 per share, for example. If the stock remains below $1 for too long (like six months), the exchange can kick them off.

Look back at Table 5.1. Notice that the average price drops 7 percent leading to the start of a reverse split. If you own the stock, that is not a happy omen. The median is even worse: a drop of 10 percent! In fact, the academic research says that stockholders view reverse stock splits as bad news, and forward stock splits as good news.

Three months after a reverse stock split, the S&P 500 index shows an average rise of 3 percent. Now look at stocks with reverse splits. They gain 11 percent. Wow! But there are two catches. First, the table does not include companies that stopped trading (were delisted or went bankrupt), and there were a lot of them for the reverse split rows. Second, the numbers are averages, pulled up by large gains. The bottom row in the table shows the median (mid range) return over time. It remains negative (loss).

How many of the 103 reverse stock splits posted gains? Answer: between 42 percent (after two months) and 45 percent (three months) of the time. Yuck! Those that gained did very well, pulling up the overall average. The average gain of those stocks rising three months after a reverse stock split was 36 percent. The average loss of those stocks dropping three months after a reverse split was 35 percent.

- Three months after a reverse split, price is down 55 percent of the time, losing an average of 35 percent.

SETUP: TRADING REVERSE SPLITS

Let us take the case of swing trading reverse stock splits. Here is a three-step trading setup based on the idea that avoids buying falling stocks, but jumps into ones that soar.

1. Place a buy stop a penny above the high on the day of the reverse split.
2. If the buy stop triggers, hold for three months.
3. Sell at the close.

Based on 83 trades, this would make an average of 15 percent, with a win/loss ratio of 49 percent. The three-month hold time is arbitrary, but it is based on the results shown in Table 5.1. It is possible that longer— or shorter—hold times might work better. To avoid curve fitting, I did not check.

I do not recommend this setup based on the few trades in the study. Why? Because the median return using this setup is actually a loss of 4 percent. That means half of all trades lost more than 4 percent. Commissions were not included, so performance was actually worse.

An alternative to this setup is to place a stop loss order a penny below the low on the day of the split. However, this reduces the average gain to 10 percent with the median turning into a loss of 7 percent, and the stop slices the win/loss ratio to just 17 percent! In other words, it may limit losses, but it kills the big winners, too. The large drop in the win/loss ratio suggests that this trading setup has large drawdowns, so be prepared for a bumpy ride.

Trend Filter

I added a trend filter to the three-step setup and results improved. If price trended upward leading to the split, then take the trade. For this filter, I just checked the price a month (31 calendar days) before the split and compared it to the closing price the day before the split.

The average gain from the 24 trades was 19 percent with a median gain of 2 percent. No commission or other charges were included. The win/loss ratio climbed to 58 percent.

If price trends downward going into the split then the average gain drops to just 9 percent (median loss of 6 percent) and the win/loss ratio drops to 46 percent. Thus the inbound trend is important to trading results.

- For better performance, only buy stocks with a rising price trend in the month before the reverse split.

Split Ratio Filter

I tried another filter, starting with the three entry rules outlined earlier. I guessed that companies that reverse split their stocks with high ratios have lower priced stocks and represent weaker situations. I found the median split ratio was 1 to 6 and used that as the difference between higher ratios (1 to 100) and smaller ones (1 to 2). I applied that filter to the trades and found that smaller ratios resulted in better performance than the higher ones.

For stocks with high split ratios (41 trades), the average gain was 17 percent, but the median was a loss of 6 percent. Trades worked 44 percent of the time. For small split ratios (42 trades), the average gain dropped to 11 percent, but the median turned into a gain of 6 percent with 55 percent of the trades being profitable. Commissions and other fees were not included.

Short Sell Trades

Since price drops after a reverse split more often than it rises, how about shorting a stock that reverse splits? Here are the four rules I tested.

1. Sell short a penny below the low on the day of the reverse split.
2. Place a stop a penny above the split day's high.
3. If the order triggers, hold for 3 months.
4. Cover at the close.

This did not test well either, making an average of 1 percent for the three-month hold time (shorter, of course, if stopped out), and that did not include commissions. The median return was a loss of 3 percent (meaning price climbed) for the 90 trades. Only 19 percent of them were profitable.

When including a trend filter to make sure price is *declining* going into the split, the average gain doubles to 2 percent (median 5 percent loss) for the 66 trades, but only 15 percent of them make a profit. Again, commissions or other charges were excluded.

CHAPTER CHECKLIST

Event patterns provide the swing trader with opportunities to make a profit using market behavior. Here are some tips to consider when trading event patterns.

☐ The best performance comes when price trends down before announcement of the common stock offering, but the breakout is upward. See "Common Stock Offerings Setup."

☐ Price tends to make lower highs for a few days, so trail a buy stop a penny above the lowest high until buying the stock. See "Common Stock Offerings Setup."

☐ Price bottoms or peaks quickly. In two weeks or less, 65 percent reach bottom after a downward breakout and 49 percent peak after an upward breakout. See "Common Stock Offerings Setup."

☐ The median recovery time for the stock to return to the pre-announcement close is 29 calendar days. See "Common Stock Offerings Setup."

☐ For a trading setup on common stock offerings, see "Trading Offers."

☐ The event decline of a dead-cat bounce sees price drop an average of 32 percent in six days. See "Surviving a Dead-Cat Bounce."

☐ The bounce phase sees price rise an average of 27 percent in 19 days. See "Surviving a Dead-Cat Bounce."

☐ The postbounce drop averages 29 percent in 40 days. See "Surviving a Dead-Cat Bounce."

☐ The larger the event decline, the larger the bounce. See "Surviving a Dead-Cat Bounce."

☐ Another dead-cat bounce follows the first one between 29 percent and 42 percent of the time within three to six months. See "Surviving a Dead-Cat Bounce."

☐ Avoid buying a stock showing a dead-cat bounce within the past six months. See "Surviving a Dead-Cat Bounce."

☐ The belief that the event decline is oversold creates buying demand that pushes price higher for a time. See "DCB Example."

☐ Price averages a drop of 18 percent below the event decline low. See "Trading the DCB."

☐ Price in an inverted dead-cat bounce jumps up by 5 to 20 percent or more in one session. See "The Inverted Dead-Cat Bounce Setup."

☐ If you bought at the closing price the day before the Dutch auction's announcement and sold at the tender price, you would make money 85 percent of the time. See "Trading Dutch Auction Tender Offers."

☐ After the auction ends, price often trades outside of the auction's high-low price range within the first month. See "Trading Dutch Auction Tender Offers."

☐ Nearly all of the time (95 percent), price drops below the tender price within three months of the auction's end. See "After the Auction."

☐ Price rises above the tender price 79 percent of the time within three months of the auction's end. See "After the Auction."

☐ Buybacks more than 14.6 percent of shares outstanding tend to see price decline after the auction ends. Small buybacks tend to see price rise. See "After the Auction."

☐ For tips on selecting and trading earnings surprises, see "Earnings Surprise Setup."

☐ Price peaks three weeks after the announcement of good earnings. See "Earnings Surprise Setup."

☐ Review the section titled "Bad Earnings" for the scoop on identifying and trading a bad earnings event pattern.

☐ After a bad earnings announcement, price drops and continues lower for two to three weeks before rebounding somewhat and then continuing lower. See "Bad Earnings."

☐ See "Earnings Flag Setup" for identification details on the earnings flag.

☐ For tips on trading the earnings flag, see "Earnings Flag Example."

☐ Ignore stock upgrades in a bear market. See "Stock Upgrades and Downgrades."

☐ Downgrades in a bull market tend to be less effective than downgrades in a bear market. See "Stock Upgrades and Downgrades."

☐ For a list of trading tips, see "Stock Upgrades and Downgrades."

☐ Neither a forward nor a reverse stock split has any effect on the value of a holding. See "Stock Splits."

☐ Stocks gain 3 percent during the month before a stock split, climbing higher than the S&P 500 index 62 percent of the time. See "My Results."

☐ Three months after a reverse split, price is down 55 percent of the time, losing an average of 35 percent. See "Reverse Stock Splits."

☐ For better performance, only buy stocks with a rising price trend in the month before the reverse split. See "Trend Filter."

CHAPTER 6

Swinging Tools and Setups

This chapter discusses tools that may help you swing trade or create ideas upon which you can build new tools and new techniques for success in the stock market. The first tool is the chart pattern indicator, and it is an important one.

THE CHART PATTERN INDICATOR

In 2007, I thought about chart patterns and wondered if bearish patterns appear just before price tumbles and bullish ones appear just before price rises. When you think of a classic double top, it is a bearish top. Price rises up to it and drops afterward. Those twin peaks mark a sentiment change from bullish to bearish.

Likewise, double bottoms do not appear at the top of a price trend. Rather, they appear when price bottoms. Price drops into the double bottom reversal and rises after it.

What would happen if we built an indicator that found all bullish chart patterns and all bearish chart patterns in large numbers of stocks? The bullish patterns would predict higher prices and the bearish ones would signal disaster. The indicator would act as a predictor of a trend change. That is what I did; I made an indicator that shows when the general market is going to change trend, and I call it the chart pattern indicator.

- The chart pattern indicator helps determine when the market changes trend.

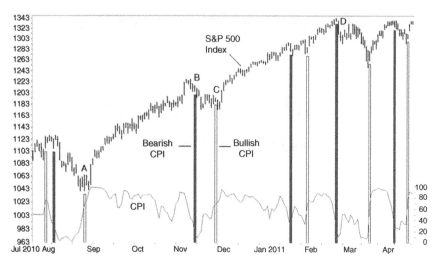

FIGURE 6.1   The chart pattern indicator confirms changes in trend.

Figure 6.1 shows an example of the result. The wavy line near the bottom of the chart is the chart pattern indicator. It bounces between 0 percent and 100 percent (right scale) with signal thresholds at 35 and 65. The vertical white and black lines show where the signal changes occur.

For example, at A, notice that the indicator turns bullish just as a straight-line run begins. At B, weakness sets in. B is not a timely signal, meaning it should have occurred a few days earlier, at a higher price. At C, the indicator says that the uptrend will resume, and it does a few days later. At D, the very day that price peaks, the indicator signals a trend change and down the S&P index goes.

As good as these signals appear, they are not as timely as the chart leads you to believe. Point D, for example, signaled a trend change as shown, but the signal actually occurred two price bars later. It is a lot like driving down the freeway and having your GPS say, "You should have turned left 300 feet ago." Knowing that you should have turned is a lot better than driving off the approaching cliff.

How Does It Work?

With the creation of personal computers and pattern recognition, the quest to build such an indicator became doable. I set out to test the idea that bullish chart patterns appear just before the market rises and bearish ones appear just before the market falls.

Using a computer program I wrote, I turned on all of the chart patterns and counted the bullish ones and the bearish ones. It did not work.

Chart patterns often take months to form and even if you look at thousands of stocks, a consensus does not form in a timely manner. Some stocks will be bottoming and show bullish patterns. Others will be pricey and show bearish patterns. Most will show nothing at all as they transition between bull and bear, or will create unreliable patterns—those that breakout in one direction and quickly reverse. I spent a month trying to find the right combination of chart patterns to get this idea to work.

What about just assigning bullish or bearish counts to patterns that we know are bullish or bearish? A double top is 100 percent bearish since price *always* breaks out downward to *confirm* a valid chart pattern. I tried that method, discarding chart patterns that had no dominant breakout direction. A symmetrical triangle, for example, breaks out upward just 54 percent of the time (about random) whereas a confirmed double bottom has a 100 percent upward breakout rate.

That scheme did not work either.

Next, I tried candlesticks. What a perfect opportunity for candles to show their worth! Large numbers of bullish candles would point the way to higher prices and bearish ones would signal a coming decline. I turned on 103 candlestick patterns and tried to build an indicator from that. It did not work. Then I tried the best performing candles, ones I knew to be reliable. Still no luck. I tried individual candlesticks and combined candles with chart patterns, and still I could not get it to work. That killed another two months.

I automated the test procedure to cycle through each candlestick and each chart pattern, looking for the right combination that would give me an indicator that worked. And that is when I found the answer. It was not a candlestick nor was it a classic chart pattern that spelled success. It was an obscure pattern called the NR7—narrow range 7.

The NR7

The narrow range 7 is a chart pattern that compares the high to low price range each day and finds the shortest price bar of the past six (for a total of seven bars). In other words, the seventh price bar is the shortest of all seven. The seven contiguous price bars need not be lined up like soldiers at attention. Rather, price will bounce up and down each day as it normally does in stocks. It is just that the most recent bar in the pattern has the smallest high-low price range of the seven.

When an NR7 appears, it suggests (but does not guarantee) a large price swing ahead. You can think of the pattern as showing the move from high to low volatility in the NR7 followed by a swing back to high volatility.

When price closes above the highest high logged by the seven bars, the stock stages an upward breakout. When price closes below the bottom of the seven bars, it makes a downward breakout.

The beauty of the NR7 is that it occurs frequently and the breakout direction points to a short-term move. When you look for the pattern in large numbers of stocks, you begin to get a consensus of which way price is going to move over the longer term.

Before I go any further, yes, I did try the NR4—narrow range 4. And I also tried other combinations of narrow ranges, but found that the NR7 worked best.

Once I found a pattern that worked, it was just a matter of pulling out my concrete mix and building an indicator around it.

- The narrow range 7 pattern predicts higher volatility ahead and the breakout gives the direction of the move.

The CPI Equation

The equation for the indicator is simple enough, and here it is.

$$CPI = 100 \times BullTotal \div (BullTotal + BearTotal)$$

BullTotal is a count of the NR7s with upward breakouts each day.
BearTotal is a count of the NR7s with downward breakouts each day.
CPI is the chart pattern indicator, expressed as a percentage, each day.
Bullish is a CPI above 65 percent. Bearish is a CPI below 35 percent. Neutral is between 35 and 65 percent.

If you program your computer to find NR7s and look for upward and downward breakouts each day in hundreds or even thousands of stocks, you will be disappointed. The actual implementation is not that simple. Even if you use every stock traded on the exchanges, the result will not be consistent enough to be useful (a friend tested it for me).

To get the indicator to work, I placed a time limit on the breakout of seven calendar days (not trading days). I tested the various combinations and found that a week worked best. If price did not breakout from an NR7 within a week, I threw away the pattern.

After locating the breakout, I increase the bullish or bearish count *for each day from the end of the pattern until the breakout.* For example, if an NR7 ends on Tuesday and breaks out upward on Wednesday, I will add 1 to the bull count total for Tuesday and 1 for Wednesday. If the sum of all bullish counts on Tuesday is 1 and there were no bearish counts, then the indicator would be 100 percent. If Wednesday showed 1 bullish count and 1 bearish count, then the CPI would be 50 percent, or $100 \times 1 \div (1 + 1)$.

One justification for doing this is that the "smart money" buys or sells over time. It is rare that they dump a few hundred thousand shares of a stock in a single day, especially when it represents many days of a stock's trading volume. Dumping (or acquiring) their shares at one time would move the stock too much, costing them money.

For example, if the smart money believes that the next earnings announcement will be wonderful, they ease into a stock to avoid disrupting the price. Other investors and traders may do the same, and that behavior helps create the chart patterns shown on our charts.

Another reason for adjusting the totals is to give the indicator more opportunity to signal a trend change without scanning every security in the market. I can get an accurate read with a few hundred stocks.

Unfortunately, this method has a drawback. Tuesday's bullish signal, for example, could change to bearish if many NR7s are waiting to signal and the market makes a large drop on Wednesday. Thus, signals can and do change up to a week later, but are usually set after three days.

Because old signals can change up to a week, the indicator *should not be used* as a trading tool. Use it only as a sentiment indicator. Rely on signals only after they are a week old (or at least three days old).

Some of you will want to improve on this mechanism. One trader reported that he tried over a billion combinations and could not get it to work as a trading tool. Others have tried their own variations, but I have not heard of anyone improving on the technique. Go ahead and try if you want, but you will have an easier time trying to eat a bowling ball.

- The chart pattern indicator is a daily ratio between bullish and bearish NR7s in hundreds of stocks.
- Do *not* use the chart pattern indicator as a trading tool, but as a sentiment indicator.
- A new signal is often set three days after it occurs.

The Patternz program, available free on my website (http://thepattern site.com/patternz.html), will calculate the chart pattern indicator for you. My website also provides daily readings for the indicator and has an enhancement to help determine how reliable the signal is (one to three up or down arrows).

THE SWING RULE

Stan Weinstein (McGraw-Hill, 1988) writes about what he calls the *swing rule*. The swing rule determines where price is going to encounter overhead resistance. In other words, where price is going to stop rising.

Figure 6.2 shows how the rule works. Measure the decline from peak A to valley B and add it to the price of A to get C. To put numbers

FIGURE 6.2 The swing rule uses the swing from A to B to predict C.

to letters, the swing from A (high price) to B (low price) is 17.27 – 14.50, for a height of 2.77. Add 2.77 to 17.27 (A) to get a target of 20.04. In this example, C tops out at 19.50, so the stock misses its target by 3 percent. That is very good.

- Use the swing rule to predict how far price might rise. Measure a drop from peak to valley and project that height above the peak to get a target price.

Does testing show that the swing method works? Yes. The test used 926 stocks and over 32,000 samples from March 2000 to April 2011. That period included two bear markets and two bull ones.

I measured the AB move and projected that above A to get the target price (C). I found the peak closest to the target in a stair-step series of moves higher. The test mimicked a trader holding an up-trending stock until it came as close to the target as it could. The test used significant turning points only (the highest high within 5 days on either side of a peak or valley, for a total of 11 days).

Table 6.1 shows what I found.

TABLE 6.1 Swing Rule Accuracy for Uptrends

How Close?	Window ±5%	Below Target −10–0%	−5–0%	Target 0%	Above Target 0–5%	0–10%
Bull market—all swings	80%	41%	38%	29%	72%	83%
Bear market—all swings	66%	34%	30%	23%	59%	78%
Bull market—small swings (<10%)	86%	43%	40%	32%	77%	86%
Bear market—small swings	79%	39%	35%	27%	71%	86%
Bull market—large swings (>10%)	53%	31%	27%	20%	45%	71%
Bear market—large swings	46%	25%	23%	16%	40%	65%

Let us begin with the Target column near the center of the table since the other columns reference it. I looked at swings in a bull market and found that 29 percent of them hit their target exactly. That means price reached point C in Figure 6.2, formed a peak, and declined thereafter. An additional 43 percent sailed past the target by no more than 5 percent, giving a total for the two columns of 72 percent. The 72 percent number appears in the 0–5 percent column. Eighty-three percent of swings peaked between 0 and 10 percent above the target.

Moving in the other direction, we find that 38 percent fell between 0 and 5 percent short of the target. By short, I mean 29 percent hit the target exactly and an additional 9 percent (for a total of 38 percent) did not climb far enough to reach the target price.

To put it another way, 80 percent (9 percent + 29 percent + 43 percent less round off) were within ±5 percent of the target. The 80 percent number appears in the Window column. The Window column shows how accurate the method is if you allow a window 10 percent tall (5 percent on either side of the target). It is the most important column in the table.

The Window column shows that the swing rule works best for small swings in a bull market (86 percent reach the target window) and works worst in a bear market after a large swing (46 percent reach the target window). I will explain what is meant by small and large swings later.

The bear market result makes sense since we are counting price moving up in a stair-step rise when the bear market current is pushing against the stock. It is like swimming against the current.

- For up trends, price tends to exceed the swing rule target rather than fall short of it.
- The swing rule for up trends works best in a bull market.

Weinstein writes that this technique works best for "an important decline." I have no idea what *important* means, so I used 10 percent as the benchmark. Declines (the move from A to B in Figure 6.2) of less than 10 percent were considered small; those more than 10 percent were large declines.

Table 6.1 shows that stocks with small swings (the AB decline) were more likely to reach their target than were large swings. For example, in a bull market, 86 percent of the stocks with small swings peaked within ±5 percent of the target (the Window column), but only 53 percent of those with large swings hit their mark.

That result makes intuitive sense since it is easier for a stock to rise by a small amount than a large one.

I conducted another test using 10 days (price bars) to mark peaks and valleys (10 days on either side of a peak or valley which gives the highest peak or lowest valley in about a month) and changed the AB drop to 15, 20, and 25 percent. The higher the drop, the fewer the samples, and the worse the results. For declines larger than 15 percent, price is within ±5 percent of the target 42 percent of the time. Using 20 and 25 percent declines, just 38 percent of the samples fit within the ±5 percent window. Large price drops seem to be less effective at predicting similar moves above a prior peak, at least by the method I tested.

- The swing rule works best when the decline used in the measure is less than 10 percent.

Swing Rule for Downtrends

Does the swing rule also work for downtrends? Yes, but they are not as accurate as for uptrends. **Table 6.2** shows the results. The columns labeled, "Below Target," show numbers where price dropped far enough to reach the target and kept going down. "Above Target" means price did not drop far enough to reach the target. The "Window" column is the total of how often price reaches a target, ±5 percent. The table is the same as Table 6.1 except it applies to downtrends.

Figure 6.3 shows an example of the swing rule for downtrends. Price bottoms at A (24.07) and peaks at B (25.93) for a swing of 1.86. That height subtracted from A gives a target of 22.21. C bottoms at 22.24, just three cents above the predicted target. That is how the swing rule for downtrends is supposed to work, but does testing show that it works well? No.

Returning to Table 6.2, the Window column shows that the best performance of the swing rule comes with swings smaller than 10 percent. That means the rise from A to B in Figure 6.3, when less than 10 percent, will correctly predict a downward price target (C) 78 percent of

TABLE 6.2　Swing Rule Accuracy for Downtrends

How Close?	Window ±5%	Below Target −10–0%	−5–0%	Target 0%	Above Target 0–5%	0–10%
Bull market—all swings	67%	30%	27%	21%	61%	79%
Bear market—all swings	49%	32%	26%	16%	39%	54%
Bull market—small swings (<10%)	78%	33%	31%	24%	72%	88%
Bear market—small swings	67%	41%	34%	23%	56%	72%
Bull market—large swings (>10%)	36%	19%	17%	11%	31%	55%
Bear market—large swings	34%	24%	19%	11%	26%	41%

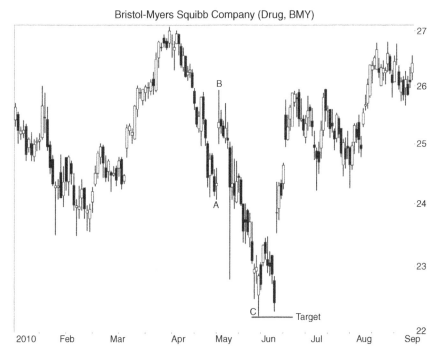

FIGURE 6.3　The swing rule for down trends accurately predicts a turning price near C.

the time, ±5 percent on either side. Just 36 percent of swings larger than 10 percent see price squeeze within the window.

You would think that the swing rule for downtrends would work best in a bear market, but that is not true. In each of the three comparisons (all, small, and large swings) shown in Table 6.2, the bear market result is less accurate than the bull market prediction.

- The swing rule for downtrends works best for small swings (less than 10 percent) in a bull market.

PUMP UP THE VOLUME OR NOT

For every share sold, one is purchased. Price does not rise because more people are buying shares, and they do not fall because more people are selling them. Rather, price moves because of buying *demand* and selling *pressure*. If buying demand overwhelms selling pressure then the price will rise. If buying demand is less than selling pressure, the price will drop.

Is it true that above-average volume on the breakout day means a better performing chart pattern? Surprisingly, the answer is mixed, and **Table 6.3** shows why.

I used double tops and bottoms, triple tops and bottoms, and rectangle tops and bottoms—chart patterns with defined breakouts. Each of those patterns has a breakout that is obvious—it is either above the top of the chart pattern, or below the bottom of it. There are no slanting trendlines where it might be difficult to determine when price has actually closed outside of the pattern (such as in a diamond top or symmetrical triangle).

I found 8,147 samples, starting from July 1991 to May 2011. That includes the two bear markets of 2000–2002 and 2007–2009. Each of these patterns I found manually, meaning I did not use automated tools to find these patterns. In other words, they are valid chart patterns that I have catalogued for my books.

I measured the gain or loss from the breakout day to the ultimate high or low (when the trend changes) and compared that to the breakout day volume versus the average volume over the prior 31 days. Table 6.3 shows the results.

TABLE 6.3 Breakout Volume versus Average Rise or Loss Post-Breakout

Breakout Volume	Bull Market, Up Breakout	Bull Market, Down Breakout	Bear Market, Up Breakout	Bear Market, Down Breakout
Above average	37.6%	15.1%	22.4%	23.6%
Below average	35.8%	15.7%	22.9%	24.5%

For example, in a bull market, after an upward breakout from a chart pattern, those chart patterns with volume above the 31-calendar-day average saw price climb 37.6 percent before the trend reversed. Those with below-average volume saw price climb just 35.8 percent. That is the only time that above-average volume worked better than below-average volume. Regardless, the numbers are close enough that you are not going to see a difference in your swing trading.

To be fair, I have run this test using other chart patterns and found that there is a slight advantage to breakouts with above-average volume. The next two tables provide additional color.

• Above-average breakout day volume does not mean substantially better performance.

Failure Rates by Volume

If you read some books, they will say something like, "a chart pattern that breaks out on weak volume is more likely to fail," and yet they offer no proof.

We saw that if you ride price after a chart pattern breakout until the trend changes, there is little difference in performance, regardless of the breakout volume. What about failures, when price moves less than 5 percent after the breakout before reversing? Do we see more failures if breakout volume is below average?

Table 6.4 shows the percentage of chart patterns with price that fails to travel more than 10 percent in the breakout direction (I chose 10 percent instead of 5 percent to boost the number of samples qualifying, but the 5 percent numbers show the same trend). Of the 3,384 chart patterns with upward breakouts in a bull market, 2,500 had above-average volume, and 884 sported below-average volume.

Sorting by the rise to the ultimate high (or a close below the bottom of the chart pattern, both of which end the price trend), we find that 14 percent with above-average breakout volume rise less than 10 percent after the breakout, but 5 percent fail with below-average breakout volume.

TABLE 6.4 Breakout Volume versus 10 Percent Failure Rates

Breakout Volume	Bull Market, Up Breakout	Bull Market, Down Breakout	Bear Market, Up Breakout	Bear Market, Down Breakout
Above average	14%	28%	16%	13%
Below average	5%	11%	8%	5%

In each column, Table 6.4 shows that breakouts with below-average volume results in fewer failures than those with above-average volume!

• Chart patterns with above-average breakout volume fail twice as often as do those with below-average volume.

Throwback and Pullback Rates by Volume

I checked the data to see how often a throwback or pullback occurred. Recall that a throwback occurs when price breaks out upward, but then turns around and returns to the breakout price or trendline boundary within a month. A pullback is the same looping maneuver, except it occurs after a downward breakout. Table 6.5 shows the throwback and pullback results sorted by breakout volume.

For example, chart patterns with upward breakouts in a bull market throwback 57 percent of the time when breakout volume is above average. That compares to a throwback rate of just 18 percent when breakout volume is below average. In all cases, fewer throwbacks or pullbacks occur when breakout volume is below average.

If a throwback is less likely to occur, then that means price stands a better chance of embarking on a straight-line run. Those runs are what swing traders dream about (but that could just be me). Knowing that price has a higher likelihood of reversing after five days (which is the average for throwbacks and pullbacks) means I will want to take profits quickly. I can also wait for the throwback or pullback to complete before taking a position.

• Throwbacks and pullbacks are three times more likely to occur after a high volume breakout.

For swing traders, a breakout with above-average volume is a big yawn where performance is concerned. The numbers show that failures double and the risk of a throwback or pullback triples after a high volume breakout. Throwbacks and pullbacks rob the stock of upward momentum, resulting in underperformance (I proved that in a study) and they increase the likelihood of a losing trade.

TABLE 6.5 Breakout Volume versus Throwback or Pullback Rate

Breakout Volume	Bull Market, Up Breakout	Bull Market, Down Breakout	Bear Market, Up Breakout	Bear Market, Down Breakout
Above average	57%	47%	19%	27%
Below average	18%	17%	6%	9%

SELECTING WINNERS USING INDEX RELATIVE STRENGTH

Have you ever heard of relative strength? I am not talking about Wilder's relative strength index but strength relative to the Standard & Poor's S&P 500 index.

Figure 6.4 shows an example of the stock's closing price divided by the closing price of the S&P 500 index (line A). A 22-trading-day (about a calendar month) simple moving average of that line appears as B, a smoothed version of line A.

Notice how the relative strength drops going into the start of the symmetrical triangle, at C. After the breakout, the stock is stronger than the index, resulting in a rising relative strength line (D). The line(s) continues rising, following price higher. The turn from down to up—a reversal—in the relative strength line is important. It can signal a lower risk trading opportunity.

IRS Study

To study the behavior of this line, I used 1,094 stocks with data from July 1991 to January 2009, and found 15,763 chart patterns that I used in

FIGURE 6.4   The chart shows stock relative strength plotted against the S&P 500 index.

TABLE 6.6 Index Relative Strength versus Performance

Trend before Chart Pattern	Trend before Breakout	Gain	10% Failures
Rising	Rising	32%	19%
Rising	Falling	29%	22%
Falling	Falling	33%	17%
Falling	Rising	34%	16%
Upward Breakout Above, Downward Below			
Rising	Rising	19%	28%
Rising	Falling	21%	28%
Falling	Falling	18%	29%
Falling	Rising	21%	28%

the test. Not all stocks covered the entire period. I looked at the slope of the line at two points: the day before the start of the chart pattern, and the day before the breakout.

Table 6.6 shows the results using the 22-day moving average of the relative strength line. For example, for upward breakouts (the top half of the table) if the slope of the line was rising at the start of the chart pattern and the day before the breakout it was still rising, price gained an average of 32 percent (measured from the breakout to the ultimate high). Nineteen percent of the chart patterns failed to rise at least 10 percent after the breakout.

The best performance occurred when the relative strength line reversed trend, from down to up. Price gained 34 percent on average and 16 percent failed to rise at least 10 percent. This is like having your cake and eating it too: Performance improves and the risk of failure drops.

- For the best performance, look for the relative strength line to reverse from falling to rising from the day before the start to the day before the breakout of a chart pattern. Avoid chart patterns with a relative strength line that turns from rising to falling.

The bottom half of the table shows the results for downward breakouts. The best performance occurred after a reversal in the relative strength line, from either down to up or up to down. Continuations performed worst.

- For the best performance from downward breakouts of chart patterns, look for a reversal in the relative strength line from the day before the start of the chart pattern to the day before the breakout.

The results suggest that looking at the slope of the relative strength line the day before the start of the chart pattern and the day before the breakout can help select stocks that will outperform in the future. The best performance comes when the relative strength line changes from falling to rising over those two measurement periods (with rising/falling coming in a close second).

Trading implications: Before buying a stock, check the relative strength going into the start of the chart pattern and the day before the breakout (or the most recent day). Compare your findings with those in Table 6.6. A falling then rising pattern is best for performance, regardless of the breakout direction.

THREE SWING TRADING SETUPS

Writing a book is like having an argument with yourself. Should you describe trading setups by others that do not work well? (My answer: No.) How about your own setups? Yes, because it might save others countless hours of testing when they may not have the breadth of data that I do. What follows are test results for setups with upward breakouts that I tested on ascending triangles, rectangle tops, and rectangle bottoms.

I used 1,559 stocks in the tests with data beginning in July 1991 and ending in mid-2010. Not all stocks had data covering the entire period. Commissions were $10 per trade ($20 round-trip) using an initial stake of $10,000 *per trade.* Profits were not accumulated from one trade to the next. I ranked eight performance factors (such as win/loss ratio, profit per trade, and so on) and those with the lowest rank total became the best performing.

Ascending Triangle Setups

An ascending triangle has price bounded between two trendlines. The top one is horizontal, or nearly so. The bottom one slants upward as if pointing the way to the breakout. In fact, price breaks out upward 67 percent of the time in this chart pattern.

I do not particularly like this chart pattern since it fails so often. The failure rate is 14 percent. That may not sound like much, but it pales when compared to other chart patterns like double bottoms which have failure rates of 8 percent. To put it another way, ascending triangles fail almost twice as often as double bottoms!

The setups described below try to take advantage of the upward move before a reversal occurs.

The best performing setup uses a buy stop a penny above the top of the triangle and exits three days later (on day 4), at the close. Here are the results, and an abbreviated list also appears in **Table 6.7** as Test 1. All of

TABLE 6.7 Results of Various Tests on Ascending Triangles

Rank	Per Trade Profit/(Loss)	% Wins	Profit/Loss Ratio	Hold Time Loss	Hold Time (Days)
1—Best	$201	65%	3.14	18%	5
2	$187	67%	3.14	18%	5
3	$200	65%	3.12	18%	5
4	$225	62%	3.03	14%	5
5	$174	64%	3.11	18%	4
6	$193	65%	2.99	18%	5
7	$186	64%	2.73	13%	5
8	$218	65%	3.02	18%	7
9	$113	60%	1.83	10%	4
10	$220	64%	2.89	18%	8
11	$159	66%	2.65	23%	5
12	$139	59%	1.98	11%	5
13	$129	67%	1.58	18%	12
14	$250	69%	1.67	34%	38
15	$264	67%	1.65	34%	44
16	$198	73%	1.62	34%	30
17	$177	76%	1.62	31%	26
18	$152	79%	1.60	31%	21
19	$209	70%	1.59	34%	34
20	$57	52%	1.26	11%	7
21	($89)	60%	−0.74	10%	4
22	($89)	59%	−0.75	10%	5
23	$56	36%	1.19	14%	15
24—Worst	($94)	57%	−0.74	10%	6

the following results were used in ranking each test except for the number of trades—the last item in the list.

Average profit per trade: $200.97, or 2 percent
Win/Loss ratio: 65 percent
Average win: $294.90
Average loss: $93.93
Ratio of profit to losses: 3.14
Hold time loss: 18 percent
Hold time: 5 days
Number of trades: 1,026

Figure 6.5 shows the best performing setup for ascending triangles with upward breakouts. The triangle is well developed, so identification is easy as price bounces between two trendlines. Entry occurs when price rises above the top trendline using a buy stop a penny above the top of the trendline. Exit happens at the close three days later for a profit of just over $515, or 5 percent.

FIGURE 6.5 This shows the best-performing setup for ascending triangles.

All of the following tests enter the trade with a buy stop a penny above the top of the ascending triangle. They may have other entry conditions as described below. The number of each item keys to the rank in Table 6.7.

1. This is the best performing setup. Exit at the close three trading days after entry.

2. Buy only if the current price is above the 200-day simple moving average. Exit at the close three trading days after entry.

3. Buy only if the current price is above the 21-day simple moving average. Exit at the close three trading days after entry.

4. Enter if the buy price is *below* the 200-day simple moving average. Exit at the close three trading days after entry.

5. Exit at the close two trading days after buying.

6. Enter if the buy price is above the 50-day simple moving average. Exit at the close three trading days after entry.

7. Exit at the close three trading days after entry. Use the lower of today or yesterday as a stop price (adjust the stop up or down each trading day, as necessary).

8. Exit at the close four trading days after entry.

9. Exit two trading days after buying and place a stop at the buy day's low minus a penny.

10. Exit at the close five trading days after entry.

11. Exit if profit reaches 5 percent or at the close three trading days after entry.

12. Exit at the close three trading days after entry, and use a stop placed a penny below the low on the buy date.

13. Exit if profit reaches 5 percent, and use a stop halfway between the buy price and the triangle's lowest low price.

14. Exit if profit reaches 9 percent, and use a stop a penny below the triangle's lowest low price.

15. Same as 14 but use 10 percent

16. Same as 14 but use 7 percent.

17. Same as 14 but use 6 percent.

18. Same as 14 but use 5 percent.

19. Same as 14 but use 8 percent.

20. Exit if the profit reaches 5 percent, and use a stop a penny below the buy day's low price.

21. Exit at the open the day after a lower close.

22. Exit at the open the day after a lower high.

23. Exit if the profit reaches 10 percent, and use a stop a penny below the buy day's low price.

24. Exit at the open the day after a lower low. This is the worst performing setup.

Rectangle Top Setups

A rectangle top chart pattern has price that bounces between two parallel—or nearly parallel—trendlines. Price enters the pattern from the bottom to qualify the rectangle as a top, but it can exit in any direction. The breakout is upward 68 percent of the time, slightly more often than ascending triangles. The failure rate is 12 percent, meaning that 12 percent have price that fails to rise above the breakout price by more than 5 percent.

Figure 6.6 shows an example of a rectangle top. Notice that price enters the chart pattern from the bottom, qualifying this as a top. Price bounces between two trendlines. The few touches of each trendline are typical for rectangles. Price comes close, but misses actually touching both trendlines several times, so be sure to give your chart patterns the benefit of the doubt when trying to identify them. Rarely will you see a perfect pattern with numerous touches of each trendline.

FIGURE 6.6 This rectangle top has a trade that exits three days after entry.

This figure represents the best performing setup for rectangle tops, and it also appears as Test 1 in **Table 6.8**. Entry occurs when price is above the 21-day simple moving average, and price rises high enough to trigger a buy stop placed a penny above the top of the rectangle. Exit occurs at the close three days later.

Here is more information on the best performing setup.

Average profit per trade: $309.66
Win/Loss ratio: 75 percent
Average win: $360.21
Average loss: $50.54
Ratio of profit to losses: 7.13
Hold time loss: 16 percent
Hold time: 5 days
Number of trades: 599

The test makes 3 percent in 5 days, on average, but the hold time loss can be large during that time, 16 percent. That is the hit taken if exiting the trade at the very worst time—when price drops the most.

TABLE 6.8   Results of Various Tests on Rectangle Tops

Rank	Per Trade Profit/(Loss)	% Wins	Profit/Loss Ratio	Hold Time Loss	Hold Time (Days)
1—Best	$310	75%	7.13	16%	5
2	$336	76%	5.27	11%	5
3	$264	78%	6.44	16%	4
4	$305	75%	6.59	16%	5
5	$278	74%	6.52	16%	4
6	$320	79%	4.34	10%	11
7	$321	75%	6.43	16%	5
8	$297	75%	6.50	16%	5
9	$336	86%	3.95	16%	15
10	$261	70%	5.53	9%	4
11	$341	68%	5.05	9%	5
12	$298	74%	6.02	11%	5
13	$396	84%	4.13	18%	19
14	$385	75%	7.06	23%	7
15	$433	82%	3.89	18%	23
16	$352	75%	6.45	23%	8
17	$450	79%	3.35	18%	28
18	$247	63%	3.77	9%	7
19	$171	69%	2.29	8%	5
20	$332	47%	3.22	11%	16
21	$479	76%	3.17	25%	32
22	$186	68%	2.32	9%	6
23	$500	74%	3.03	25%	36
24—Worst	$178	68%	2.26	23%	5

The following explain each test and they key to the rank numbers shown in Table 6.8. **All tests enter when price rises a penny above the top of the rectangle**, but they may have other entry conditions as explained below.

1. This is the best performing setup. Buy when price is above the 21-day simple moving average. Exit at the close three trading days later.

2. Buy when price is *below* the 200-day simple moving average. Exit at the close three trading days later.

3. Exit if profit reaches 5 percent or at the close three trading days after entry.

4. Buy when price is above the 50-day simple moving average. Exit at the close three trading days later.

5. Exit at the close two trading days after buying.

6. Exit if profit reaches 5 percent, and use a stop placed halfway between the buy price and the rectangle's low.

7. Exit at the close three trading days later.

8. Buy when price is above the 200-day simple moving average. Exit at the close three trading days later.

9. Exit on 5 percent profit and place a stop a penny below the rectangle's low.

10. Exit at the close two trading days after buying, and use a stop placed a penny below the buy day's low.

11. Exit at the close three trading days later. Place a stop a penny below the buy day's low.

12. Exit at the close three trading days later. Use the lower of the two most recent price bars as the stop (adjust the stop up or down each trading day, as necessary).

13. Exit on 6 percent profit. Use a stop placed a penny below the rectangle's low.

14. Exit at the close four trading days after entry.

15. Exit on 7 percent profit. Use a stop placed a penny below the rectangle's low.

16. Exit at the close five trading days later.

17. Exit on 8 percent profit. Use a stop placed a penny below the rectangle's low.

18. Exit on 5 percent profit. Place a stop a penny below the buy day's low.

19. Exit at the open the day after a lower close.

20. Exit on 10 percent profit. Place a stop a penny below the buy day's low.

21. Exit on 9 percent profit. Use a stop placed a penny below the rectangle's low.

22. Exit at the open the day after a lower low.

23. Exit on 10 percent profit. Use a stop placed a penny below the rectangle's low.

24. Exit at the open the day after a lower high. This is the worst performing setup.

Rectangle Bottom Setups

Rectangle bottoms share the same configuration as rectangle tops except that price enters the chart pattern from the top. Price breaks out upward 59 percent of the time. The 5 percent failure rate is 10 percent (10 percent of the patterns show price failing to rise at least 5 percent). I only looked at upward breakouts in the tests that follow. Again, the idea behind these tests is to capture the explosive breakout move before a throwback occurs.

Figure 6.7 shows an example of the best performing setup for rectangle bottoms. Since we are dealing with bottoms, price enters the rectangle from the top and breaks out upward. A buy stop placed a penny above the top of the rectangle gets the trade underway just as things get interesting. Price continues moving up the next day, and the stock reaches the 5 percent profit exit. The stock would be sold then. Otherwise, a sale would occur three days after buying, just as the figure shows.

Here are the test results for Test 1, the best performing setup for rectangle bottoms.

Average profit per trade: $248.64
Win/Loss ratio: 73 percent
Average win: $313.63
Average loss: $65.00
Ratio of profit to losses: 4.83
Hold time loss: 12 percent
Hold time: 5 days
Number of trades: 261

FIGURE 6.7 The best performing setup is when price breaks out upward and the position is sold three price bars later, or if the trade reaches a 5 percent profit.

Rectangle bottoms do not perform as well as tops, but it depends on what you look at. The average profit per trade drops from $310 to $249, but the hold time loss drops from 16 to 12 percent, for rectangle tops and bottoms, respectively. However, few trades occurred because I did not find many rectangle bottoms with upward breakouts.

The following tests key to the Rank numbers in **Table 6.9**. **Entry occurs by using a buy stop a penny above the top of the rectangle bottom**, but entry might also have additional conditions as specified below.

1. This is the best performing setup. Exit after a 5 percent profit or at the close three trading days after entry.

2. The buy price must be above the 200-day simple moving average. Exit at the close three trading days after entry.

3. Exit at the close three trading days after entry.

TABLE 6.9 Results of Various Tests on Rectangle Bottoms

Rank	Per Trade Profit/(Loss)	% Wins	Profit/ Loss Ratio	Hold Time Loss	Hold Time (Days)
1—Best	$249	73%	4.83	12%	5
2	$246	68%	5.25	8%	5
3	$244	69%	4.28	19%	5
4	$246	69%	4.26	19%	5
5	$213	68%	3.86	11%	4
6	$234	71%	3.29	19%	5
7	$327	78%	3.88	16%	12
8	$309	72%	4.47	19%	8
9	$234	68%	3.99	19%	5
10	$276	70%	4.42	19%	7
11	$429	83%	3.41	36%	24
12	$200	68%	2.78	12%	5
13	$163	64%	2.40	7%	4
14	$332	86%	3.25	36%	18
15	$522	79%	3.50	36%	32
16	$370	84%	3.16	36%	21
17	$460	80%	3.26	36%	28
18	$211	61%	2.5	11%	8
19	$81	63%	1.43	6%	4
20	$180	61%	2.47	10%	5
21	$87	63%	1.47	7%	5
22	$477	75%	2.63	36%	36
23	$380	58%	2.75	24%	21
24—Worst	$93	62%	1.46	7%	6

4. The buy price must be above the 21-day simple moving average. Exit at the close three trading days after entry.

5. Exit at the close two trading days after entry.

6. The buy price must be *below* the 200-day simple moving average. Exit at the close three trading days after entry.

7. Exit after a 5 percent profit. Use a stop placed halfway between the buy price and rectangle's low.

8. Exit at the close five trading days after entry.

9. Enter if the buy price is above the 50-day simple moving average. Exit at the close three trading days after entry.

10. Exit at the close four trading days after entry.

11. Exit on 7 percent profit. Place a stop a penny below the rectangle's low.

12. Exit at the close three trading days after entry. Use the lower of the two most recent price bars as a stop (adjust the stop up or down each trading day, as necessary).

13. Exit at the close two trading days after buying, and use a stop placed a penny below the buy day's low.

14. Exit on 5 percent profit. Place a stop a penny below the rectangle's low.

15. Exit on 9 percent profit. Place a stop a penny below the rectangle's low.

16. Exit on 6 percent profit. Place a stop a penny below the rectangle's low.

17. Exit on 8 percent profit. Place a stop a penny below the rectangle's low.

18. Exit on 5 percent profit, but use a stop placed a penny below the buy day's low.

19. Exit at the open the day after a lower close.

20. Exit at the close three trading days after entry, and use a stop placed a penny below the buy day's low.

21. Exit at the open the day after a lower high.

22. Exit on 10 percent profit. Place a stop a penny below the rectangle's low.

23. Exit on 10 percent profit. Place a stop a penny below the buy day's low.

24. This is the worst performing setup of the group. Exit at the open the day after a lower low.

Notice that for ascending triangles and rectangles, tests that include a stop mechanism tend to underperform setups without stops. Several of the tests (11 and 14–17) "tune" or optimize the results, so avoid drawing conclusions on how well those tests will do in the future. I chose the 5 percent number as the profit exit of choice on all three chart patterns. Make sure you do your own tests, and expect your results to differ from those here.

TRADING SETUP: SIMPLE MOVING AVERAGE TESTS

This test is different from the others. I used rectangle tops and bottoms as the springboard for this series of tests. Entry occurred when price rose a penny above the top of the rectangle, providing that price was also above a simple moving average. The stock sold if price closed below either the moving average or a penny below the rectangle's low price. **Table 6.10** shows the results.

The idea was to ride price higher and catch it before it fell too far. With longer moving averages, price can rise far and fall without triggering a sale, so the potential profit giveback can be huge. Using the 200-day simple moving average, I would expect a larger hold time loss. The 19 percent seems to be an error, given that the others trend lower (27 percent then 23 percent). Notice that as the days in the moving average shorten, the average profit per trade drops, but the percentage of winning trades increases. The ratio of average win to average loss drops, but so does the hold time loss and hold time.

A dynamic moving average might work better in this test than the simple moving average. A dynamic one can hug price as it rises steeply and lengthen out when the price trend flattens. I did not test such a vehicle because I am not too impressed with this setup. Clearly, I like to make big bucks from a setup that wins most of the time without giving back much of my profit, and while keeping any losses miniscule. That does not describe this setup. I am not sure it describes any setup, which is why I prefer to remain a discretionary trader, not a mechanical system trader.

TABLE 6.10 Results of Various Tests on Rectangles

Simple Moving Average	Per Trade Profit	% Wins	Profit/Loss Ratio	Hold Time Loss	Hold Time (Days)	Number of Trades
200 days	$1,785	41%	5.02	19%	165	743
150 days	$1,433	43%	4.63	27%	132	780
100 days	$1,157	49%	4.58	27%	98	851
50 days	$779	52%	4.23	23%	61	964
20 days	$412	58%	3.63	23%	28	1,030

THE SMILE AND FROWN SETUP

I think this setup is nothing short of brilliant, but some of you will roll your eyes and say, "Of course. It's obvious," (and maybe even stupid in its simplicity). You may have even seen it elsewhere. Yet, how many of you look for smiles and frowns on the price chart as entry or exit conditions? Let me explain.

Figure 6.8 shows the ideal smile and frown setup. I chose those names to make identification obvious.

Price moves in waves as the line chart of the stock suggests. The ideal trade entry location is at B. That gets you into a swing trade (or any other style of trade) at the lowest price, just as the stock is about to take off.

If you buy at A, you will pull your hair out as the stock drops. If the stock continues down, you will often sell a week or two before B. That seems to happen regularly when associated with large losses. It is a catch-22 situation. If you sell, then two weeks later the stock will bottom. If you suspect the bottom is near and hold on, the stock will continue dropping.

The safest entry is at C. The rounded turn is clear. Price hits bottom at B, and is now moving up. As long as it is not too far above B, then buy.

The ABC pattern is what I call a smile. If you buy smiles, you set yourself up for a winning trade.

- A smile pattern is a rounding bottom. Enter a trade after the stock has bottomed and is moving up. Avoid buying a stock when price is still moving down.
- Buy smiles not frowns.

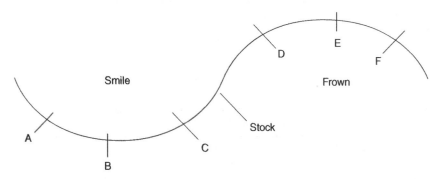

FIGURE 6.8   Can (swing) trading be as easy as finding smiles and frowns?

Frowns

The DEF pattern is a frown. It occurs when price changes direction from up to down. In chart pattern terms, it is a rounded top (but usually much narrower).

For the sell side, look at the second half of the chart. Exiting at D, while price is rising, leaves money on the table.

Point E is the optimum exit. It represents the ultimate high, the highest high where price drops away from it on either side. It is like summiting Everest: all other peaks are lower. Selling at the perfect time (E) is rare.

At F, each day that you hold the stock, the value of it drops. For my trades, I found that selling at D was more profitable than selling at F (for details, see *Fundamental Analysis and Position Trading*, Chapter 16, under the heading "Testing"). That may be because I held on too long after the E peak.

Smile and Frown Testing

I have not figured out how to test this setup using automated means, so I resorted to another method. I reviewed 400 trades covering the four styles of trading (buy-and-hold, position, swing, and day trading) from November 1987 to August 2011. That period includes two bear markets. **Table 6.11** shows what I found.

For example, buying stocks during a smile, I made an average of 16 percent and the trades were profitable 65 percent of the time. When I bought during a frown pattern, the trades lost 5 percent and were profitable only 31 percent of the time.

If I want to win twice as often, all I have to do is buy smile patterns and ignore trades showing frowns.

The sell side is less dramatic. When I have sold during a smile, I made 2 percent and won 37 percent of the time. However, when I sold during a frown, I made three times as much (6 percent) and won 53 percent of the time. Although the percentages may not seem large, the numbers include going long in a bear market and day trades.

TABLE 6.11 Smile and Frown Testing

	Buy Smile	Buy Frown	Sell Smile	Sell Frown
Wins	65%	31%	37%	53%
Average Gain/Loss	16%	−5%	2%	6%

It might be worth the time to review your trades and put them into the smile or frown categories. Doing so will indicate how your results might improve by trading smiles and frowns. As I said, this technique works for all types of trading.

- Categorize your trades into smiles and frowns to see if your results might improve by concentrating purchases during smiles and sales during frowns.

TRADING SMILES AND FROWNS

Let me show you what smiles and frowns look like by reviewing a few trades before I discuss trading tips.

Figure 6.9 shows a swing trade in Eagle Materials. I show this on the line chart to make the smile and frown easier to see. I also show a 50-day simple moving average except that the line is offset by 25 days. That means

FIGURE 6.9   A line chart with a 50-day moving average highlights two trades.

I moved the average to the *left* 25 days or about a month's worth of trading (half the moving average number. If I used a 200-day moving average, then I would plot it 100 days to the left). That helps align the moving average with price so that they both peak and valley near the same time. If your software cannot do that, then just use your imagination to move the average until peaks and valleys align.

I am not a fan of moving averages, but in this case they make finding smiles and frowns easier. For example, you can see that I bought as price climbed out of a smile. It is easiest to see the smile on the moving average. I sold after price frowned. Again, the moving average shows the frown better than price.

Including three dividend payments, I made 25 percent on the trade.

Figure 6.10 shows another example of a smile and frown trade. I bought the stock twice at the bottom of the smile. Again, a 50-day simple moving average offset to the left by 25 days shows the smile clearly. I sold it when the stock frowned.

I made 28 percent on the first trade and 23 percent on the second.

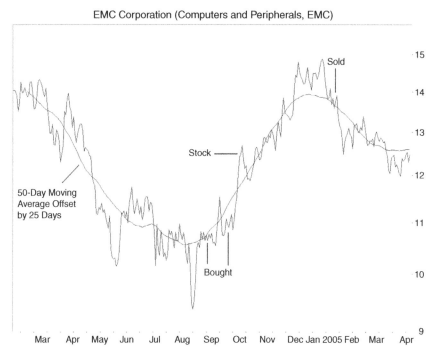

FIGURE 6.10   I bought the stock twice in a smile and sold it during a frown. The moving average is offset to the left by 25 days.

SMILE AND FROWN TRADING TIPS

How do you trade smiles and frowns? Here are some identification tips. The first is to use a line chart instead of other types of charts. The line chart makes finding smiles and frowns easier.

- Use a line chart to show smiles and frowns.

In a historical price series, using a moving average helps smooth the line chart, making smiles and frowns even easier to see.

For the daily chart, I use a 50-day simple moving average. I offset the moving average by half the wavelength to the left. In other words, I draw it pushed 25 days to the left so that the price and moving average peak at or near the same time. You can use whatever moving average works best for the time scales you trade.

In real time, of course, pushing the moving average to the left will force the program to hide the line within 25-price bars of the current position.

- For historical price charts, offset a simple moving average to the left by half the moving average length (for example, offset a 200-day moving average by 100 days).
- For real time charts, do not offset the moving average.

That covers drawing and identifying smiles and frowns. What about trading them?

You will want to avoid trading stocks that are in a long-term downtrend. That means longer than one year in a bull market. While those types of stocks do rebound, they probably will not make for good swing candidates. Why? Because any smile quickly turns into a frown as the stock resumes dropping.

In a bear market, be cautious going long unless the bear market is about 1 to 1½ years old. In other words, the bear market should be coming to an end before you consider trading smiles and frowns.

- Do not go long in a bear market. Wait for the bear market to end (about 1 to 1½ years old).
- When searching for smiles, avoid stocks that have been declining for over a year.

Instead, look for quick plunges such that if price returns back to where it was before the plunge, it would be a profitable and worthwhile trade. Quick declines can lead to quick rises (but that is rare). More often, a slow, stair-step rise follows a quick, straight-line decline.

Buying a dip is especially useful if the entire market has suffered a setback. Large plunges happen from time to time and they see stocks drop 10 to 20 percent or even more over a week or two. If the stocks recover, it can make for a good swing trade.

- Look for a sharp decline in a stock over a week or two that leads to a smile pattern.

When searching for frowns, you can exit as soon as the line chart shows price rounding over. Before selling, look at the historical price chart to see how the stock behaves. If the stock forms narrow peaks, then expect a narrow peak as well. For those stocks with wide turns, then expect a wide turn.

- When searching for frowns, look at the shape of prior peaks. Are they narrow or wide? Expect a similar shaped peak during the frown.

Practice paper trading by buying smiles and selling frowns. You can do this electronically if your software has scroll bars or print out a chart and cover it with another sheet that you slide to the right, exposing the price action.

- Practice paper trading smiles and frowns.

Avoid taking a position in stocks that show dead-cat bounces. Those stocks see their price drop at least 15 percent in one session. A stock showing a dead-cat bounce tends to bounce higher and then decline, sometimes suffering additional dead-cat bounces three and six months later (if earnings related. See "Surviving a Dead-Cat Bounce" in Chapter 5).

- Do not smile/frown trade stocks within six months of those stocks showing dead-cat bounces.

Avoid stocks whose swings are not tall enough. You are searching for stocks that travel like the moving average. Day to day, they are not that volatile but over time, they make tall price swings. To give you an analogy, trade the waves, not the ripples. The ripples (daily swings) should be small in comparison to the height of the waves. A weekly chart might help select stocks for swing trading using smiles and frowns. Look for large swings between the smiles and the frowns.

- Try using the weekly chart to find stocks for swing trading using smiles and frowns.

Look back at Figure 6.8. Avoid buying at A. Instead, buy at C, but profitability will improve and risk will drop if you keep it close to B.

To exit, you will likely be selling at F, but keep it as close to E as possible.

- Use Figure 6.8 as a template for how a trade should progress. Buy at C (as close to B as possible) and sell at F (as close to E as possible).

CHAPTER CHECKLIST

Based on findings in this chapter, here are some tips to consider when swing trading.

☐ The chart pattern indicator helps determine when the market changes trend. See "The Chart Pattern Indicator."

☐ The narrow range 7 pattern predicts higher volatility ahead and the breakout gives the direction. See "The NR7."

☐ The chart pattern indicator is a daily ratio of bullish and bearish NR7s in hundreds of stocks. See "The CPI Equation."

☐ Do *not* use the chart pattern indicator as a trading tool, but as a sentiment indicator. See "The CPI Equation."

☐ A new signal is often set three days after it occurs. See "The CPI Equation."

☐ Use the swing rule to help predict how far price might rise. Measure a drop from peak to valley and project that height above the peak to get a target price. See "The Swing Rule."

☐ For up trends, price tends to exceed the swing rule target rather than fall short of it. See "The Swing Rule."

☐ The swing rule for up trends works best in a bull market. See "The Swing Rule."

☐ The swing rule works best when the decline used in the measure is less than 10 percent. See "The Swing Rule."

☐ The swing rule for downtrends works best for small swings (less than 10 percent) in a bull market. See "Swing Rule for Downtrends."

☐ Above-average breakout day volume does not mean substantially better performance. See "Pump Up the Volume or Not."

☐ Chart patterns with above-average breakout volume fail twice as often as do those with below-average volume. See "Failure Rates by Volume."

☐ Throwbacks and pullbacks are three times more likely to occur after a high volume breakout. See "Throwback and Pullback Rates by Volume."

☐ For the best performance, look for the relative strength line to reverse from falling to rising from the day before the start to the day before the breakout of a chart pattern. Avoid chart patterns with a relative strength line that turns from rising to falling. See "IRS Study."

☐ For the best performance from downward breakouts of chart patterns, look for a reversal in the relative strength line from the day before the start of the chart pattern to the day before the breakout. See "IRS Study."

☐ For various trading setups using ascending triangles and rectangles, see "Three Swing Trading Setups."

☐ "Trading Setup: Simple Moving Average Tests" use a moving average to test rectangles.

☐ A smile pattern is a rounding bottom. Enter a trade after the stock has bottomed and is moving up. Avoid buying a stock when price is still moving down. See "The Smile and Frown Setup."

☐ Buy smiles not frowns. See "The Smile and Frown Setup."

☐ Categorize your trades into smiles and frowns to see if your results might improve by concentrating purchases during smiles and sales during frowns. See "Smile and Frown Testing."

☐ Use a line chart to show smiles and frowns. See "Smile and Frown Trading Tips."

☐ For historical price charts, offset a simple moving average to the left by half the moving average length (for example, offset a 200-day moving average by 100 days). See "Smile and Frown Trading Tips."

☐ For real time charts, do not offset the moving average. See "Smile and Frown Trading Tips."

☐ Do not go long in a bear market. Wait for the bear market to end (about 1 to 1½ years old). See "Smile and Frown Trading Tips."

☐ When searching for smiles, avoid stocks that have been declining for over a year. See "Smile and Frown Trading Tips."

☐ Look for a sharp decline in a stock over a week or two that leads to a smile pattern. See "Smile and Frown Trading Tips."

☐ When searching for frowns, look at the shape of prior peaks. Are they narrow or wide? Expect a similar shaped peak during the frown. See "Smile and Frown Trading Tips."

☐ Practice paper trading smiles and frowns. See "Smile and Frown Trading Tips."

☐ Do not smile/frown trade stocks within six months of those stocks showing dead-cat bounces. See "Smile and Frown Trading Tips."

☐ Try using the weekly chart to find stocks for swing trading using smiles and frowns. See "Smile and Frown Trading Tips."

☐ Use Figure 6.8 as a template for how a trade should progress. Buy at C (as close to B as possible) and sell at F (as close to E as possible). See "Smile and Frown Trading Tips."

CHAPTER 7

Introduction to Day Trading

Each trading day, millions of people sit down in front of computer screens to watch their favorite stocks pulse like human hearts. Many just want to see how their portfolio is fairing while others make or lose money by the keystroke as professional traders. Sandy is one of those trying to make the move from unemployed broker to day trader.

She spent thousands of dollars on books, wasted (in her words) nearly $5,000 attending a trading school, and even paid for two day traders to divulge their secrets. She picked the Ultra QQQ ProShares (QLD) as her security of choice to trade each day—an exchange-traded fund (ETF) designed to move twice as far as the Nasdaq 100 index. She liked the volatility that the fund provided.

With seed money from her last job and a spouse who worked full time, she started placing small bets over three months to learn the ropes. She made upward of 40 trades per day (a sign of overtrading), and *almost* broke even at days' end—until adding in commissions and fees. Her trading account was down only 8 percent at the end of those three months. That is good for a beginner.

An hour into the trading session, she called to talk about her progress. "I'm down a little bit today." She went long, but price reversed and headed south. Did she sell? "No. I bought more." At what she hoped was the bottom, she doubled her position (doubled down), controlling stock worth more than $72,000 with just $3,600, due to the 20 to 1 leverage afforded by her trading account (since then, the SEC has cracked down on firms that sponsor those types of trading accounts).

The maneuver worked. Price climbed, but she ended the trade as soon as it broke even instead of soaring with it into the clouds.

Was this an isolated case of doubling down, one that she was confident would pay off? No. She had used the technique several times before, and each time it bailed her out of a losing position.

Being rewarded after making mistakes is how bad habits form, habits that can spell disaster, habits that can end a trading career.

In our phone conversation, we discussed the merits of doubling down, and both agreed that it was dangerous. Did that stop her from using it? Our conversation reminded me of telling my dad to stop smoking. "I have to die of something," he said, and he was right. Not old age, but emphysema killed him. Would doubling down kill Sandy?

She cannot hold a stock overnight because she does not have the funds to cover the cost of ownership. She *has* to sell at the end of each day. If price happens to be lower after she doubles down, then she can lose a substantial amount of money.

The next day started well enough. She closed out her first trade for an 8 percent loss. Then she switched to her favorite fund, the QLDs, and started to "trade my way out of it."

In a phone call, she admitted, "I'm down 24 percent! How did I get myself into this? How did this happen?"

Less than an hour into the trading day, minor economic reports came out that flipped the market from positive to negative. She had bought shares and was unaware of the reports until later. She continued buying more as price dropped, averaging down, hoping that her buying alone would float a sinking ETF. She even doubled her position at the bottom, but the market had other ideas.

What she thought was the bottom became a shark's mouth that chewed on her position as the shark did to Quint in the movie *Jaws*. She had spent all of her money and could not buy another share to lower the cost. The 20 to 1 leverage was an anchor pulling her under water. Every *penny* that the ETF dropped cost her $10.

Did she close out the trade? No, but the market threw her a life preserver. It formed a V-bottom. Price began to rise.

"Will it make a double bottom, do you think?" she asked, and when I closed my eyes, I could visualize her hand strangling the computer mouse, hoping that it would act as a flotation device for the ETF. Her concern was that the rising price trend would stop and drop, forming a second bottom equal in value to the first.

"Is it going to double bottom? Will it double bottom?" Those questions became her mantra as the emotional stress of the trade gripped her.

Price climbed a wall of worry. "I think it's going to double bottom. What do you think?" Instead of asking questions, she should have used the rising price to sell for a smaller loss.

Price hit overhead resistance and formed a rectangle top, moving sideways like driftwood until it decided on a new direction. She must have been gripping the table, knuckles white, holding on as the shark chewed her legs—at least that is what her voice suggested. "Will it double bottom?"

Price slipped out of the rectangle, easing down into the depths. She sat paralyzed at her computer, watching it sink. "How did I get into this?"

She called again an hour later, her voice calm, quiet. "I lost 43 percent of my money," she said. "How did that happen? How did I get into this?" Coupled with her earlier loss, half her money drowned in red ink and disappeared from sight.

This is the first time that I have witnessed a trader blow out their account—or half of it. I have more horror stories to tell, but before we get there, the lessons and techniques in the following chapters will help prevent such disasters.

At the end of the trading day, it will be your judgment that counts for everything.

WHAT IS DAY TRADING?

Day trading is buying and selling securities during a session in which no open positions remain when the session completes. Many will agree with this definition, but you will find that some day traders hold positions overnight, perhaps out of the belief that the trend will continue. Novice day traders will hold on because they could not bear to close out the position for a loss.

The reasons for not closing out a trade are many, some of them bad. If a day trader has a good reason for keeping the trade open, then fine. I feel that a trader should not be tied down to a "day trader" label. Just have a valid reason for keeping the position open besides fear or greed.

- Day trading is opening and closing a position within the same day.

WHY DAY TRADE?

Many day trader wannabes will say something like, "I don't want to have a boss," or "I want to work for a few hours and then quit for the day." Rarely will you see a trader admit that they trade for the adrenaline rush, but some do. Many just want to make big bucks with little effort as if each day is like winning the lottery. The only work involved is pushing a wheelbarrow full of cash to the bank at day's end.

People who are serious about day trading know that it is a lot of work. Your day begins an hour or two before the open and your analysis answers questions like, "What stocks should I trade today?" and "What will the market do?" and most important, "What if I'm wrong?"

Following that, traders wait for setups to occur, both on the entry side and on the exit. Their day can end an hour or two after the open if they have met their quota for money lost or gained. Some will continue to monitor the market throughout the day. Once the market closes, then they prepare for the next day.

They conduct research, answering questions like, "How often has this price configuration led to an extended move?" or "Does volume have to be high, and if so, how high?"

Many day traders will tell you that they will not hold a trade overnight. They are afraid of single stock risk. I call that a dead-cat bounce, where price can drop 70 percent or more, in a single session. As I have mentioned, I have suffered through those on a number of occasions. Day trading minimizes—but does not eliminate—that risk.

Successful day trading is collecting a paycheck at the end of the trading day. Unsuccessful day trading is writing a check to someone you have never met. The size of that check is based on skill and luck. The difference between blowing out an account like Sandy or making a million can be just a few price bars away, every day.

- Day trading can reduce, but not eliminate, single stock risk.

IS DAY TRADING FOR YOU?

I already mentioned some of the perquisites of day trading, but let us go through them individually.

- *No driving involved.* This is my favorite. For the past five years, I have averaged 372 miles on my car annually. That is *not* 372,000 miles, but 372. My trading day commute takes 10 seconds as I walk from my bedroom to my office. I do not have to worry about road rage, car jackings, being stuck in traffic, or being stranded because my car broke down. The only time I need to drive now is to fetch groceries. That also means my car can last decades. Can you imagine looking down at your odometer 10 years from now and watching it roll over to (wait for it)

5,000 miles? Wow. Another five years and you will be due for the first oil change (based on mileage, anyway).

- *Lower auto insurance costs.* Since you are not driving your car, your insurance cost drops. Why? Because insurance companies give a discount to "pleasure" drivers, those people that do not put much mileage on their cars.
- *No customers.* I hate dealing with people. I paid my way through college in the 1970s by running a shift at a gas station. The station did not have digital pumps but analog ones. People overshot their target by nearly a penny. Nearly. That meant I had to ask for the penny or else it came out of my pocket. That fraction of a cent added up to dollars on a Friday evening when you have two gas attendants working and hundreds of cars gassing up. People would argue for that penny as if their life depended on it.

  Then there were the cheats. One man filled up the company jeep from the business behind the station. "Oops! I forgot my wallet. Bye!" Off he went, never to be seen again. Guess whose pocket the money came out of? Mine. And how about the other gas attendant who decides to slip a $20 bill into his pocket? Yes, I paid for that, too, since I was the shift manager.
- *No employees.* If you are in charge and an employee fails to come to work, how do you cope? What if several are out with the flu? Disagreements and fights among employees who act as children can spoil the fun in life. What happens when you have to fire one of them?

  An employee of mine who applied for the position I was hired into became a continual thorn in my side. I remember him saying that building a database would take two weeks. The person I hired to replace him took just three days to do the job.
- *No boss.* Sometimes you work for wonderful people and sometimes not. I recall working as a manager for a man with an exceptional memory in which every word out of his mouth was a lie. I spent an hour each day making notes to be sure I had protected myself. There is a joke that goes, "Monday is a hell of a way to spend one-seventh of your life." Monday lasted all week in that job, but I loved every minute of it.
- *Small startup and operating costs.* The cost of starting a trading business is small. All you need is seed money. You do not need a computer. You do not need a data feed or a direct access broker or a gazillion monitors lining the walls of your office. Those are optional. Phone your order into a broker and hope he does not live up to his name (that is, make you broker). That is how I traded years ago. It is not a route I recommend, but it can be done.
- *Set own hours.* If you do not want to work today, then go play golf. I have read numerous accounts of traders that say, "As soon as I meet

my profit target for the day, then I'm done." Or how about, "If I get stopped out of three trades in a row, I quit for the day. If I lose three days in a row, I am done for the week." And so on.

If you do well, you can quit early. If you do not do well, then you can leave anyway. What kind of a job is that? It sounds as if you will be spending more buying golf balls than on trading.

- *Unlimited income.* As an engineer, I was always on salary. When I put in a 60-hour week, the corporation paid me as if I worked 40. I knew what I would be earning each year. With trading, you do not have a fixed or limited income. You can make as much money as your skill allows.

WHAT ARE THE PROBLEMS OF DAY TRADING?

Like any job, day trading is not without its own set of problems. Here are several to consider.

- *Risk of failure.* To succeed in this business means you have to learn to fail. A failed trade is the cost of doing business. If you keep losses small and profits large, you can accumulate wealth.
- *Leverage.* One mistake can wipe you out. Leverage is the downfall of many traders, amateurs and professionals alike. If you limit the use of leverage (like none at all), then this is not a problem. Of course, if you have enough losing trades, then they can wipe you out, too.
- *Hours.* Despite what you may have heard or expect, day trading well takes long hours. The concentration of watching multiple computer screens during the day takes a toll, knowing that one sharp move could spell the difference between having three exotic vacations this year or none at all. But after the trading day ends, there is the analysis that follows. What went right or wrong, and why? Are bad habits forming? What will tomorrow be like?

  An hour or two before the market opens the next day, there is the search for stocks to trade. Which ones are gapping open or showing signs of trending? Which markets deserve my money today?

  You may only trade for two hours each morning, but the stress makes it feel like more, and after-hours analysis piles on additional time.
- *Financial pressures.* The mortgage is due and you have lost thousands. How do you recover? You may ponder how long you can survive without eating.
- *Social isolation.* Let me tell you Janet's story. She was a stockbroker who sold the dream of making money. Each day, she talked to people she never met into doing business with the firm she represented. The

people she called were often corporate executives who controlled pension or retirement funds entrusted to them by their employees.

She was good at bringing in business, but not good enough. After a year with the company, they fired her but gave her a generous severance. With a portion of the money, she decided to become a day trader.

Fast-forward four years. Janet is still struggling to become profitable. After the day's trading session ends, she runs through a list of friends and acquaintances and calls a few of them up, chatting with them for as long as two hours each. She rotates through the list so she does not call any of them too often.

Despite being married, when she has finished with the calls, she hops into her car and visits a bar. Why? Because she hates the solitude of trading by herself. She is happiest when surrounded by people. She *needs* the connection of being with people.

Contrast Janet with me. My mom pushed out boys every two years until I came along. I was the third of four. By the time I arrived, she knew the ropes and was tired of lavishing attention on me—at least that is how I felt.

I learned to live with that. I stayed in my room and played with Tinker Toys, erector sets, or wooden building blocks. I experimented. I explored. I became an engineer and was comfortable being my own best friend; being alone never bothered me because I was used to it.

Those characteristics of my youth carried over into adulthood. I am comfortable being by myself and do not need the company of others to be happy. Give me a book to read or give me an idea to explore in the markets and I am off, happy with the voyage of discovery.

If Janet does not talk to someone every day, she gets withdrawal symptoms like a heroin addict in need of a fix.

Which of us will likely be more successful as a trader or investor? Which of us will be happier?

Day trading is a very lonely business. If you cannot handle the solitude then do not become a day trader.

- *Stress.* The most stress so far in my life was when a teenager ran a stop sign, and I totaled his car with mine. How was I going to drive to work (that was when I was an engineer)? For me, trading stress does not come close to that event, but over time, even moderate stress can affect your health.

Traders need to learn stress reduction techniques such as meditation or daily exercise. Another way is to prevent stress from happening in the first place. One easy way to do that is to use mechanical setups. You decide in advance what conditions will trigger an entry and an exit. Once the order triggers, the trade will either make money or not. You can turn off your computer and let the trade unfold naturally without fear or greed playing a part.

- *Reliable setups break.* A setup making big bucks today can break tomorrow. That happened to one trader I know. It has been five years and the once-reliable system still has not turned a profit.

  The markets change from bull to bear and back again. Industries are seasonal or cyclic. Volatility changes daily. All of those factors can influence how successful setups are. For example, chart patterns built for trending markets fail miserably in trading ranges. What happens if the market is range bound for six months?

  Setups require maintenance. They need tuning to keep their edge. When they stop working, other setups in a trader's tool bag replace them. That means traders must have new setups available or they risk sliding into unprofitability.

- *Interruptions.* When I started day trading, I quickly learned to shut my blinds to keep out the morning sun. The glare made it impossible to read the screen. Any interruption can cost money.

- *Resources.* If you have a problem with your trading setup, emotional issues have infected your trading, or your money management rules seem to have gone nuts, to whom do you turn?

  I think it feels like driving down the highway and your car suddenly dies. Or how about when your computer starts rebooting unexpectedly? Here is one I had when I drove a Firebird. You walk out of the grocery store and scan the lot for your car. It is gone! Did you forget where you parked, or did someone steal it?

- *Health insurance costs.* One of the big benefits of working for a large corporation is having group health insurance. As a single trader, you have an individual plan. One insurance company I used went bankrupt just a few months after I joined. Another company took over the plan and started raising rates. Every three months, I received a letter saying my premium was going up by 25 to 40 percent. I repeat, *every three months!* I fired them and joined a new company. In just *seven* years, my monthly premium went from $118 to $423, with a $5,000 deductible—an increase of 350 percent. If you are just starting your trading career at a young age, imagine what your health insurance costs will be as you near retirement.

- *No pension or retirement plan.* This is another benefit of working for a large corporation. Although I have never had a pension, I did have a 401(k) to which the corporation contributed.

As a trader, you run your own business, so you can set it up to fund a retirement plan. However, if you have a losing year, will you contribute to your retirement? How will you fund it? Some trade from within their retirement accounts. Do you really want to risk draining that account?

The next chapter begins our review of day trading basics. Imagine that you have a job that pays you $50,000 annually. A survey of 1,000 traders' tax returns says that just 4 percent of them made more than that. Will you be one of them?

CHAPTER CHECKLIST

Here are some considerations for day trading.

- ☐ Day trading is opening and closing a position within the same day.
- ☐ Day trading can reduce, but not eliminate, single stock risk.
- ☐ See "Is Day Trading for You?" for a checklist.
- ☐ See "What Are the Problems of Day Trading?" for a checklist.

CHAPTER 8

Day Trading Basics

T he following is what I wrote when I first started day trading years ago.

I feel lost. That is the best way to describe how it feels to transition from swing trading, or one of the other phases in a trader's life, to day trading. Nothing seems to work. All of the rules I spent years learning just do not apply in this universe.

The feeling of foundering reminds me of how I felt when I first started trading. There was so much to consider, so many methods to try. Which one should I begin with?

Day trading is the same way. Should I play the 1-minute or 5-minute scale? Gaps on the daily chart that I considered rare happen on every stock at the market open. Should I trade with them or fade them?

What about indicator settings, candlesticks, or chart patterns? How well do they work in this universe? There are so many options, I do not know where to begin.

A day trader I watched operate for a few days told me that he spent four years and tens of thousands of dollars buying almost every course offered. Remember seeing those infomercials for trading programs on late night TV? Forget red and green signals. The programs do not work, and they cost $5,000 or more. Trading schools? You cannot buy experience, and they only teach you the basics anyway.

What should I do?

I often feel lost when tackling a large project, but I have found that breaking it down into small steps and creating a plan to tackle the project helps overcome the feeling. Let us approach day trading in a similar manner, beginning with expectations.

MANAGING EXPECTATIONS: HOW MUCH CAN YOU REALLY MAKE?

I received an email that asked, "I want to trade full time for a living. When do I know it's time to quit my day job?" My answer was simple: When profit from trading replaces your income from the day job, then consider switching. In most cases, that will never happen.

In *Trading Basics*, Chapter 2, in the section titled "Trading: How Much Money, Honey?" I dissected the question by looking at the cost of living and arrived at a value of $50,000. Your trading capital needed to be at least $50,000 to get started day trading stocks. That is not income I am talking about, but savings that you can use to fund trading activities.

What if your day job pays $60,000 annually? That is the income that you will need to replace. The average annual return (with dividends reinvested) of the S&P 500 index, based on an Internet search using data from 1950 and 1926 (two sources with different start and end dates), is 11 percent. Assume that you want to earn that kind of return. How much money would you need to start with to make $60,000 annually? Answer: 60,000 ÷ 0.11 = $546,000. In other words, if you started with a portfolio valued at $546,000 and made 11 percent trading the markets, then you would gross $60,000. That is *gross*, not net.

Do you think an annualized rate of return of 11 percent is too low? Then let us double it, to 22 percent. That would cut the required portfolio value in half, to $273,000.

I looked at actively managed (not indexed) Vanguard mutual funds to see what kind of return the professional mutt fund drivers earn over time. On average, the 23 stock funds I looked at using data from fund inception (1958 to 2005) to May 31, 2011, returned 8.9 percent annually. Using that in our equation means you would need a starting portfolio value of $675,000 to gross $60k a year.

To be fair, the discussion assumed that the mutual funds engaged in day trading. They might, but that is not their primary focus.

In Chapter 7, I told you about a study that looked at over 1,000 trader's tax returns and found that only 4 percent made more than $50,000 annually. Based on the numbers above, my guess is that few of them have large trading accounts. That means they use leverage, and since only 4 percent succeed making big bucks, they are either unlucky, unskilled, or undisciplined, and leverage magnifies the problem.

- Just 4 percent of traders make over $50,000 annually.
- To make $60,000 annually from trading requires a portfolio valued at $546,000, based on the S&P's average annual return of 11 percent.

Stock traders can leverage their portfolio 2:1 and traders qualifying as pattern day traders can increase that to 4:1. Thus, an 11 percent return on a $546,000 portfolio can effectively shrink it to $136,500, but it quadruples the risk. When things go bad, they do so four times as fast. That can mean the difference between running your car into the back of a truck at 20 mph or 80 mph. At which speed would you rather crash? The answer, of course, is to avoid the crash altogether.

If you hold overnight, factor in interest rate charges of 7 percent on the loan, based on a major brokerage firm as of mid-2011. If you were to borrow $136,500 for a year that means you would pay almost $10,000 in interest. You would have to make $70,000 to net $60,000 (excluding other charges).

The point is this: The odds of making big money are stacked against you. Even if you become profitable, you probably will not make much. The outliers who earn $100,000 or more annually on tiny stakes, are just that, outliers—the exceptions to the rule. They are the ones who stand beside huge yachts on marketing brochures. Those pictures feed dreams but not reality.

I asked a day trader what the expected annual return is for people day trading stocks. She said that a successful day or swing trader could make "many times the multiple of the S&P's return." They key word in her reply is *successful*.

- If you want to become a day trader, keep your expectations realistic, your living expenses low, and be well capitalized.

Day trading is just another business. It takes years of study to become a doctor and even more years to have the experience to get good at it. Should day trading be any different? Do not expect to make six figures the first year. There is an old joke that says, to make a small fortune in the stock market, start with a big one. That happens all the time in this business.

Enough with the scare tactics. Let us begin building a home office where we can day trade.

BUILDING THE HOME OFFICE

Setting up a home office is both exciting and seeded with many decisions, but it need not be expensive. One day trader uses a laptop, and that is all he needs. His office is wherever he happens to be.

Each month *Active Trader* magazine interviews a trader for a column called "The Face of Trading." For years now, I have been tracking the trading setups used by those traders. In a poll of 94 traders, here is what I learned.

Number of Computers

Table 8.1 shows the distribution of computers. Just over half (55 percent) of the setups I surveyed used one computer, 36 percent had two, and the rest had more than two machines powering their trading systems. One setup used five computers!

The setups used 85 desktops machines, 31 laptops, and 2 hand-held devices.

For those with multiple computers, many traders run one system dedicated to order entry and the rest for charts. Those with laptops often use them as backup devices in case their desktop crashes or they lose their Internet connection.

Computer Speed

The central processing unit (CPU) is the brains behind a computer, and speed ranged from slow, 0.6 gigahertz, to fast, 3.6 gigahertz. The most recent machines are the fast ones, as you can imagine. **Table 8.2** shows the distribution of processor speed to the percentage of setups involved.

Over half of the trading setups (60 percent) had fast machines, above 2 gigahertz.

TABLE 8.1 Number of Computers

Computers	Count	Total
1	52	55%
2	34	36%
>2	8	9%
Desktop	85	72%
Laptop	31	26%
Hand-held	2	2%

TABLE 8.2 CPU Speed

Speed (gigahertz)	Total
0 to 1	5%
1 to 2	35%
2 to 3	44%
3 to 4	16%

Computer Memory

Since the survey began in mid-2000, the amount of memory has changed dramatically. The more memory a computer has, the faster the computer tends to run (but other factors come into play, too).

Table 8.3 shows the memory size by the number of setups with that configuration. The amount of random access memory (RAM) varied from 256 megabytes for the oldest machines to 16 gigabytes. Many of the recent machines use 2 gigs or more.

Monitors: Number and Size

Do traders have a monitor for each eye? Yes, and some have more. The number of monitors varied from 1 to 13. The trader with 13 probably has a power generating station with a cooling tower in his back yard.

Table 8.4 shows the number (and size) of monitors that traders use. For example, 28 percent of the setups have only one monitor, but a surprising number have four (20 percent).

The monitor's size varied from 15" to 57" with the most common being a 19" screen followed by a 17" screen. As the price of monitors declines, expect the diagonal measure to increase. I use 23" monitors, for example, and I love them.

TABLE 8.3 Computer Memory

Size (megabytes)	Total
256	3%
512	20%
1,024	27%
2,048	22%
4,096	17%
8,192	7%
16,384	3%

TABLE 8.4 Computer Monitors

Monitors	Total	Size	Total	Size	Total
1	28%	15˝	6%	23˝	2%
2	23%	17˝	18%	24˝	9%
3	14%	18˝	4%	Over 24˝	2%
4	20%	19˝	23%		
5	7%	20˝	15%		
6	3%	21˝	8%		
More than 6	4%	22˝	12%		

Connections: Type and Number

The majority of traders connect to their broker by cable modem (63 percent). Following that, 31 percent use DSL or another type of broadband connection. The remainder use satellite (3 percent), T-1 lines (2 percent), or dial up (1 percent).

Most setups (61 percent) use brokers with direct access, but that is misleading since some setups did not report the type of connection. Direct access means the broker routes orders to the market through electronic communications networks (ECNs) or similar systems, often allowing better pricing and faster execution.

Brokers and Software

The number of brokers and software packages varied from setup to setup. However, a consensus appeared. For brokers, the most often used were TradeStation (16 setups), Interactive Brokers (15), and thinkorswim (9).

For software, TradeStation comes in first place with 32 setups, followed by RealTick (9) and eSignal (8).

For additional information on brokers and software packages, I direct you to the bonus issue of *Technical Analysis of Stocks & Commodities* magazine. They hold the Reader's Choice Awards each year and subscribers vote on their favorites. If you want to know what other traders recommend, read that issue.

The Ideal Trading Setup

If I were to build the ideal trading setup, it would contain the following (but recognize that any numbers will likely change with time as computer technology advances):

- Two desktop computers, with external hard drives for backups, and uninterruptible power supplies. Both computers would be able to trade on the Internet, so if one crashed, the other would be available. Optionally, I would also have a laptop with wireless capability. In a pinch, I could take it somewhere with wireless Internet access.
- Both computers would have processors faster than 2 gigahertz, preferably faster than 3 gigahertz.
- Two gigabytes of RAM or more, per computer.
- Two to four LCD monitors, each 23" or larger (diagonally measured). One to three screens would show the indices and stocks I traded most often with one dedicated to open trades and order entry.
- A quad-head graphics card with plenty of on-board memory.

- Support to mount the monitors if more than two screens are used.
- Broadband connection by cable, DSL, or fiber optic.
- A discount broker with direct access.

This would be a dedicated setup, used for trading only. A separate computer would handle email, web surfing, and other nontrading activities to help minimize computer viruses, spyware, and such.

That wraps up the technology involved in a trading setup, but what about everything else?

Ergonomics: Furniture

When I was a teenager, I placed an old door on two piles of newspapers and used that as a workbench. Now that I am older with money to spend, I can afford better. Here are my tips for office furniture. The following applies to desktop computers and less so for laptops. These recommendations are especially true for desktops when I discuss keyboards and preventing repetitive motion injuries.

- Look for an office chair with good lower back support. When you sit in the chair, your feet should be flat on the floor and weight should be on your feet and not on the front of your chair. With hands on the keyboard or mouse, your forearm should be horizontal, so adjust the chair accordingly. Instead of lowering your chair, perhaps a footrest would work better to help raise your feet.
- Select a desk (or two desks in an L- or U-shape) with a keyboard platform slung below the top of the desk (because the desktop is too high to be comfortable). The keyboard platform should be wide enough for both a keyboard and a mouse, so measure them before you go shopping. If you do not have a platform for the keyboard, then those can be purchased separately and bolted to the underside of the desk.
- The office supply stores also sell thick, plastic rug protectors that your chair slides on. I do not use one, but if you need to reposition your chair frequently, then one may help save your wooden floor or carpet.

  This may sound stupid, but avoid running over your pets with the chair. My dog likes to nap near me and it is a continual problem. Even after years of being chair road kill, she has not learned to keep her distance, and I often forget to look before I move. Well, her hair will grow back, and the vet cut off her tail before I got her.
- Place your monitor a comfortable distance away, usually between 18" and 24" from your eyes. If you have a monitor the size of a wall, then you will want to sit in the bleachers and not two feet away.

- For those setups without a monitor stand, when you sit erect in the chair, the monitor *top* should be level with your eyes. This means you will be looking slightly down at the screen. Instead of buying a shelf to raise the monitor, I just use two old phone books.
- Position the monitor that will get the most use directly in front of you. Position additional monitors to each side or above, if needed.
- For multiple computer setups, the keyboard and mouse you use most often should be directly in front of you. For that computer, the keyboard table should be lower than the top of the desk. You can place additional keyboards on the desk, where space allows.
- Adjust the position and tilt of the monitor so little or no glare and few reflections appear on the screen.
- If you buy a new monitor, it will probably look as bright as the sun when you turn it on. You may find that clicking on the brightness control does not dim the screen as much as expected. The secret to dimming the screen is to adjust the contrast as well as the brightness controls.
- Have a wrist pad (a cushion placed between you and the keyboard) that spans both the keyboard and mouse pad. In a pinch, I used a rolled up towel to support my wrist as I typed until I visited my nearby office supply store and bought a gel-filled one. These pads are almost a necessity if you handle your mouse a lot. Supporting your wrist is necessary to prevent repetitive motion injuries.
- Each summer, I install a window air conditioning unit in my office. That sure beats running the central air and it dramatically lowers the electric bill. In the winter, I stow the window unit and bring out a small space heater. The specifications of my desktop computer say to keep the temperature between 50°F and 95°F, so keep that in mind. Computers do not like extreme heat or cold.

OFFICE SETUP COST

The cost of becoming a day trader varies depending on the markets and exchanges traded. Certainly, the computer systems and office furniture can cost a bundle depending on how extravagant you want to be. I suggest keeping your startup costs as low as possible. If you need to add another monitor or computer, then do so only when it becomes necessary. Spending big bucks on a gold-plated setup is foolish when you do not know if you can make it in this business. Keep as much money as possible for trading capital.

A bare-bones office setup will run about $2,500 to $4,000, and most of that will be for a computer with two monitors. The cost of the computer equipment continues to spiral down, so your dollar should go further. A chair will run $200 and a desk about $300 unless you go nuts or status is important to you.

You will want to protect your computer with security software. Some of that will be free (like a firewall). Expect to spend $100 for an antivirus program, spyware program, and firewall annually.

Broker commissions have been dropping when trading online. The pay-per-trade discount brokers will charge about $7 to $10 *per trade*, but that includes research and free real-time data, depending on the size of the account. A pay-per-share broker advertises a *minimum* $1 per trade and $0.005 per share with a maximum charge of 0.5 percent of trade value. Thus a 1,000-share trade of a $50 stock will cost $5.

You can lower your commission charges by paying for exchange, clearing, transaction, and data-feed fees separately. The cost of some of those services depends on volume of shares traded and whether you are adding or removing liquidity from the exchange. Yes, it can get complicated, so ask your broker for details.

Margin loan rates vary by the size of the loan. Fees range from about 6 percent to over 8 percent for a $25,000 loan.

Since these costs can change over time, be sure to ask questions for the most recent numbers. What some traders do is open a small account with a major discount broker (such as Ameritrade, Fidelity, or Schwab) and use them as data providers, news sources, and for other bells and whistles. Then they use a deep discount (pay-per-share) broker, like Interactive Brokers, to consummate the trade.

- Creating a home office need not cost a lot of money. Start small and add equipment as necessary.

PATTERN DAY TRADING RULES

When you begin day trading, your broker may warn you about pattern day trading rules. Non–day traders may trip the rules in the following circumstances:

- When they make four or more round-trip day trades (buying and selling or selling short and covering the same security during the same day) within any rolling five-business-day period.
- When the number of day trades is at least 6 percent of all trades within the same five days in a margin account.

Accounts classified as *pattern day trading* have a minimum equity restriction imposed.

- Maintain a minimum equity value of $25,000 at the start of any day in which day trading occurs.

Accounts that fall below the $25k minimum will not be allowed to day trade. If you manage to execute a day trade in violation of the rule, you will be limited to closing trades only for 90 days or until the equity rises to at least $25,000.

Day traders are provided up to 4:1 margin on their trades (less what is called the SRO, that is, Self-Regulatory Organization requirements), based on the equity at the prior business day's close. If you exceed that margin rate then the same trading penalty applies (limiting trading to closing transactions for 90 days, and so on).

There are other rules associated with margin that are too complicated to discuss here. Be sure to talk to your broker for any regulatory changes to pattern day trading rules or brokerage-specific rules that they may impose.

- Keep the value of your trading account at least $25,000 at the start of each trading day and do not abuse leverage.

WASH SALE RULE

The wash sale rule says that a loss is disallowed if *within* 30 days of a sale you buy substantially *similar securities* or a put or call option on such securities.

The word *within* means just that: from 30 days before to 30 days after the sale (61 days total), if you buy back the shares, the loss is barred. You cannot escape the wash sale rule by first doubling your position and then selling half of it for a loss within 30 days.

Similar securities means the same stock (buying and selling General Electric, for example). It does not mean selling Ford and buying Chrysler. If you sell Ford for a loss and your wife buys it within 30 days, then that will also trip the wash sale rule. The loss is disallowed.

The wash sale rule does not apply to gains.

If a loss is disallowed because of the wash sale rule, add the loss to the cost of the new shares. In this manner, the loss is not really thrown away but merely postponed.

For example, suppose I buy 100 shares of DuPont for $5,000 and sell them for $4,000 on March 10 for a $1,000 loss. A few days later, I buy 100 shares of DuPont for $3,500. The second transaction triggers the wash sale since it occurs within 30 days of a loss on the stock. The $1,000 loss from the first sale is disallowed and the cost of the second sale becomes $4,500 ($3,500 + $1,000).

IRS Publication 550 explains the details of the wash sale rule, so consult that for the latest tax code changes.

* The wash sale rule only postpones a loss.

EIGHT TIPS FOR PICKING STOCKS TO DAY TRADE

How do you decide which stocks to day trade? That is not an easy question to answer because it depends on whom you ask. Here are my answers.

Trading Volume

Answers to the question, "To properly day trade a stock, how much volume should the stock have?" seem to depend on the number of traders asked. One told me a million shares and another says 500,000 while a third source uses 1.5 million as a minimum. Which is right?

I decided to do some investigating. I looked at 10 days of price data on the 1-minute scale and compared that to the average volume over those 10 days. For various volume levels, I looked for infrequent trading—gaps on the chart or what looked like sand sprinkled on a map.

The gaps appear when trades do not occur. The sand appears when a narrow high-low price range happens.

I found that stocks with 10-day average volume of at least 500,000 shares are good for day trading. Below that, and you may want to sell during the day and find no takers, or they will buy your shares at rates well below the last sale price.

Using 500,000 as an average means that some days will trade much more than 500k and some days will trade less. Those days with lower volume mean wider spreads or times when you want to trade and cannot because no one wants to come out and play.

To eliminate that concern, use stocks with 10-day average volume of at least 1 million shares.

* Look for stocks with a 10-day average volume of at least 1 million shares.

Trading Range

If a stock has a high to low daily trading range of 20 cents and another has a range of $1, which would be easier to peel off a profitable trade? Clearly the one with the larger range. What about a stock that has a $15 range?

If a stock has a huge trading range (whatever *huge* means), the stock may be too volatile to get good fills. In other words, before your trade is executed, price has shot up too far, too fast, and your order fills at the top of the price bar. That is an example of slippage. The stock is too volatile to trade.

That happened to me on Intel. The company released earnings the day before, and I day traded in the opening minutes. Price was so volatile that the whiplash felt worse than being rear-ended in a car.

I asked some traders about how much of the day's trading range they were able to capture. One novice day trader trying to make a profit for three years told me that on winning trades, she routinely captured 20 percent of the day's range. A successful day trader told me that he was able to capture 25 percent of the day's range if the trend stalled, and 50 percent if the trend continued throughout most of the day (in one trade, not a cumulative total).

As a beginning day trader, if you can make more than 10 percent of the day's trading range after the first year, then you are doing well. Part of that is because price does not rise or fall in a straight line. You grab what you can from each trend trade (not scalping) and hope that at day's end, the result is a profit. More seasoned pros learn to hold longer and tend to capture more of the day's range.

How much of the day's range a trader captures depends on style. One trader buys 100 shares of stocks priced over $100 each. He tries to take no more than 15 or 20 cents per trade and executes 30 to 40 trades per day. His goal is to average $400 per day. The 15- or 20-cent swings are small compared to the high-low range, and yet he makes consistent money by nibbling away at the stock. He also uses a pay-per-share broker, so his commissions are small.

The taller the day's range, the higher the profitability. If you capture 10 percent of a stock that has a $1 daily swing, then that is a dime profit. If you capture 10 percent of a $5 swing stock, then you pocket 50 cents. Thus, look for a daily average high-low move of $1 to $5. If price swings more than that, it could be too volatile and too stressful to trade profitably.

- Select stocks with a large ($1 to $5) high to low daily trading range.

Stock Price and Volatility

Stocks priced below $10 are more volatile than are those priced higher. I proved that when I did research on beta adjusted trailing stops (which was an early attempt to create a volatility based stop).

I prefer to trade stocks in the $10 to $70 range. Above that and the number of shares I am willing to trade drops. If I have my keyboard set up to trade 1,000 share blocks at the touch of a button, then I have to make a special effort to trade a high-priced stock to avoid buying too many shares and risking too much capital.

Below $10 and the volatility is often too high and the stock will move too fast to trade. In fact, I did a frequency distribution of stock price versus profit and found that 67 percent of my trades with stocks below $10 were unprofitable. Trades in the higher range (between $10 to $70) made money.

- Avoid trading stocks below $10. Low priced stocks show higher volatility.

As to volatility, some people recommend checking beta. Beta is a measure of how a stock fluctuates when compared to the market. It changes over time, so to be accurate, you need to monitor it periodically (which becomes a pain).

I do not care about beta or other volatility measures. What I care about is that the stock has a heartbeat (often measured by the daily high-low range, as already explained). If the stock moves nowhere during the day then it is not worth trading. If it makes moves that are too fast (too steep) then that is no good either. Slippage (the difference between placing an order and the price at which it fills) will be too great. The volatility sweet spot is somewhere in between. Unfortunately, I do not have a better guideline than that. If you want to use beta, then the guidelines suggest keeping it between 1.0 and 4.5.

- Avoid stocks that are too volatile or not volatile enough.

Time Scale

Which time scale should you use to trade? If you love the excitement of quick action then try the 1-minute scale. If you hate feeling as though you overdosed on caffeine, then try the 5-minute scale.

I started trading the 1-minute scale and found it noisy and volatile. It caused too much stress as price bounced and formed untradable patterns without a clear direction.

Once I switched to the 5-minute scale, it felt as if I could break for lunch, come back, and see only one additional price bar appear. Using the 1-minute scale, I was losing money. After I switched to the 5-minute scale, I started making money.

- If you have difficulty making money, try switching to a longer time scale (from 1 minute to 5 minutes, for example).

Trend

Once the above conditions have been met (volume is high enough, the stock makes a tall daily trading range, and so on), then look at the intraday chart on the scale you wish to trade. How often does price trend? Compare its trendiness, for lack of a better word, with other charts. Select stocks that trend the most (have long straight-line runs). Avoid stocks that are choppy and trendless.

Why? Because you make money by trading with the trend. The longer price trends, the easier it will be to jump in and stay in. Even scalpers are looking for trends long enough to capture a profit.

- Select stocks that trend. Avoid choppy stocks.

Tradable Chart Patterns

In your search for stocks that trend, look for tradable patterns. When stocks stop trending, do they move sideways, forming rectangle tops or bottoms? When stocks make their move by forming straight-line runs, do flags and pennants appear along the way?

Here is a short list of tradable chart patterns to look for.

- Support and resistance
- Rectangle tops and bottoms
- Ascending, descending, and symmetrical triangles
- Double tops and bottoms
- Flags and pennants
- Tight consolidation regions

The breakout from these chart patterns should result in strong moves, either higher or lower. If throwbacks or pullbacks appear, which is common after a breakout (especially when accompanied by above average volume), does price resume trending, or does it wobble up and down in a trendless manner?

- Select stocks with tradable price trends after the breakout from chart patterns.

Bid/Ask Spread

When you look at a price chart and see something that resembles the Great Wall of China running from left to right, you know that the bid/ask spread is too wide. This type of price movement often appears on low-priced stocks, because of the difference between the bid price and what is asked.

If you choose to trade such a stock, recognize that you could be buying at the asking price and selling at the bid. If that spread is 5 cents and you are trading 1,000 shares, then that means a loss of $1,000 \times 0.05$, or $50 for each way ($100 for a round-trip). That is far greater than the broker's commission you are paying.

- Look at the difference between the bid and ask prices. If they are wider than a penny or two apart, consider looking for another stock to day trade.

Building Core Holdings

Once you have found a stock with the above features, then look for another. Continue searching until you find several (up to six), creating a core list of stocks. They will be the ones you trade most often. They will become your best friends, stocks that bare their intimate secrets because you study them for hours each day.

When your profitability drops, review your core selections and see if other stocks should take the place of a core holding. If another stock has consistent straight-line runs in a hot industry, then swap it for one of the core members struggling to find a trend each day. Do not fall in love and marry any core stocks. Trade them, sure, but look for emerging stocks that might lead to better profit.

When you do make a substitution to a core holding, be careful trading your new friend. You do not know how it behaves, so cut the position size until its price movements become more predictable.

- Build a core list of stocks that you trade each day.

If you keep track of all of your trades, you should be able to tell which of the core stocks make you the most money. The ones that fail to live up to expectations are the ones that should be phased out.

Which stocks do best when the market trends higher? Which outperform when going down, based on your trades? What time of day gives the highest profit (within a half hour of the open, two hours in the morning, during lunch, just before the close and so on)? All of that can be revealed by an analysis of your trades.

- Log each trade and analyze the results to determine the stocks that do best going long, going short, the best time of the day to trade, and so on.

PRICE REVERSAL TIMES REVEALED!

If price has been trending for 20 minutes since the opening bell, is it time to sell? Probably. Why? Because the chances improve that in the next minute price will reverse. That is the conclusion I made after analyzing almost 21 million one-minute price bars (which is the equivalent of 205 years' worth of daily price bars).

I used two sets of 1-minute data: February 3, 2003–December 30, 2005 (bull market) and February 1, 2007–February 13, 2009 (mostly bear market). I found all peaks and valleys within that data and sorted them by the minute in which they occurred.

I also used two tests, one that found the highest peak within 5 bars (5 bars before to 5 bars after for 11 bars total) and another test that used 10 bars. Both showed the same results, or nearly the same. The point of this explanation is that the reversal should be sustained for a length of 5 to 10 bars (5 to 10 minutes), at a minimum. That varies from situation to situation, but it should be a good rule of thumb.

A frequency distribution of the top 3 reversal times for each hour of the trading day appears in **Table 8.5**. The percentage is how often the reversal appears for that minute among all samples for that minute. For example, the 9:31 minute (all times are Eastern Standard) had 9,385 reversals out of a possible 39,895, or 24 percent.

Most of the hourly reversal periods fall into three slots. **Hourly:** Near the top of each hour, such as 10:01, 11:01, and so on, expect a reversal. Usually it happens a minute after the hour except for the 3:00 hour, although the 3:01 slot ranked fourth (and so does not appear in the table).

Half hour: A minute after the half hour, such as 9:31, 10:31, and so on, expect a reversal. In fact, the 9:31 slot shows the most reversals of any minute during the trading day. This also suggests that you avoid taking a position going into the opening minutes of the session. The first three minutes for peaks and the first two minutes for valleys cluster near the top

TABLE 8.5 Top Three Reversal Times per Hour for Stocks

Peaks				Valleys			
Morning	%	Afternoon	%	Morning	%	Afternoon	%
9:31	24%	12:01	8%	9:31	22%	12:01	8%
9:46	7%	12:16	8%	9:46	7%	12:21	8%
9:51	7%	12:31	8%	9:54	7%	12:31	8%
10:01	9%	1:01	8%	10:01	8%	1:01	9%
10:31	8%	1:31	8%	10:31	8%	1:31	8%
10:46	8%	1:51	8%	10:46	8%	1:51	8%
11:01	8%	2:01	9%	11:06	8%	2:01	9%
11:31	8%	2:31	8%	11:11	7%	2:16	8%
11:51	8%	2:46	8%	11:31	8%	2:31	8%
		3:31	8%			3:31	8%
		3:51	9%			3:51	8%
		4:00	10%			4:00	11%

of the reversal times. In other words, the opening is especially volatile, but it ends quickly.

- Avoid taking a position during the first minute of the trading day.

The last reversal slot is a range, from **46 to 51 minutes after the hour** (such as 9:46, 9:51, 10:46, 11:51). Reversals at 51 minutes past the hour beat the 46-minute slot by two counts (7 to 5) in the table, so I view it as a more reliable value.

- Price is most likely to reverse direction a minute after the hour, a minute after the half hour, and 51 minutes after the hour.

What I find striking about the numbers is that it does not matter whether price is trending up (a peak) or down (a valley). I separated the numbers into bull and bear markets and they had no effect on results, too.

- The reversal times are the same regardless of price trend (up or down) and market condition (bull or bear).

The second most frequent reversal period for the trading day was the close, 4:00, followed by 10:01 (peaks) and 3:31 (valleys).

A chart of the peaks and valleys looks like a picture of an electrocardiogram. The reversal peaks are regularly spaced with lots of noise filling the space between. A line chart using a 30-period average (since the tallest peaks are 60 minutes apart—use half for a complete up/down cycle) shows that after 1:30, the number of peaks and valleys increases. In other words, the afternoon session is more volatile with a higher reversal rate. If you want sustained trends, favor the morning session.

- Price trends more often in the morning session than in the afternoon.

WHAT TIME SETS INTRADAY HIGH AND LOW?

I read an article in *Active Trader* magazine (May 2011) that discussed research on the time of day most likely to find the day's high and low for *futures*.

I programmed my computer and used 60,801 days of intraday *stock* data to catalog at what minute price posted the day's high and low. My test included both bull and bear markets and significantly more data than the magazine, and yet we arrived at similar conclusions.

I excluded half days (such as the half day before major market holidays).

TABLE 8.6   Intraday Highs and Lows

Time Period	High	Low
First minute	10%	9%
First half hour	40%	37%
First hour	49%	46%
Last half hour	14%	14%
Last hour	19%	20%
Last minute	3%	3%

Table 8.6 shows the results of tests where only the first time the stock reached the intraday high or low was counted. For example, if the intraday high was $10 and price reached it during the first minute and again at 11:00 and 12:00, only the first touch counted.

By far, the first minute saw the most occurrences of the stock setting the day's high or low, at 10 and 9 percent of samples, respectively. The last minute of the trading day also showed a spike, but it was not nearly as popular as the first minute.

The opening minutes tended to see price post the day's high or low most often. Looking at longer periods, we find that 40 percent of the time, price set the day's high within a half hour of the open and 49 percent of the time within the first hour. The last half and full hour showed lesser counts of setting the day's high or low.

- Most often, stocks set the day's high (10 percent) or low (9 percent) within the first minute of trading.

Combining the periods, we can say that there is a 68 percent chance (49 percent + 19 percent) that the day's high will be set within the first or last hour of trading. For the day's low, the probability is 46 percent + 20 percent, or 66 percent, that a new low will occur within the first or last hour of trading.

- Within the first and last hour of trading, stocks post the day's high or low between 66 percent (for lows) and 68 percent (for highs) of the time.

When looking at multiple hits of the day's high or low, I found that they happen 38 percent of the time for both highs and lows. In other words, 38 percent of the time, price will reach the day's high or low at least once more. Often, price will tie the day's high or low an average of 2.7 times each. Let me be clear: On 38 percent of the days, price will tie the day's high or low an average of 2.7 times. The average time between touches is 41 minutes for highs and 40 minutes for lows.

- Price will tie the day's high or low 38 percent of the time, on average, sometime during the day.

INSIDE LEVEL II QUOTES

The Nasdaq quotation system has three levels of service. Level I offers the "inside quote," the highest bid and asked prices along with the number of shares offered (the "size") with the last sale information. The Level II display represents trading activity in a stock. It shows a range of bid and asked prices and sizes along with market maker IDs and exchanges. Level III has the same information as level II, but with more statistics and the ability to post and change bid and asked prices. Institutions making markets in stocks use Level III.

The usual configuration for Level II shows a color-coded list box of bid prices on the left and asked prices on the right. Each color groups together the same bid or asked prices. Small charts above the list box show price and size distributions of the bid and asked information.

There is debate among traders as to whether Level II quotes add value since a trader or market maker can make a bid or offer at any price only to remove it seconds later (providing it has not been accepted).

For example, I have seen a bid for 3,000 shares appear and disappear repeatedly (at a price below the current best bid) as if a market maker were flashing a signal that he had a large position he wanted to *buy*. Those traders wanting to sell withdrew their offers in the belief that price would rise on the buying demand. When selling pressure evaporated, the unchanged buying demand made price climb. Then the market maker reappeared and dumped his 3,000 shares at a higher price (remember, he first wanted to *buy* it).

In my trading, I used to watch Level II to help time entry and exits, but found myself scratching my head over the direction price moved. For example, when I thought Level II was pointing the way higher, price would drop instead. With all the games market makers play, I now find the tool to be entertaining to watch, but almost useless for trading.

- Should you use Level II quotes?

Level II Games

What kind of games do market makers play with Level II? Let us begin with the classic interpretation of how the display *should* work, and assume that the *size* of each bid or offer is similar.

When the top color group shrinks on the bid side and expands on the ask side, then look for the stock to drop. This clockwise movement says that fewer traders are bidding (demand) and more want to dump the turkey (selling pressure).

When the color movement goes counter-clockwise, with the top color expanding on the left (more bidding at the same price) and shrinking on the right (fewer offering), then look for the stock to rise.

- Clockwise movement from shrinking bids to expanding offers suggests a falling stock. Counter-clockwise movement of bids and offers means a rising stock.

Knowing who is behind the market marker IDs can provide valuable intelligence about how the stock is going to behave. Watch the electronic communication networks (ECNs) for activity representing day traders. If a number of day traders *offer* a stock through their ECNs, then that is a sign the stock is going to tumble. The same applies to bids before a stock rises.

Before trading in the direction of the ECN orders, make sure that others are following, too. You want to see brokers and the smart money trading in the direction of the new trend. Otherwise, you could drown by jumping in.

- ECNs that cater to day traders can signal market direction, providing others follow their lead.

Look at the bids or offers further down the list. Are those prices at or near pivot points, whole numbers (prices that end in zero or double zero), or perhaps at the previous day's high or low? Those prices can help identify technical turning points. They tell where traders think the stock will reverse.

- Bids or offers further down the list help identify technical turning points.

In less active and low cost stocks, market makers can stack the Level II display, making it look like there are more offers than bids, suggesting that price will drop. Once it does, they jump in and buy the stock on the cheap, forcing price to move higher and beginning a strong up trend.

The reverse also happens with more bids than offers. Price rises, making it look like a strong rally, only to make a sustained move down when market makers begin dumping the stock.

The size of the bid or offers is the key. Many times, you see a large number of small lots (100 shares) bid or offered, tricking traders into thinking that buying demand or selling pressure is higher than it really is.

- Watch for market markers to manipulate the Level II display with numerous small-sized bids or offers. The market will move in an unexpected direction, trapping players on the wrong side.

Market makers can also bid/offer 100 shares (or whatever size they want) and as soon as someone takes the bait, they bid/offer another 100 shares at the same price. They continue doing that until exhausting their supply (which could number thousands of shares). This "parking" tends to freeze the bids or offers at the same price.

When these types of games occur, look at the market maker ID and watch which ones tend to manipulate the market. Over time, you will get a sense of the reliability of the quotes by seeing that the ECNs play by the rules, but other market makers do not.

- Use the market maker ID to identify participants that frequently manipulate the stocks you commonly trade. The ID may vary from stock to stock because a different individual from the same firm may handle the other stock.

HEARTBEAT OF THE MARKET: TIME-AND-SALES TICKER

The time-and-sales ticker tape is what others call the last sale screen or time-and-sales window. The scrolling display lists each sale's price, time, and size.

The speed of the transactions demonstrates how liquid the stock is. A fast moving ticker means many traders are vying for position and actively trading the stock. A slow moving ticker means traders are out to lunch and bid-ask spreads may be too wide for a good fill.

- The speed of the time and sales ticker shows the stock's liquidity.

I have the time-and-sales ticker displayed on my screen. When I am looking to make a trade, often trying to time the exit, I watch how fast the scrolling occurs. When the scrolling slows or even stops, then that is the signal for a reversal. That is when I sell the stock.

Of course, using the ticker tape in this manner only works in highly liquid stocks and only at certain times of the day (avoid lunchtime). However, you may be surprised at how often this unique momentum indicator works. It reminds me of putting a car in neutral and coasting up a hill. The car slows to a stop before beginning to coast back down the hill.

- A slowing time-and-sales ticker can indicate a coming price reversal.

PRE-MARKET CHECKLIST

I complete a checklist of items before I start day trading each morning. Here is that list.

- ☐ **News.** For the stocks that I day trade most often, I check the news on yahoo.com to see if any new development might influence their price.
- ☐ **Earnings.** Checking for earnings announcements is especially important if I intend to swing trade the issue and hold it overnight. I do *not* want an earnings announcement to take the stock down before the next day's open.
- ☐ **Economic reports.** Almost every business day, the government releases economic data that is reported on websites such as yahoo.com. Finding out the times and importance of those releases can help prepare a trader for market reactions.

    For example, if the Federal Reserve announces an interest rate increase on Wednesday, you can be sure that the market is going to react. Knowing that the announcement is coming means that you prepare by exiting open positions. Not knowing about an important announcement means taking an increased risk.
- ☐ **Futures.** I check the futures reading on yahoo.com to get a feel for the opening direction. If futures are down 10–20 points, then the market is likely to open lower. If the futures are up 10–20 points, then I look for a gap up open. The futures number is a reliable way to determine the direction of the stock market in the opening minutes of trading. It does not tell you how the market will close, and often the effect lasts only a few minutes after the open.
- ☐ **Heatmap.** The Nasdaq pre-market heatmap shows the Nasdaq 100 stocks using a color code to illustrate significant price changes premarket. You can find links to the heatmap at the Nasdaq website: http://www.nasdaq.com. Look under the "Extended Trading" tab for "Pre-Market Heatmap" or do a site search.

    The heatmap is useful for finding gap plays.

☐ **Pre-market trading.** When I select a stock, especially if it is from the heatmap, I look at the pre-market activity. I look at prior trading (days and weeks) to see where major support and resistance levels are. I have found intraday support and resistance to be almost useless to predict where a stock might turn. Daily support and resistance is more reliable.

☐ **Closing price prediction.** I know that many of you will not be able to do this, but I will tell you anyway because I find it valuable. I wrote a program that computes the high-low range of the prior day, looks back through history, and counts how many times the stock closed higher or lower the next day. If the analysis says that in 100 out of 150 times the stock closed higher, then I want to concentrate on the long side during the day. I may even use a market on close order to exit open positions.

This technique works well for the indices, too. It accurately predicts whether the market will close higher or lower. It is not always right, and it is more accurate when the probabilities are highest, of course. If the reading is 50-50, then that might mean it will be a good day to spend gardening (or whatever floats your boat). It could be a nontrending day.

With some work, you can do the same analysis with an Excel spreadsheet. Download the historical data and compute the high-low range of each day as a percentage (no decimal). Then count how many times a particular move has occurred in the past and what the next day's outcome was.

AFTER-MARKET ANALYSIS

Once the session is over, analyze your trades. How many times have you heard that you learn more from your mistakes than your winners? Winners have lessons to teach, too.

For example, did a trade win because you canceled a stop loss and rode out a decline? That type of behavior leads to bad habits. So, *do* look at your winning trades as well as your losers.

One key question to ask is how many trades followed your trading plan? I have mentioned before that you should ignore the money and instead focus on technique. If you have a winning setup and follow that setup, then over time you should make money. Deviations will likely cost money. Try to trade better by planning the trade and trading the plan.

• Did each trade follow the trading plan?

You want to get to a point where your trades are executed as if by machine. Buy only when the conditions are right, when they show the highest probability of winning. Sell when price hits a target, you get an exit signal, or are stopped out. Always use a stop, by the way.

Get to a point in your trading where confidence in your ability replaces fear or greed. Remove stress by using mechanical orders (limit orders, buy stops, stop loss orders) to enter and exit trades based on tested setups.

CHAPTER CHECKLIST

Here is a checklist to help get started day trading stocks.

- ☐ Just 4 percent of traders make over $50,000 annually. See "Managing Expectations: How Much Can You Really Make?"
- ☐ To make $60,000 annually from trading requires a portfolio valued at $546,000, based on the S&P's average annual return of 11 percent. See "Managing Expectations: How Much Can You Really Make?"
- ☐ If you want to become a day trader, keep your expectations realistic, your living expenses low, and be well capitalized. See "Managing Expectations: How Much Can You Really Make?"
- ☐ See "Building the Home Office" for tips on creating your own trading space.
- ☐ Creating a home office need not cost a lot of money. Start small and add equipment as necessary. See "Office Setup Cost."
- ☐ "Pattern Day Trading Rules" outline the regulations for day traders.
- ☐ The wash sale rule only postpones a loss. See "Wash Sale Rule."
- ☐ Look for stocks with a 10-day average volume of at least 1 million shares. See "Trading Volume."
- ☐ Select stocks with a large ($1 to $5) high to low daily trading range. See "Trading Range."
- ☐ Avoid trading stocks below $10. Low-priced stocks show higher volatility. See "Stock Price and Volatility."
- ☐ Avoid stocks that are too volatile or not volatile enough. See "Stock Price and Volatility."
- ☐ If you have difficulty making money, try switching to a longer time scale (from 1 minute to 5 minute, for example). See "Time Scale."
- ☐ Select stocks that trend. Avoid choppy stocks. See "Trend."
- ☐ Select stocks with tradable price trends after the breakout from chart patterns. See "Tradable Chart Patterns."

☐ Look at the difference between the bid and ask prices. If they are wider than a penny or two apart, consider looking for another stock to day trade. See "Bid/Ask Spread."

☐ Build a core list of stocks that you trade each day. See "Building Core Holdings."

☐ Avoid taking a position during the first minute of the trading day. See "Price Reversal Times Revealed!"

☐ Price is most likely to reverse direction a minute after the hour, a minute after the half hour, and 51 minutes after the hour. See "Price Reversal Times Revealed!"

☐ The reversal times are the same regardless of price trend (up or down) and market condition (bull or bear). See "Price Reversal Times Revealed!"

☐ Price trends more often in the morning session than in the afternoon. See "Price Reversal Times Revealed!"

☐ Most often, stocks set the day's high (10 percent) or low (9 percent) within the first minute of trading. See "What Time Sets Intraday High and Low?"

☐ Within the first and last hour of trading, stocks post the day's high or low between 66 percent (for lows) and 68 percent (for highs) of the time. See "What Time Sets Intraday High and Low?"

☐ Price will tie the day's high or low 38 percent of the time, on average, sometime during the day. See "What Time Sets Intraday High and Low?"

☐ Should you use Level II quotes? See "Inside Level II Quotes."

☐ Clockwise movement from shrinking bids to expanding offers suggests a falling stock. Counter-clockwise movement of bids and offers means a rising stock. See "Level II Games."

☐ ECNs that cater to day traders can signal market direction, providing others follow their lead. See "Level II Games."

☐ Bids or offers further down the list help identify technical turning points. See "Level II Games."

☐ Watch for market markers to manipulate the Level II display with numerous small-sized bids or offers. The market will move in an unexpected direction, trapping players on the wrong side. See "Level II Games."

☐ Use the market maker ID to identify participants that frequently manipulate the stocks you commonly trade. The ID may vary from stock to stock because a different individual from the same firm may handle the other stock. See "Level II Games."

☐ The speed of the time and sales ticker shows the stock's liquidity. See "Heartbeat of the Market: Time-and-Sales Ticker."

☐ A slowing time-and-sales ticker can indicate a coming price reversal. See "Heartbeat of the Market: Time-and-Sales Ticker."

☐ See "Pre-Market Checklist" for a shopping list to help profit from the day's trading.

☐ Did each trade follow the trading plan? See "After-Market Analysis."

CHAPTER 9

Opening Gap Setup

The first part of this chapter takes a systematic approach to building a trading setup for opening gaps. What I discovered during research is that the opening gap is profitable, but not by much. When you are right, you can make 50 cents to 75 cents a share. That may not sound like much, but multiply that by 1,000 shares and it means $500 to $750 for each day trade. Annualized, that is between $125,000 and $200,000. You can make that kind of money after about three minutes of screen time, watching the charts. Wait for the entry signal and place another order to sell at the close with a stop in place, too. Then spend the day golfing, fishing, or in a glider, pretending you are a bird.

As glowing as that sounds, winning is just half the picture. Losses average about 20 cents a share, which is what I consider a maximum for a day trade. That still leaves a payoff ratio of up to 5 to 1, depending on the setup. Unfortunately, you will be stopped out about 70 percent of the time, which is not fun. Still, the numbers say that this setup is profitable. Perhaps you can find ways to improve it, such as using other types of market indicators to boost performance or season it with experience.

After that, I review three other opening gap setups that traders use, but my tests show that the skill of the trader, not the setup, is what leads to profits. How do you test experience? The answer reminds me of the time when our knowledge of aerodynamics suggested that bumblebees should not be able to fly. The three trading setups fit that category. Some traders may find that they work even if they cannot explain why.

OPENING GAP TEST DATA

The tests that follow use two databases, one composed of 54 stocks and intraday data on the 1- or 5-minute scale, from February 3, 2003, to December 30, 2005, and February 1, 2007, to February 13, 2009. Those two periods cover a bull and bear market, respectively. The stocks are split into two groups: in-sample (28 stocks) and out-of-sample (26 stocks). I felt this division was better than splitting the group along time periods. The data is the same as used in prior tests, and it includes the equivalent of 205 years' worth of daily price data.

The second database uses daily price data from 555 stocks beginning with the March 2000 bear market until July 1, 2011. That period includes two bear markets and two bull ones.

For both databases, not all stocks covered the entire period.

SETUP: FADING THE OPENING GAP

Traders define an opening gap as one in which the opening price gaps away from the prior day's close, leaving a hole on the chart—at least temporarily. The gap definition is different from the one we explored in Chapter 5 of *Trading Basics* (under the heading Identifying and Trading Gaps; see Figure 5.8).

One of the differences between day trading and the other types of trading is that opening gaps appear on almost every stock at the opening bell. On the daily chart, gaps such as area, breakout, continuation, and exhaustion gaps are rare by comparison. To be fair, though, opening gaps also appear on the daily charts, but they are as difficult to see as fleas on a dog.

Figure 9.1 shows the four types of opening gaps for day traders. A full gap up occurs when price opens higher (C), gapping above the prior day's close (B) and above the day's high price (A). The opening gap is between B and C, but it must also clear A to be a full gap up.

Let me be clear. The dot at C is the *opening* price of the next day and the tall candle (adjacent to A) represents the *entire* day's price range, not just the last candle on the 1-minute scale.

A full gap down is similar except it applies when price gaps lower. The low at E is above the opening price at F. D is the prior close, so the opening gap is between D and F. Again, the prior day's trading range is compared to the opening price of the next day. The opening price must clear (gap below) the prior candle, including the lower shadow, for a full gap down.

A partial gap up is more complicated and difficult to see. Point I represents the opening price with G being the prior day's high and H is the prior

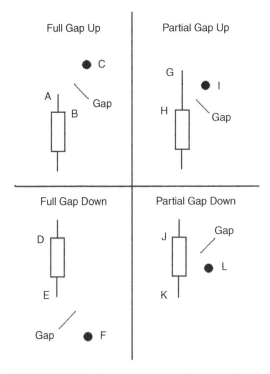

FIGURE 9.1 The various opening gap types for day traders.

close. The opening gap appears between H and I (the close and open, respectively), but I does not clear the high at G. It is a partial gap up because the opening price has not opened above G.

A partial gap down is similar with the opening price represented by L. It gaps below the prior day's close (J), but remains above the day's low (K). The gap is between J and L.

For the tests that follow, I ignore the shadows of the candles and just compare the opening and closing prices unless otherwise stated. When I search for a gap to close, I mean that price returns to the value of the prior close. I ignore the shadows when contemplating closing or filling the gap.

Do Bull or Bear Markets Matter?

If you ask enough day traders, some will say that they fade the opening gap and others trade with the trend. Fade means to go against the prevailing trend, like trying to spit into the wind. These opposing groups can both be right (though not at the same time) when trading gaps, but their setups differ.

If you want to trade the opening gap, the main question is this: How often does the opening gap close each day? In other words, if price gaps open lower, what is the probability that price will climb back up to the level of the prior day's close? Using Figure 9.1 as a reference, how often will the price at F or L climb back up to the close at D or J during the day?

I decided to answer that question by using my 555 stock database, but starting from March 2000, the start of the bear market. Searching backward in time, I excluded price data for stocks that dropped below $3 (meaning I used data from the present—above $3—and stopped if price moved below $3 in the past). I found 435,410 up gaps and 356,820 down gaps.

I wanted to know how the bull or bear market affected the closure rate. I found that up gaps closed 73 percent of the time in a bull market and 74 percent of the time in a bear market. Down gaps closed 75 percent of the time in a bull market and 72 percent of the time in a bear market. I concluded that the market condition (bull or bear) had almost no effect on the closure rate of opening gaps.

- Bull or bear markets have almost no influence on the closure rate of opening gaps.

Since we can ignore the bull or bear market distinction for day trades, I let the test run (regardless of the bull/bear market condition) using all of the data I have on the 555 stocks (meaning the start date was as old as January 1990, and perhaps earlier). The data amounted to over 1.6 million opening gap samples. The result is that 72 percent of up gaps closed and 72 percent of down gaps closed by the end of the trading day.

- In stocks, 72 percent of opening gaps (either up or down) closed by day's end.

Another test on exchange-traded funds found that just 56 percent of up and down opening gaps closed by day's end (up and down gaps both scored 56 percent). That test used 88 long-only ETFs and found just over 207,000 gaps.

- ETF opening gaps (either up or down) closed just 56 percent of the time.

Closure Rate for Full and Partial Gaps

It makes sense that partial gaps close more frequently than full gaps, but let us check this to be sure.

I switched databases to use intraday data on the 1-minute scale. I found that full gaps closed 77 percent of the time (the same rate for full up and down gaps), 78 percent closed for partial gaps down, and 79 percent closed for partial gaps up. In other words, the closure rate for full gaps versus partial gaps is not much different.

- The closure rate for full and partial gaps is similar: 77 percent versus 79 percent, respectively.

What Gap Size Works Best?

The smaller the gap, the easier it is for price to close the gap. To test the closure rate, I measured the gap size from the prior day's close to the open the next day and followed price throughout the day to determine how often it closed the gap (meaning price moved far enough to reach the prior day's closing price).

I used intraday data on the 1-minute scale. **Table 9.1** shows the results, seasoned with two flavors that I will describe in a moment.

Let me give you a few examples to show how to read the table. I used the prior day's open-to-close price trend to see if momentum helped or hurt when price gapped open a day later. The "Any" column ignores the prior day's price trend.

TABLE 9.1 Gap Size versus Closure Rate

Prior Day's Open to Close Price Trend				Price to 50-Day Simple Moving Average (SMA)	
Up Gaps					
Gap Size	Down	Up	Any	Below SMA	Above SMA
7%	27%	26%	26%	39%	14%
6%	35%	34%	35%	46%	24%
5%	33%	37%	35%	46%	22%
4%	38%	49%	43%	53%	33%
3%	52%	47%	50%	56%	46%
2%	54%	56%	55%	60%	51%
1%	67%	69%	67%	71%	66%
Down Gaps					
Gap Size	Down	Up	Any	Below SMA	Above SMA
1%	68%	67%	68%	70%	67%
2%	60%	55%	58%	61%	55%
3%	47%	47%	47%	48%	44%
4%	46%	47%	46%	51%	40%
5%	43%	35%	40%	41%	38%
6%	41%	32%	37%	40%	32%
7%	28%	26%	27%	29%	17%

Begin with the first row of numbers, a gap size of 7 percent. When price gapped up 7 percent and the prior day's trend was down, there was a 27 percent chance that the stock would drop far enough to close the gap. If the prior day's trend was up, then there was a 26 percent probability of a gap closure. If you ignore the prior day's trend, then the gap closure rate was also 26 percent.

I consider a gap size of 2 percent to be a minimum, and it represents 20 cents a share for a $10 stock. Unfortunately, only about half of the gaps up (55 percent) will see price drop far enough to close the 2 percent gap by day's end.

For 2 percent gaps downward, the highest probability is to wait for an open-to-close drop the day before price gaps open lower. There is a 60 percent chance that price will close the gap.

As the "Any" column shows, the direction of the prior day's price trend does not significantly change the gap closure rate. Down gaps tend to do slightly better if the prior day's price trend swung downward from open to close. Similarly, up gaps tend to outperform slightly better after a prior day's uptrend.

- The closure rate for *up* gaps increases if the prior day's open to close price trend was also up.
- The closure rate for *down* gaps increases if the prior day's open to close move was downward.

Think of these two scenarios as momentum running out of steam. In the case of an up gap after an up day (open to close, not close to close), price trended higher the prior day and gaps upward. That buying enthusiasm evaporates like drops of sweat on concrete in the hot Texas sun, and selling pressure takes price down, closing the gap.

The same fear and greed influence occurs after a downward price trend and downward gap. The selling pressure gives way to buying enthusiasm, as if price is so low, it is a steal. That forces price upward to close the gap.

Keep in mind that the closure rate is not as important as how much money you can make by trading the opening gap. Testing shows that profit increases by using larger gaps, not smaller ones. Even though the closure rate for gaps 3 percent or higher is small (compared to 1 percent gaps), the move becomes tasty since the gap is so large. The gap might not close, but selling at day's end can result in moves of 50 cents a share, or higher.

Use a Simple Moving Average?

Let us discuss using a moving average, the results of which appear in Table 9.1. I tried a 50-day simple moving average (SMA) to see if the closure rates changed. I used a moving average on *daily* price data, not intraday data. Using a 50-period SMA on intraday data means you only get part of the last hour's worth of trading, and the gap often flings price well outside of that range. Using daily data for our moving average gives a longer-term price trend, which is what we want.

For closure rates, I used 1-minute intraday data and the same method as described for the prior day's move (open to close). I used the closing price of the first minute of each trading day and compared that to the 50-*day* SMA. The first minute is the one that gaps from the prior day's close. I did not test other moving averages.

From Table 9.1, if price gaps up 7 percent, but remains below the moving average, then 39 percent of those gaps close by day's end. Think of this scenario as an upward gap in a short downtrend. Price fades the trend and closes the gap.

Similarly, for 7 percent up gaps that were *above* the moving average, just 14 percent of those gaps closed by the end of trading. This scenario occurs when price is in a rising price trend and gaps higher. That bullish enthusiasm makes it less likely that price will close the gap.

In all but two cases, price below the moving average beats the results of the prior day's open to close price trend. When price is *above* the moving average and it gaps, the closure rate is *worse*.

In many instances, the differences between the numbers are not significantly different. However, if you want a trading edge, then only fade gaps below the 50-day SMA and forget about the prior day's price trend. I confirmed that with testing.

- For fading the opening gap, the prior day's price trend is less significant than the gap being below the 50-day simple moving average.
- Fade only when price gaps below the 50-day simple moving average (it works for both up or down gaps).

Should You Hold Longer Than a Day?

Let me tell you a quick story that I read in a magazine (Pugliese, 2012). A day trader held 1,000 shares of stock. At the end of the first day, he was down $1,500, so he decided to hold the trade open to the next day and hope for a recovery.

The next day the stock plummeted by $50 a share. That meant he had lost a heart stopping $50,000. He decided to hold on for a bounce. In fact, he used his remaining cash and bought more of the stock.

It took a few weeks, but the stock declined an additional 80 percent, wiping the day trader off the board. The moral of the story is this: If you are a day trader, think twice about holding longer than a day.

If you hold a day trade open overnight, what are the chances that the gap will close the next day or the next? To find out, I used my database of stocks covering 1.6 million opening gaps (daily price data). I found that 72 percent of the gaps closed on the day of the gap, 80 percent within the first two days, and 84 percent closed within three days.

If the gap does not close on the day price gaps open, then the chance of it closing diminishes with each passing day. In fact, tests show the chance that a gap still open on the second day closes on that day is 28 percent and it is 18 percent the next day.

- There is a 28 percent chance that price will close a gap on the second day and 18 percent on the third day. Holding a trade open for an additional day and hoping for the gap to close is a mistake.

Gap Closes. Hold On or Sell?

When a gap closes, should you hold on for additional gains? To answer that, I ran another test using 1.6 million opening gaps. Of those gaps, 72 percent of them closed—a rate I have already discussed. Then I looked at how often price either closed higher for a down gap, or closed lower for an up gap. In other words, if you fade the gap and it closes, should you hold the position until the end of the day anyway?

Price closed the day higher than the previous day after a down gap 47 percent of the time. In other words, price gapped down, closed the gap, and then remained above the prior day's close 47 percent of the time.

Similarly, 48 percent of the time price gapped upward then dropped to close the gap and remained below the prior close at day's end.

- Fading the gap and holding on for additional gains until the day's close works 47 to 48 percent of the time.

Trade Entry Details

Perhaps by now you are wondering where this discussion is leading. Let us take these observations so far, mix in a few more, and construct a trading setup.

I logged how often price gapped down and counted the number of price bars in which the high price dropped after the gap. Why is that important? Because it tells you when to enter a trade.

Figure 9.2 make this clear. Suppose that candle A is the one that gaps lower at the day's open. The high of that candle is at A. Place a buy stop a penny above A and trail it lower as the high price drops.

When candle C begins forming, lower the stop to a penny above B. When candle D begins forming, drop the stop to a penny above C. Candle D triggers the buy stop and the trade begins.

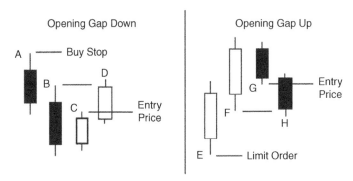

FIGURE 9.2 A trailing buy stop gets you into the trade when the trend reverses.

I studied the low price for upward gaps in a similar manner. The right half of Figure 9.2 shows this situation. Trail a limit order a penny below the low as price rises from E to F to G. When the turn comes at H, the order triggers and shorts the stock, opening the trade as price retraces the gap.

Research shows that the number of price bars that follow the direction of the opening gap is between 1 and 2, regardless of the gap direction. After price gaps down (A), expect one or two minutes of lowering prices (candles B and C) before the stock reverses. The same applies to up gaps. Expect one or two minutes of rising prices (candles F and G) before the turn. Since these are averages, your results will vary, but the tailing stop methodology is sound for *strong* trends.

- Expect one to two minutes of price continuing in the gap direction before a reversal begins.

The smaller the gap, the more there is a slight tendency for price to continue the trend, at least for upward gaps. Tall gaps tend to show quicker reversals than short ones. For example, when price gaps up 5 percent, it takes an average of 1.5 bars before a reversal begins. When the gap is 1 percent, the average number of bars is 1.8 before a reversal occurs.

Downward gaps seem to reverse at about the same rate: a gap 5 percent tall means an average of 1.8 bars before a reversal occurs. A 1 percent gap also means 1.8 price bars before a reversal.

- Tall upward opening gaps tend to see price reverse quicker than short ones.

How Many Gaps Close in First Minute?

The first few minutes of the trading day can be volatile and hazardous to your wealth when trading during that time (see Chapter 8, "Price Reversal

TABLE 9.2 First Minute Gap Closings

Gap Size	Up Gaps	Down Gaps
5%	0%	0%
4%	0%	0%
3%	1%	1%
2%	3%	3%
1%	20%	20%
0%	76%	75%

Times Revealed!"). How often does a gap close during the first minute? Answer: 17 percent for up gaps and 19 percent for down gaps.

What is the frequency distribution of closure rate by gap size? **Table 9.2** shows the answer.

For example, 0 percent of the gaps 5 percent tall closed within the first minute. Out of 5,267 up gaps that closed during the first minute, just five of them were 5 percent tall.

As the table suggests, most of the gaps that closed were small ones, either 1 percent or smaller for both up and down gaps. Just 3 percent of the gaps 2 percent tall closed within the first minute. Although it would be nice to be in and out of a trade quickly, I would rather watch from the sidelines until I received a proper entry signal.

This table suggests that gaps 2 percent or taller are the ones to trade. They do not close in the first minute, leaving time to assess the situation before jumping in and riding the new trend.

- Few gaps taller than 1 percent close within the first minute.

Trade Anyway If Gap Closes?

If the gap closes before the entry signal occurs, should you enter the trade anyway and ride price to the close for the day? The answer to that question is not easy to discern by looking at the trading results, shown in **Table 9.3**. These are in-sample tests on stocks using 1-minute data.

Commissions were $5 per trade ($10 round trip) on a fixed $10,000 investment per trade. Gap size ranged from 1 to 2 percent, using both up and down gap directions, with a buy stop or limit order to enter the trade and an initial stop loss in place. I will explain the entry and stop techniques later.

The profits and losses in cents per share ($.04) were the same regardless of whether you entered a trade or skipped it because the gap had already closed. The average win per share is higher if you skip the trade, and

TABLE 9.3 In-Sample Tests of Skipped or Completed Trades

	Skip if Gap Closed	Trade Anyway
Net profit	$213,267	$278,807
Profit per share	$0.04	$0.04
Profit per trade	$19.79	$21.67
Number of trades	10,774	12,866
Winning trades	2,594	3,267
Average win	$222	$234
Average win/share	$0.42	$0.40
Losing trades	8,180	9,599
Average loss	($44)	($50)
Average loss/share	($0.09)	($0.10)
Win/Loss	24%	25%
Number stopped out	8,057	9,369
Number sold at day's end	2,717	3,497
Payoff ratio (average profit/average loss)	5	4.6

so is the payoff ratio. The numbers suggest that skipping the trade is the better choice.

- If the gap closes before entry, skip the trade.

Trade Exit: Five Popular Selling Prices

During gap research, I found something quite extraordinary and exciting. I found the most popular locations that traders choose to sell after an opening gap.

Before I give you the results, let me discuss the methodology. I used my intraday database of 54 stocks. I compared how far the closing price moved within the opening gap (prior day's close to the opening price of the current day). If price gapped down, for example, and retraced halfway up the gap, then I would log 50 percent for that gap. I did this type of frequency distribution for all large and small, up and down opening gaps. I show the results in **Table 9.4.**

If price gaps open upward, for example, the most popular selling point is midway down the gap (50 percent) followed by two-thirds of the way down (67 percent) and then one-third.

For downward gaps, the three most popular sell locations are the same: 50, 67, and 33 percent, in that order.

If you are trading a gap and see price stall halfway across the gap, then consider selling. Midway and thirds are the most popular selling points in the gap; it is where price reverses most often.

TABLE 9.4 Five Most Popular Selling Locations as Percentage of Gap Size

Frequency Rank	Up Gaps	Down Gaps
(Highest frequency)		
1	50%	50%
2	67%	67%
3	33%	33%
4	80%	25%
5	75%	83%

- If price stalls one-third, midway, or two-thirds of the way across an opening gap, then sell.

Testing the Opening Gap Setup

I used my intraday data for in-sample and out-of-sample tests. Here are the parameters I used for testing.

- Allocate $10,000 per trade. Profits were not reinvested.
- Commissions were $5 per trade, $10 per round-trip.
- No allowance for slippage or other fees.
- Close all open trades at day's end at the closing price.

Entry Order Location

There are several ways to open a trade using gaps.

1. One is to check the pre-market activity and see where the stock is trading and place a market order to buy the stock at the open (for simplicity, assume price gaps down). That guarantees a fill, but the fill price is unknown.

2. Another method is to use a limit order. If you want to catch gaps at least 3 percent below the prior day's close, and if price gaps down far enough at the open, your order will trigger. You can use conditional orders such as an open-only sell stop (short a gap up) and open-only limit order (buy a gap down) 3 percent away from the prior close. If one order triggers, have it cancel the other.

3. Finally, you can watch price and adjust the trigger price (trailing it) as explained for Figure 9.2.

Option 3 is the technique I used for testing, and the one I prefer for trading. An example of the entry technique appears in **Figure 9.3.**

This is a chart of Amgen on the 1-minute scale. Price gaps open lower (A) at the start of the day on February 8. The inset shows a

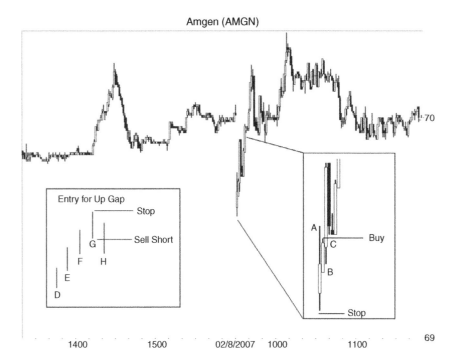

FIGURE 9.3 A buy stop is used to enter the trade.

clearer picture of the action. Place a buy stop a penny above the high at A (69.76) when trading begins at B. The next minute, when price makes a lower high, adjust the order price to a penny above the high at B (69.72). When price rises to hit the stop, the order completes, opening the trade. In other words, trail the buy stop lower by a penny above the high until it fills.

Stop Location

When a stop loss order is used, place a stop a penny below the lowest of the day's open to the entry bar. In this case, entry occurs on bar C and the day's open is on bar A. The lowest low of those three bars is at A, the opening bar. Place a stop a penny below the low (69.54). The reason I use a penny below the low is that sometimes price will match the low (or high) exactly and you do not want to be stopped out in those situations.

For upward gaps, I show the setup in the left inset. Price gaps higher at D, so place a sell stop a penny below the low when candle E forms. When price moves to candle F, raise the stop to a penny below E. Continue to raise the stop as price climbs at F and G. When price drops to trigger the sell stop at H, the trade opens with a short sale. Place a stop a penny above the highest bar from the day's open to the order entry. Since price peaks at G, locate an order to close the trade a penny above the high.

Opening Gap Setup Rules

Based on the tests discussed, here are the rules for the opening gap setup.

1. Trade only down gaps using 1-minute data.
2. Gaps must be 3 percent or larger.
3. Price must gap below the 50-*day* (not 1-minute price bar, but day) simple moving average.
4. If the gap closes before entry, skip the trade.
5. Trail a buy stop a penny above the high as price drops.
6. Place a stop a penny below the lowest low from the opening bar to the entry bar.
7. Sell at the day's close.

Table 9.5 shows the results of in-sample and out-of-sample tests. The out-of-sample uses two fewer stocks so the total profit is less. Notice that when the setup wins, it tends to do well: $0.67 to $0.72 per share. When it loses, it drops an average of 16 to 18 cents a share. Unfortunately, it wins only about a third of the time.

TABLE 9.5 Test Results for Fading the Gap

	In-Sample	Out-of-Sample
Net profit	$58,708	$42,891
Profit per share	$0.14	$0.15
Profit per trade	$102.28	$96.38
Number of trades	574	445
Winning trades	183	148
Average win	$554	$509
Average win/share	$0.67	$0.72
Losing trades	391	297
Average loss	($109)	($109)
Average loss/share	($0.16)	($0.18)
Win/Loss	31.9%	33.3%
Number stopped out	380	289
Reached prior close	0	0
Number sold at day's end	194	156
Payoff ratio (average profit/average loss)	5.1	4.7

Notice that in both tests, the gap is not closed. That is because the gap size is at least 3 percent. Since traders like to sell at 33, 50, and 67 percent of the gap, I ran tests to measure those take-profit points. The results are what you would expect. You win more (48, 46, and 42 percent for targets of 33, 50, and 67 percent, respectively) but make less money per trade (7, 9, and 10 cents per share).

• Fading the gap, if done carefully, can lead to profitable trades.

SAMPLE TRADE

To show how this setup would work, I dug out a popular company, Apple Computer, illustrated in **Figure 9.4**.

On the daily chart (not shown), the stock was in freefall from its peak in May 2008 and going into the bottom in 2009, following the bear market lower.

The stock closed at 85.35 on January 14, 2009 (A), and opened 5.6 percent lower, at 80.57 (B). The gap fulfilled the minimum 3 percent size.

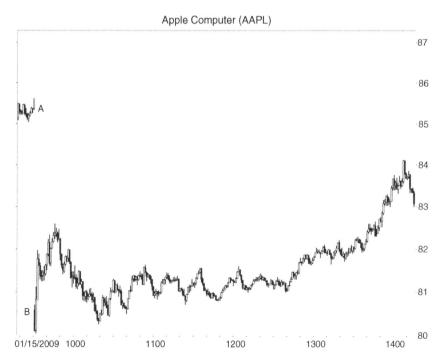

FIGURE 9.4　Price gaps open lower but closes higher, leading to a profitable trade.

Not shown on the 1-minute scale, but the 50-day simple moving average was above price, as required by the setup.

When the second candle after B began forming, a buy stop placed above B would get you into the trade at 80.71, a penny above the high. That triggered during the candle after B.

Place the stop at 80.04 (a penny below the entry bar).

The stock recovered during the day but came close to stopping out the trade just after 10:00 a.m. However, the recovery going into the close saw the stock close at 83.42. That would be the sell price. The close is not shown on the chart because of space limitations. The trade made $2.71 a share (83.42 − 80.71).

CHAPTER CHECKLIST

I used to discuss additional setups by other authors that either faded the gap or traded with the opening gap trend. They did not test well, so I removed them. What remains is the opening gap setup as I have described it above. It is not perfect and may not work in your market or under different market conditions. However, it is based on research. Perhaps you can use that research to build a setup that works for your trading style.

Use this setup not as a list of unbreakable rules to follow on your way to making your first million, but as a roadmap for constructing your own setup. No setup will work all of the time, and few will provide the comfort and trust of a well-tested setup that fits your trading style.

Markets change over time and that tends to break setups. Be sure to test the ideas in this chapter before using the setup.

Here are some tips to consider when day trading the opening gap.

☐ Bull or bear markets have almost no influence on the closure rate of opening gaps. See "Do Bull or Bear Markets Matter?"

☐ In stocks, 72 percent of opening gaps (either up or down) closed by day's end. See "Do Bull or Bear Markets Matter?"

☐ ETF opening gaps (either up or down) closed just 56 percent of the time. See "Do Bull or Bear Markets Matter?"

☐ The closure rate for full and partial gaps is similar: 77 versus 79 percent, respectively. See "Closure Rate for Full and Partial Gaps."

☐ The closure rate for *up* gaps increases if the prior day's open to close price trend was also up. See "What Gap Size Works Best?"

☐ The closure rate for *down* gaps increases if the prior day's open to close move was downward. See "What Gap Size Works Best?"

☐ For fading the opening gap, the prior day's price trend is less significant than the gap being below the 50-day simple moving average. See "Use a Simple Moving Average?"

☐ Fade only when price gaps below the 50-day simple moving average (it works for both up or down gaps). See "Use a Simple Moving Average?"

☐ There is a 28 percent chance that price will close a gap on the second day and 18 percent on the third day. Holding a trade open for an additional day and hoping for the gap to close is a mistake. See "Should You Hold Longer Than a Day?"

☐ Fading the gap and holding on for additional gains until the day's close works 47 to 48 percent of the time. See "Gap Closes. Hold On or Sell?"

☐ Expect one to two minutes of price continuing in the gap direction before a reversal begins. See "Trade Entry Details."

☐ Tall upward opening gaps tend to see price reverse quicker than short ones. See "Trade Entry Details."

☐ Few gaps taller than 1 percent close within the first minute. See "How Many Gaps Close in First Minute?"

☐ If the gap closes before entry, skip the trade. See "Trade Anyway If Gap Closes?"

☐ If price stalls one-third, midway, or two-thirds of the way across an opening gap, then sell. See "Trade Exit: Five Popular Selling Prices."

☐ Fading the gap, if done carefully, can lead to profitable trades. See "Opening Gap Setup Rules."

CHAPTER 10

Day Trading Chart Patterns

D ay trading chart patterns is an exercise in patience. If you use the opening gap setup to trade in the morning, chart pattern setups will occupy the afternoon. Chart patterns take time to form and confirm as valid patterns. Thus, they appear around noon or later. By using the measure rule along with pattern recognition, you can determine how much money you are likely to make and gauge the risk before trading. That is valuable information. Let us take a closer look at several setups. All of the charts in this chapter use the 5-minute scale.

DAY TRADING DOUBLE TOPS

Figure 10.1 shows a chart pattern called a double top at A and B. The two peaks are uneven, but close enough to be worth trading. Perfect patterns are rare, but imperfect ones, like that shown, are as plentiful as hair on a gorilla.

The double top confirms as a valid one when price closes below the bottom of the pattern (F), which happens at C. I drew a horizontal line beneath the pattern's low price to highlight confirmation.

An order to short the stock placed a penny below the line gets you into the trade in a timely manner.

How far might price drop? Use the height of the chart pattern to help gauge the decline. Take the difference between the top at B (the higher of the two peaks) and the low at F (the lowest valley between the two peaks).

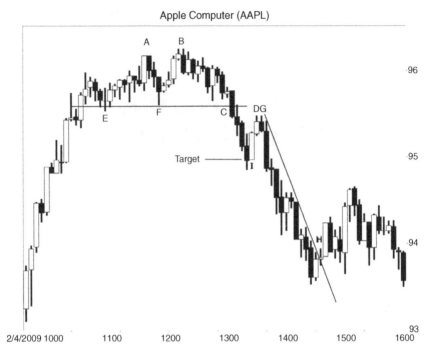

FIGURE 10.1   A double top tells that the stock is going down.

Subtract the result from F to get a price target. Plugging in the numbers, the pattern's top is at 96.25, the low is at 95.60 for a height of 65 cents. Subtract the height from the bottom of the pattern to get a target of 95.60 – 0.65, or 94.95. I show the target on the figure.

- Use the measure rule to predict how far price may drop. Compute the height of the chart pattern and subtract it from the lowest price in the chart pattern to get a price target.

How often does the measure rule work for double tops intraday? Due to limitations in my software, I cannot answer that directly. However, I have researched chart patterns on the daily scale extensively and they give us a clue. For double tops, the measure rule works 44 percent of the time based on 1,658 double tops in bull markets. I will report the accuracy of the measure rule for the other chart patterns in this chapter, but remember that it applies to the daily charts, not intraday.

The stock climbs up one side of the hill and runs down the other (which is what some friends and I did on Mt. Washington. Have you ever *run* down a mountain?). In this example, the EFC line represents a long support area in the shape of a gentle rounded turn. Once price drills through that support, then expect a large decline. That is what happened.

Keep an eye on the clock. Since you are day trading, you will want to exit all positions by the close. Because chart patterns confirm in the early afternoon, there must be enough time for price to move in the expected direction, otherwise, you could be forced to sell prematurely.

- Watch the clock to be sure you have enough time to complete the trade before the day's close.

In this example, price made a strong move down that quickly hit the target. The stock pulled back to D and once price resumed moving down, you could have shorted the stock again.

For entry, trail an order to short the stock as each white candle forms during the pullback (meaning below candle I and then below D and G). A penny or two below the candle's low would work well in this situation. That would get you into the trade the candle after G. Exit when price closes above the down-sloping trendline. That happens to the right of H. The candle below H marks the close above the trendline, but it may be difficult to see.

Of course, this looks easy in hindsight, but in real time, it is more difficult. Patience is the key to day trading chart patterns.

- If a pullback occurs, consider adding to an existing position or entering a new one.

Notice that price moves up from the day's open in a strong uphill run and then rounds over at the top. The key is the straight-line run. After the breakout from the double top, price drops, mirroring the morning's rise. In these cases, the stock often stops declining above the launch price (the morning's low). You can use this as a guideline to how far price might drop.

- After a strong move up, look for the stock to remain just above the launch price.

Here are the rules for day trading double tops

1. Wait for a double top to appear, two peaks near the same price.
2. Measure the height of the double top from highest peak to lowest valley between the two peaks. Subtract the height from the lowest valley in the pattern to get a target price.

3. Is the height of the pattern large enough to be worth trading?

4. Is there enough time remaining for the stock to reach the target before the close (estimate this based on prior price movement)?

5. If yes to questions 3 and 4, then place an order to short a penny below the double top's low price (F in Figure 10.1).

6. Place an initial stop loss a penny above the top of the chart pattern.

7. Cover the stock when price reaches the target or at the day's close.

To trade a pullback, here are the rules.

1. If a pullback occurs, enter when price stops rising. An order to short the stock a penny below the prior candle's low or a penny below the lower of the prior two candles also works.

2. Place a stop loss order above the top of the pullback.

3. For an exit, use the height of the chart pattern subtracted from the entry price to get a target. Exit when price hits the target, at the day's close, or other exit mechanism.

Do You Have the Time?

You may be rolling your eyes at step 4. How can you know if price will reach the target before the close? You cannot. But you can guess based on how fast price typically moves. Look at prior trading days to see what happened during the last hour or two of trading. Does the stock move horizontally or does it make a strong advance going into the close? Trading chart patterns intraday often means having to making this kind of guess.

Another approach is to take the trade and hope that the stock moves in your favor before the close. If it does not, then close out the trade and try again the next day.

I did research and found that the velocity of a stock leaving a chart pattern mirrors the velocity leading to a chart pattern. That is how it works on the daily charts, but you can see similar behavior on the intraday charts. Look at the slope of the inbound and outbound price trends. Use those trends to help determine if you have enough time before the close to make money.

- Use historical price movement to help gauge if there is enough time to complete a trade by day's end. The slope of the trend before and after a chart pattern can help determine if price will reach the target before the close.

DAY TRADING TRIPLE TOPS

Triple tops are rarer than double tops, but common enough on the intraday scale. **Figure 10.2** shows an example.

The triple top forms at ABC, from noon onward, and confirms as a valid chart pattern when price closes below the lowest valley (D) between the three tops. I show that at E. An order to short the stock a penny below D would open the trade two hours before the close.

The height of the pattern, from peak B to valley D, measures 32 cents for a target of 19.98. Price reaches the target as shown, right before a pullback begins. The measure rule works 48 percent of the time in 600 triple tops on the *daily* scale. That should give you a hint of how well it works intraday.

If you have the courage, you could wait for the pullback to end, short the stock again, and ride the stock lower going into the close.

Notice that there is not much of an up trend for the chart pattern to reverse. Starting at F, the stock climbed, but not far. For an effective reversal, there has to be something to reverse. Do not expect a large

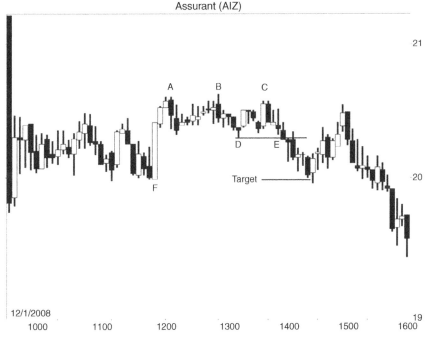

FIGURE 10.2 A confirmed triple tops means an opportunity to short the stock.

decline after a small rise. Notice that price returned to the launch price (F) before pulling back.

- A reversal chart pattern needs something to reverse. After a small rise leading to a reversal chart pattern, expect a small decline after the breakout.

Here are the setup rules for trading triple tops.

1. Find a triple top, three peaks near the same price.
2. Measure the height of the chart pattern. If the pattern is tall enough to be worth risking a trade, then subtract the height from the bottom of the chart pattern to get a target price.
3. Place an order to short the stock a penny below the lowest valley between the three peaks.
4. After the order executes, place a stop loss order a penny above the top of the chart pattern. You can also use a penny above the third peak if it happens to be lower.
5. Cover when price hits the target or at day's end.

DAY TRADING SYMMETRICAL TRIANGLES

Symmetrical triangles are difficult patterns to make money trading and yet they are as prolific as ants at a picnic. I show an example of one in **Figure 10.3.**

This symmetrical triangle started forming just after the market opened and by noon, price had broken out downward (C). Price moved almost horizontally until just over an hour before the day's close when it plummeted like a toy rocket missing its parachute.

The measure rule applies to symmetrical triangles by taking the height of the chart pattern (A – B) and subtracting it from C, the breakout price. In this example, the rule gives a target of 13.98 – (14.30 – 13.85), or 13.53. I marked the target on the figure. The measure rule works 46 percent of the time in 825 symmetrical triangles with downward breakouts in bull markets on the daily charts.

If the stock makes a strong move down (such as the one after 2:30 p.m., or 14:30 on the chart), a straight-line run when each bar's high is below the prior bar, place a stop a penny above the prior bar's high. Lower the stop as price drops. I show the new exit as Target 2. I like to see three consecutive lower highs (and lower lows) to mark a straight-line run before I trail the stop lower using this method.

FIGURE 10.3 A symmetrical triangle with a downward breakout leads to a profitable trade.

- After a straight-line run forms (three consecutive lower highs and lower lows), trail the stop lower by placing the stop a penny above the prior bar's high. Lower the stop as price drops, but do not raise the stop.

Here are the rules for day trading this setup.

1. Find a symmetrical triangle, a pattern with lower highs and higher lows that follows two converging trendlines.

2. Measure the height of the pattern near the start of the triangle (the two tallest swings). If the pattern is tall enough to risk making a trade, then short when price pierces the bottom trendline (a downward breakout) providing there is enough time to reach the target by the close.

3. Place a stop loss order above the top of the chart pattern, but many times the triangle's apex will work. Check historical patterns to see how they behaved in the past under similar situations.

4. Subtract the height of the chart pattern from the breakout price to get a target price.

5. Cover the short at the target or near the close of trading.

6. However, if price makes a straight-line run downward, trail a stop a penny above the prior bar's high until stopped out.

DAY TRADING HEAD-AND-SHOULDERS TOPS

Head-and-shoulders tops are rarer than many other chart patterns, and yet they pose a profitable opportunity for day traders. **Figure 10.4** shows an example. Price forms the left shoulder at A, head at B, and right shoulder at C.

Use the height of the pattern for the measure rule. Compute the height from the highest peak at A to the neckline (D) directly below. I show that as a vertical line. Subtract the height from the breakout price (E) to get a target.

If the neckline slopes downward, then use the value of the right armpit (F) as the breakout price. The armpit is the lowest valley between the head and right shoulder. The neckline joins the left and right armpits. The reason for using the right armpit for the breakout price is because price may never

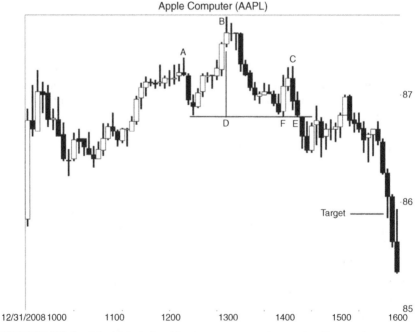

FIGURE 10.4 A head-and-shoulders top suggests the stock will move lower, and it does.

cross a steeply sloping neckline. Bypass that concern and use the right armpit's price, but only when the neckline slopes downward.

- If the neckline slopes downward in a head-and-shoulders top, use the right armpit's low as the breakout price.

In this case, the head tops out at 87.74, the neckline directly below that is at 86.81, for a height of 93 cents. Subtract the height from the breakout price (86.81) to get a target of 85.88. The measure rule works 53 percent of the time on the daily charts (using 1,340 samples from bull markets). That means price reaches the target just over half the time.

The figure shows another example of a strong move down, so a trailing stop placed a penny above the prior candle's high would work well. You could cover the short before the close and smile on the ride to the bank.

Here are the rules for day trading head-and-shoulders tops.

1. Find a head-and-shoulders top, a three-peak pattern with the middle peak well above the other two.

2. Measure the height of the pattern from the highest price in the head to the neckline directly below. Is the height of the pattern tall enough to be worth trading?

3. Is there enough time remaining in the session for the stock to reach the target before the close?

4. If yes, then short the stock when it pierces an up-sloping neckline. For a down-sloping neckline, use the price of the right armpit as the trigger price.

5. Place an initial stop loss order a penny above the right shoulder peak.

6. Cover the short when price reaches the target or at the day's close.

DAY TRADING DOUBLE BOTTOMS

The chart patterns discussed so far in this chapter have been bearish ones. Here are the bullish ones that commonly appear intraday. Let us begin with double bottoms.

Figure 10.5 shows a double bottom at AB. It confirms as a valid chart pattern when price closes above C. For day trading, however, a buy stop placed a penny above the top of the chart pattern works better as an entry signal. The target price is the height of the chart pattern added to the breakout price. In this example, that is, (3.88 − 3.73) + 3.88, or 4.03. I show the target on the figure. It is only 15 cents away, so maybe this is a trade to avoid (not enough profit potential).

Advanced Micro Devices (AMD)

10/16/2008   1600

FIGURE 10.5 A double bottom is a bullish chart pattern. After the breakout, price rises.

Double bottoms on the *daily* charts reach or exceed the target 67 percent of the time in 2,211 double bottoms in a bull market. Based on this finding, bullish patterns are more reliable than bearish ones (meaning the 67 percent number is higher than others reported so far).

Here are the rules for trading this setup.

1. Find a double bottom chart pattern, two bottoms near the same price.
2. Measure the height of the pattern from the highest peak to the lower of the two bottoms. Is the height of the pattern tall enough to be worth trading?
3. Is there enough time remaining in the session for the stock to reach the target before the close?
4. If yes, then place a buy stop a penny above the peak between the two bottoms.
5. Place a stop loss order a penny below the lowest bottom in the chart pattern.
6. Sell when the stock reaches the target or at the day's close.

DAY TRADING HEAD-AND-SHOULDERS BOTTOMS

Head-and-shoulders bottoms are rare intraday patterns, but you may come across them. When you do, here is how to trade them.

Figure 10.6 shows an example of a head-and-shoulders bottom at ABC. On the intraday scale, the patterns may not look as good as they do on the daily charts, so be flexible. Here, the shoulders and head are price spikes.

The height of the pattern measures from the lowest low in the head to the neckline directly above. I show that as distance BD. It measures 16.70 – 16.52 or 18 cents. Since the neckline slopes upward, I use the right armpit as the breakout price. I show that as horizontal line E. The target would be 16.88. The stock reaches the target just a few minutes before the close.

In 1,286 head-and-shoulders bottoms on the daily scale, price reaches the target 72 percent of the time. That should give you a good clue as to how often it works intraday.

- If the neckline slopes upward in a head-and-shoulders bottom, then use the right armpit as the breakout price.

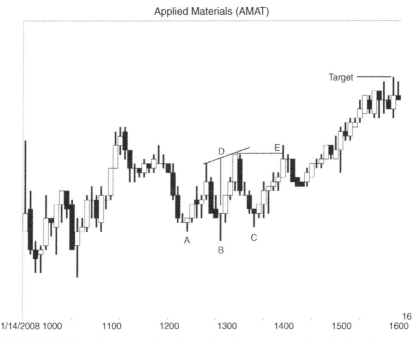

FIGURE 10.6 A bullish head-and-shoulders bottom has a head below the adjacent shoulders.

Here are the rules for trading head-and-shoulders bottoms.

1. Find a head-and-shoulders bottom, a three-valley pattern with the middle valley below the adjacent ones.

2. Measure the height of the head-and-shoulders from the lowest price in the head to the neckline directly above it. Is the height of the pattern tall enough to be worth trading?

3. Is there enough time remaining in the session for the stock to reach the target before the close?

4. If yes, then buy the stock when it pierces a down-sloping neckline. For up-sloping necklines, place a buy stop a penny above the right armpit. The right armpit is the highest peak between the head and right shoulder.

5. Once into the trade, place an initial stop loss order a penny below the right shoulder.

6. Sell the stock when price reaches the target or at the day's close.

DAY TRADING TRIPLE BOTTOMS

Triple bottoms, like ABC shown in **Figure 10.7**, are bullish chart patterns. The middle valley (B) is below A by just 6 cents, which is close enough for government work. In other words, it is not a head-and-shoulders bottom.

The height of the chart pattern helps us find a target price. Measure the height from the highest peak to the lowest valley in the pattern and add the result to the highest peak. In this example, that means, (13.09 − 12.60) + 13.09, or 13.58. Price confirms the chart pattern at D and rises beyond the target. The target price can serve as a minimum move, not a maximum.

Price reaches the target 67 percent of the time in 609 triple bottoms on the daily scale, bull markets.

- The measure rule target often serves as a minimum price to which the stock rises.

Here are the rules for trading triple bottoms.

1. Find a triple bottom, a three-valley pattern with bottoms near the same price.

2. Measure the height of the pattern from the lowest bottom to the highest peak between the three bottoms. Is the height of the pattern tall enough to be worth trading?

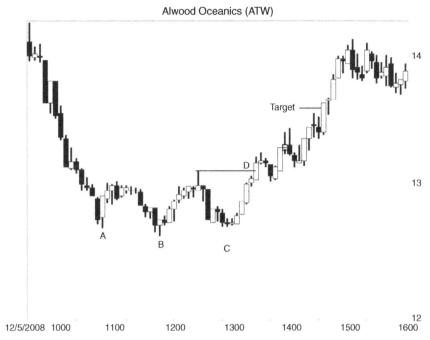

Alwood Oceanics (ATW)

FIGURE 10.7 A triple bottom is a bullish chart pattern which leads to a good rise.

3. Is there enough time remaining in the session for the stock to reach the target before the close?

4. If yes, then buy the stock as it climbs above the breakout price. The breakout price is the highest peak in the pattern.

5. Once into the trade, place an initial stop loss order a penny below the lowest valley in the pattern.

6. Sell the stock when price reaches the target or at the day's close.

OTHER TRADING TIPS

If you have difficulty day trading chart patterns in stocks like those that I show here, try trading them in exchange traded funds. ETFs based on a major market index often provide a smoother ride.

- Try trading ETFs based on a major market index, like DIA (Long Dow), DOG (short Dow), SPY (long S&P 500), SH (short S&P 500), QQQ (long Nasdaq 100), PSQ (short Nasdaq 100).

I find that the 5-minute scale works well. The 1-minute scale makes me feel as if I have overdosed on caffeine and longer scales put me to sleep. The 5-minute scale is a good compromise.

- Trade using the 5-minute scale.

Either visit my website (http://thepatternsite.com/CPIUpdate.html) or compute the chart pattern indicator. If it shows a bullish reading and you are continually shorting, then that could be your problem. Trade with the prevailing market trend (daily or weekly scale).

- Use the chart pattern indicator to show market sentiment.

If you can calculate the likelihood of a higher or lower close as I discussed in Chapter 8, under the heading "Closing Price Prediction" in the "Pre-Market Checklist" section, then that may prove helpful, too. Check to see how well the prediction works for securities you trade. I found it works well for ETFs but less so for stocks.

- Run the calculation to predict tomorrow's close.

Review the material in this book for swing trading because it may help you with day trading.

CHAPTER CHECKLIST

The setups discussed in this chapter are standard, without gimmicks attached. If you find that a moving average adds value, for example, then use it. I have found that many indicators are not worthwhile, but you may disagree. Take the basic setup and add any condiments that sweeten the setup to your liking.

Based on findings in this chapter, here are some tips to consider when day trading chart patterns.

☐ Review each chart pattern for specific trading setups.

☐ For bearish chart patterns, use the measure rule to predict how far price may drop. Compute the height of the chart pattern and subtract it from the lowest price in the chart pattern to get a price target. See "Day Trading Double Tops."

☐ Watch the clock to be sure you have enough time to complete the trade before the day's close. See "Day Trading Double Tops."

☐ If a pullback occurs, consider adding to an existing position or entering a new one. See "Day Trading Double Tops."

☐ After a strong move up, look for the stock to remain just above the launch price. See "Day Trading Double Tops."

☐ Use historical price movement to help gauge if there is enough time to complete a trade by day's end. The slope of the trend before and after a chart pattern can help determine if price will reach the target before the close. See "Do You Have the Time?"

☐ A reversal chart pattern needs something to reverse. After a small rise leading to a reversal chart pattern, expect a small decline after the breakout. See "Day Trading Triple Tops."

☐ After a straight-line run forms (three consecutive lower highs and lower lows), trail the stop lower by placing the stop a penny above the prior bar's high. Lower the stop as price drops, but do not raise the stop. See "Day Trading Symmetrical Triangles."

☐ If the neckline slopes downward in a head-and-shoulders top, use the right armpit's low as the breakout price. See "Day Trading Head-and-Shoulders Tops."

☐ If the neckline slopes upward in a head-and-shoulders bottom chart pattern, then use the right armpit as the breakout price. See "Day Trading Head-and-Shoulders Bottoms."

☐ The measure rule target often serves as a minimum price to which the stock moves. See "Day Trading Triple Bottoms."

☐ If you are having trouble making money day trading, try trading ETFs based on a major market index. See "Other Trading Tips."

☐ Trade using the 5-minute scale. See "Other Trading Tips."

☐ Use the chart pattern indicator to show market sentiment. See "Other Trading Tips."

☐ Run the calculation to predict tomorrow's close. See "Other Trading Tips."

CHAPTER 11

Opening Range Breakout

The research and setup I describe in these pages goes by other names, depending on whom you ask. I call it the opening range breakout. In short, when price leaves a trading range, then trade with the trend. Let me show you an example, and then I will discuss the particulars.

Figure 11.1 shows an example of the opening range breakout. I used the first 20 minutes of trading in this example to highlight the high-low range. The range is the highest high (A) and lowest low (B) made by the stock in the first 20 minutes of trading.

Notice that price hugs the top of the range (circled, at C) more than it does the bottom of the range. Research shows that such behavior leads to better gains. The reverse is also true. When price walks along the bottom of the range more than it does the top and then breaks out downward, the drop is larger than if price were to hug the top of the range and break out downward.

- For upward breakouts, look for price to hug the top of the range more than it does the bottom of the range. For downward breakouts, look for the reverse: Price should hug the bottom of the range most often.

I show a target based on the round number 10. Often in day trading, round numbers (those ending with a zero or double zero) represent support and resistance areas that make good profit targets.

- Prices ending with zero make good profit targets.

Let us look at the research behind the setup.

237

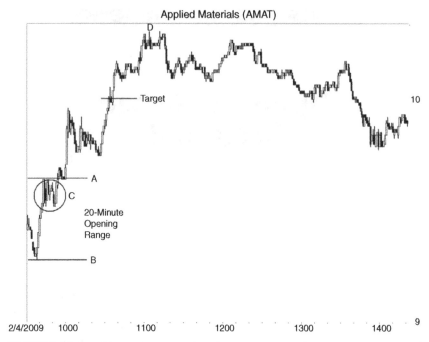

FIGURE 11.1   The opening range breakout, with price clustered near the top of the range, leads to a good gain.

WHAT IS BEST RANGE TIME?

In Figure 11.1, I used a 20-minute range, but is that the best? To find out, I used intraday bull and bear market data on 55 stocks, each several years long.

I selected the day's range in 5-minute intervals up to 30 minutes and ran another test using a 60-minute range. When price closed outside of that range, I assumed a trade began and closed out the trade when it reached the highest high or lowest low for the day.

Using Figure 11.1 as an example, I found the range high and low made during the first 20 minutes of trading, which I show as horizontal lines A and B. Since price broke out upward from the range, I used the day's highest price as the target (D) and measured the gain from A to D.

In a similar manner, I computed the range and target for downward breakouts. If price did not exceed the range during the remainder of the day's trading, then no trade occurred.

The results do not depend on how well a stop loss order works or other exit mechanism. Thus, the numbers shown in **Table 11.1** are the result of thousands of *perfect trades.*

TABLE 11.1 Range Determination Excluding Commissions

	Bull Market		Bear Market	
Minutes	Up	Down	Up	Down
5	$0.32	$0.33	$0.71	$0.77
10	0.30	0.30	0.67	0.72
15	0.30	0.30	0.61	0.66
20	0.29	0.29	0.65	0.71
25	0.28	0.27	0.59	0.65
30	0.28	0.27	0.60	0.66
60	0.29	0.28	0.60	0.66
Total	$2.06	$2.04	$4.43	$4.83

The left half of the table shows the results for bull markets, up and down breakouts, from February 2003 to December 2006. The right half covers the bear market from October 2007 to February 2009.

For example, using the first 5 minutes to set the breakout range in a bull market, upward breakouts climbed an average of 32 cents to reach the day's high. Downward breakouts dropped an average of 33 cents to reach the day's low.

Using the 60-minute range in a bear market (bottom right), price climbed 60 cents after an upward breakout and dropped 66 cents to reach the day's low after a downward breakout.

The results are interesting. First, the sooner you get into the trade, the more profitable it is. For example, in a bull market after an upward breakout, the profit averages 32 cents for a 5-minute range and 29 cents for an hour's range. For both bull and bear markets, the highest profit comes with the smallest range (5 minutes) and the lowest profit comes with longer ranges.

- The quicker you enter a range breakout trade, the better.
- The shortest opening range (5 minutes) results in the best profit for opening range trading.

Second, compare the bull and bear market results. Notice that for both up and down breakouts, results are best in a bear market. In fact, profits are about twice as large in a bear market than they are in a bull market. Why?

I can only speculate. The bear market data is more recent than the bull market, so maybe the volatility in the stocks changed during the gap between the two periods (the same stocks were involved in both periods). It is possible that the opening range trade is more profitable now than it was in 2003 to 2005.

Also, notice that upward breakouts in a bear market earn less than downward breakouts. This makes sense since it pays to trade with the prevailing primary trend (downward in a bear market and upward in a bull market). This relationship is weaker in a bull market. To make this clear, I show the total of the columns at the bottom of Table 11.1.

The bull market total for upward breakouts is $2.06, which is slightly higher than the $2.04 total for downward breakouts. Bear markets perform best after a downward breakout by dropping $4.83 compared to $4.43 for upward breakouts.

- Trade with the trend. In a bear market, downward breakouts tend to make more money than upward breakouts in intraday trading. In bull markets, upward breakouts make more money.

Table 11.1 shows the best-case scenario, that of selling at the day's high or low. **Table 11.2** shows the results after selling at the day's *close*. The left up and down columns are in cents *per share* excluding commissions and the right includes $20 round-trip commissions and is *per trade*.

For example, trades using a 5-minute range lose an average $14.34 per trade (after commissions) for upward breakouts and lose of $3.37 after downward breakouts. Excluding commissions, the *per share* amounts are shown in the table as $0.00 and $0.06 for up and down breakouts, respectively.

For upward breakouts, the 30-minute range works best (it loses least after commissions). The 5-minute range shows the smallest loss for downward breakouts.

The difference between the profits on the left of the table and the losses on the right emphasize the effect of commission charges. You might think that all you have to do is trade in the opposite direction (sell short after an upward breakout, buy after a downward breakout, and hold to the close). How would that do?

TABLE 11.2 Range Breakout with Selling at Day's End

Minutes	Per Share		Per Trade	
	Up	**Down**	**Up**	**Down**
5	$0.00	$0.06	$(14.34)	$(3.37)
10	(0.03)	0.05	(17.74)	(5.69)
15	(0.02)	0.05	(18.56)	(6.59)
20	(0.00)	0.05	(15.35)	(6.89)
25	0.01	0.05	(14.64)	(8.22)
30	0.01	0.06	(12.47)	(7.16)
60	0.00	0.05	(14.40)	(7.74)

Using the 30-minute range breakout, the system lost $25.03 per trade for upward breakouts and lost $33.88 for downward ones.

The gains shown in Table 11.1 suggest that there is a way to profit from the range breakout idea if you can sell close to the day's high or low. What would that setup look like? I have no idea. Here is why.

THE ORB SETUP

The idea for the ORB setup (open range breakout) is easy enough to understand. Buy if price moves outside of the opening high-low range and sell at or before the day's close. Finding a profitable setup is where the problem begins.

Since the bear market data is more recent and shows higher profits, I used that to explore a trading setup while reserving the bull market data for out-of-sample tests.

All tests included $10 per trade commissions ($20 round trip, which is high for day trading, but consider it a conservative estimate of all charges, like data feeds and so on). If a trade did not complete by the market's close, I ended the trade at the day's closing price. *Each* trade started with $10,000 in capital. That means profits or losses were not accumulated.

Each test began with a range breakout (that is, of varying arbitrarily chosen 5-, 15-, and 30-minute ranges), depending on the test. I used the longer periods to give price a chance to cluster along the top or bottom of the trading range using 1-minute data. The exit methods varied.

Here is a list of the methods I tested.

1. Price should hover near the breakout.

2. Use a 10-period exponential moving average to confirm entry.

3. Offset the entry by 5 cents.

4. Round number exit.

5. Initial 10-cent stop.

6. Trailing 10-cent stop.

7. Three-bar exit.

A discussion of the tests and trading results follows.

Price Should Hover near Breakout

In Figure 11.1, I discussed how price outperformed when it stayed closer to the top of the range than the bottom of it. To test this, I counted the position of closing prices (1-minute scale) within an opening range of 30 minutes. **Table 11.3** shows the results.

TABLE 11.3 Position of Price during First 30 Minutes

Measure	1×	3×
Up breakout, above midpoint	$0.61	$0.58
Up breakout, all trades	$0.58	$0.56
Up breakout, below midpoint	$0.54	$0.43
Down breakout, above midpoint	$0.64	$0.51
Down breakout, all trades	$0.64	$0.61
Down breakout, below midpoint	$0.64	$0.56

I averaged the two range high and low prices posted during the first 30 minutes of trading and counted how often price closed above or below the midpoint. For the 1× column, if price closed more often above the midpoint and price broke out upward, the setup made an average of 61 cents. This is the scenario shown in Figure 11.1. If price rested below the midpoint more often but still broke out upward, it made an average of 54 cents ("Up breakout, below midpoint" row).

In other words, upward breakouts do best when price closes above the middle of the range.

Downward breakouts were a tie at 64 cents regardless of where price clustered. To break the tie I used a three multiplier (3× column). That means trades occurred only if three times as many prices closed above (or below) the midpoint. For example, if price closed below the midpoint once and above it 29 times, then the trade would occur (regardless of the breakout direction). If price closed below the midpoint 10 times and above it 20 times, the system would skip the trade (because the ratio is only 2:1, not 3:1).

The 3× column shows performance differences that eluded the 1× column. Upward breakouts do best when price hovers near the top of the range (0.58 versus 0.43, respectively). Downward breakouts outperform when price rests below the middle of the trading range (0.56 versus 0.51, respectively).

The two "all trades" rows include those trades that did not show price clustering near the range high or low *as well as those that did.*

- For upward breakouts, trade only those situations where price closes above the middle of the opening range most of the time.
- Downward breakouts from the opening range do best when price resides below the range's midpoint most often.

The 3× column had many trades that failed to qualify (almost 9,000), but not the 1× column (110 out of over 7,000). The numbers show that performance improves only when price clusters near an upward breakout (for both 1× and 3× columns).

Notice the difference between the 1× and 3× columns. When more prices hover near the breakout price (the 3× column), performance deteriorates compared to 1×. That is not what I expected. It appears that the method removes trades that make big gains or allows more trades that are stinkers.

Ten-Period EMA

The next idea qualifies the entry only if price is above the 10-period exponential moving average (EMA) when it breaks out above the range. Does this idea make sense?

Look at Figure 11.1 again. When price breaks out above the top horizontal line, do you think it will be above the 10-period EMA? Yes. Except for large opening gaps, the moving average will almost always be inside the range when price pokes its head outside the range.

I used a 30-minute opening range and price had to be above the midpoint at least three times as often as it was below it to consummate a trade. Then I looked at the value of the 10-period EMA compared to the buy price. In just 18 cases, price was below the EMA. In the other 7,101 cases, price was above the EMA.

In other words, using a moving average in this manner is a useless gimmick. In fact, it removes profitable trades. Those 18 trades made an average of $37.44 per trade. The 7,101 lost an average of $14.86 per trade.

- Do not use a short moving average (based on intraday data) with this setup.

When testing an indicator to see if it adds value, but sure to test both directions. By that, I mean if you add a rule that says price must be *above* a moving average before trading, be sure to test price when it is *below* the moving average. You may be surprised to learn that performance improves when price is below a moving average or other indicator!

Offset Entry by 5 Cents

The offset entry idea helps assure that price will trend after the breakout. The thinking is that a trader can avoid those situations where the breakout occurs and price then reverses or goes sideways. Does this idea work?

Look at Figure 11.1. Instead of having a buy stop at the price of line A, the stop would be a nickel higher (or 10 cents or whatever you chose to use).

I did not visually qualify each of the 16,565 trades to see if they were trending. However, the results should be obvious. Delaying entry is costly. The average loss for trades using no entry offset (that is, buying at line A, in Figure 11.1) is $14.42. Delaying entry by a nickel per trade means a loss of $16.45. In other words, you lose more money by waiting.

• Do not delay entry.

Let me give you a more intuitive example. If price is going to top out at $10 and you have a range breakout at 9.50, does it make sense to delay entry until price rises to 9.55 to assure you that a trend has formed?

If you buy at the breakout of 9.50, price will either go up, down, or move sideways. The maximum profit is 50 cents a share. If you delay entry by a nickel to 9.55, price will either go up, down, or sideways. The maximum profit drops to 45 cents a share and yet you face the same trend variables: up, down, or sideways. Nothing has changed except the maximum profit has dropped. Delaying entry is a mistake.

Round-Number Exit

I used a round number (a number ending in zero), such as 10, as a sell signal providing it was more than 10 cents away from the buy price. For example, a trade would exit at 10.00 providing the buy price was lower than 9.90 (more than 10 cents away). The actual exit occurred at the open of the next price bar.

The test used a 30-minute opening range, but only if three times as many closing prices were above the middle of the range (upward breakouts) or below the middle (downward breakouts). There were 14,805 trades logged. None of the tests used a stop loss order. **Table 11.4** shows the results.

Perhaps the biggest surprise is that the opening range breakout setup produces a loss of $7 (downward breakouts) to over $14.50 (upward

TABLE 11.4 Trading Results for Round-Number Exit

Measure	Up Breakouts	Down Breakouts
Number of trades	7,158	7,647
Average gain or loss	$(14.51)	$(7.33)
Percentage of winning trades	54%	57%
Average gain of trades open at day's end	$(93.23)	$(92.64)
Average gain of trades exiting at round number	$98.95	$104.56
Largest loss	(21%)	(19%)

breakouts) per trade. That is without any type of stop loss in place. What happens when we use an initial stop?

• Round numbers, those ending in zero, are support and resistance areas that make good price targets for day trades.

Initial 10-Cent Stop

After placing the trade, I used an initial stop of 10 cents and kept it there throughout the trade, never raising or lowering it. This setup is the same as in the prior test.

1. A 30-minute opening range breakout.

2. Three times as many closing prices must be above the middle (upward breakouts) or below the middle (downward breakouts) of the range.

3. Round-number exit.

4. Close any open trades at day's end.

There were 13,807 trades logged. **Table 11.5** lists the results.

Using an initial stop loss order leads to worse performance. Upward breakouts without stops lost $14.51 (from Table 11.4) but using a stop increased the loss to $16.28 per trade. Downward breakouts show worse performance, too, with losses climbing from $7.33 (no stops) to $13.65 per trade (with stops). The number of winning trades drops by more than half from the prior test. However, the largest loss drops in half, from 21 to 9 percent for upward breakouts and from 19 to 10 percent for downward breakouts.

In the prior test, trades open at day's end lost $93.23, but in this test, the trades gained $111.20 (upward breakouts). Losing trades that used to remain open until the market close in the prior test were sold in this

TABLE 11.5 Trading Results for Initial Stop

Measure	Up Breakouts	Down Breakouts
Number of trades	6,663	7,144
Average gain or loss	$(16.28)	$(13.65)
Percentage of winning trades	22%	24%
Average loss of trades stopped out	$(59.79)	$(62.16)
Average gain of trades open at day's end	$111.20	$126.35
Average gain of trades exiting at round number	$116.49	$117.14
Largest loss	(9%)	(10%)

test, allowing the gainers to continue to the close. A similar flip occurs for downward breakouts.

Profits for trades exiting at a round number also improve by climbing from $98.95 to $116.49 (upward breakouts) and $104.56 to $117.14 for downward breakouts.

- Range breakouts that use an initial stop perform worse but limit losses.

Trailing Stop

The prior test used a fixed stop. What do the results show after using a trailing stop? **Table 11.6** shows them. After opening a trade, I placed a 10-cent stop. I raised the stop if the stock made a higher low (upward breakouts) or lowered the stop if the stock made a lower high (downward breakouts). The stop was never moved in the adverse direction (never lowered for upward breakouts or raised for downward breakouts).

The trailing stop improved results by cutting the average loss from $16.28 to $14.25 after upward breakouts, but increased the loss from $13.65 to $14.62 after downward breakouts. The trailing stop cut the average gain for trades open at day's end (upward breakouts only) and for those exiting at a round number (both breakout directions). The largest loss improved from –9 percent to –8 percent (upward breakouts) and –10 percent to –7 percent (downward breakouts).

- A trailing stop can help trim losses and salvage profits.

Three-Bar Exit

The idea behind a three-bar exit is that when price stops trending, it will close lower (upward breakouts) or higher (downward breakouts)

TABLE 11.6 Trading Results for Trailing Stop

Measure	Up Breakouts	Down Breakouts
Number of trades	7,158	7,647
Average gain or loss	$(14.25)	$(14.62)
Percentage of winning trades	26%	26%
Average loss of trades stopped out initially	$(54.73)	$(56.86)
Average loss of trades stopped out trailing	$(1.42)	$(4.20)
Average gain of trades open at day's end	$77.88	$137.93
Average gain of trades exiting at round number	$75.42	$75.94
Largest loss	(8%)	(7%)

TABLE 11.7 Trading Results Using Three-Bar Exit

Measure	Up Breakouts	Down Breakouts
Number of trades	7,158	7,647
Average gain or loss	$(18.33)	$(19.95)
Percentage of winning trades	23%	24%
Average loss of trades stopped out initially	$(51.96)	$(53.49)
Average loss of trades stopped out trailing	$(3.79)	$(9.41)
Average gain of trades open at day's end	$72.18	$63.18
Average gain of trades exiting at round number	$67.12	$66.49
Largest loss	(6%)	(7%)

at least three price bars in a row. I tested this idea and **Table 11.7** lists what I found.

The test uses a 30-minute range breakout, 10-cent trailing stop, and price has to cluster above the midpoint three times as often as below it (upward breakouts) or the reverse for downward breakouts. In other words, it is the same test as the prior section except for the three-bar exit.

As the table shows, the results are worse, which surprised me. The average loss increases from $14.25 to $18.33 for upward breakouts and increases even more for downward breakouts. Other measures changed as well, but the largest loss narrowed from 8 percent to 6 percent for upward breakouts and held constant at 7 percent for downward breakouts.

- The three-bar exit resulted in larger losses.

DOES THE ORB SETUP WORK?

These tests show that although profits are theoretically possible, I could find no mechanical exit mechanism to capture those profits. Of course, I did not test more complex exits like moving average crossovers, overbought relative strength index (RSI), or other indicator signals. Additionally, a commission charge of $20 for a round-trip is high (it should be half that with a good discount broker), but you can consider that a conservative estimate. A working system should be able to tolerate such charges.

Discretionary traders make money using the opening range breakout. However, that may be because they are disclosing only profitable trades and hiding losses or using unquantifiable methods for entry and exit, such as intuition, luck, or skill.

One trader, for example, exits trades around 11:00 a.m. I tested this using a 5-minute opening range breakout and found that trades exiting before noon made 46 cents per share and those exiting after noon saw profits accumulate to 95 cents per share (upward breakouts). For downward breakouts, the profit was 51 cents per share before noon and 99 cents after noon. Trades that last into the afternoon are about twice as profitable as those exiting in the morning.

It is also possible that other times of the day might work well for the opening range breakout (say the first half hour after lunch). However, that would give the trade less time to actually break out and trend before the close.

Again, take the ideas I discussed and apply them to your setup. Maybe you can get ORB to work.

CHAPTER CHECKLIST

Here is a checklist of what we learned about the opening range breakout.

☐ Before an upward breakout, look for price to hug the top of the range more than it does the bottom of the range. Before a downward breakout, look for the reverse: Price should hug the bottom of the range most often. See chapter introduction.

☐ Prices ending with zero (round numbers) make good profit targets. See chapter introduction.

☐ The quicker you enter a range breakout trade, the better. See "What Is Best Range Time?"

☐ The shortest opening range (five minutes) results in the best profit for opening range trading. See "What Is Best Range Time?"

☐ Trade with the trend. In a bear market, downward breakouts tend to make more money than upward breakouts in intraday trading. In bull markets, upward breakouts make more money. See "What Is Best Range Time?"

☐ For upward breakouts, trade only those situations where price closes above the middle of the opening range most of the time. See "Price Should Hover near Breakout."

☐ Downward breakouts from the opening range do best when price resides below the range's midpoint most often. See "Price Should Hover near Breakout."

☐ Do not use a short moving average with the opening range breakout. See "Ten-Period EMA."

☐ Do not delay entering a trade. See "Offset Entry by 5 Cents."

☐ Round numbers, those ending in zero, are support and resistance areas that make good price targets for day trades. See "Round-Number Exit."

☐ Range breakouts that use an initial stop perform worse but limit losses. See "Initial 10-Cent Stop."

☐ A trailing stop can help trim losses and salvage profits. See "Trailing Stop."

☐ The three-bar exit resulted in larger losses. See "Three-Bar Exit."

CHAPTER 12

Ten Horror Stories

I began this trilogy with how I was able to retire at 36 after saving my money and investing it in stocks like Michaels Stores, which then soared 5,000 percent. It seems fitting that I end it with horror stories, trading disasters that snuck up on the people involved. The emotional toll on an individual or family far exceeds the monetary loss.

The trades were made by men and women who will remain anonymous. They gave me permission to discuss their stories and share their pain with others. I edited their emails only for clarity and style.

THIS IS A WINNER, MOM. BUY IT!

You often hear the saying that a successful first trade can make a novice trader or investor think that making money in the markets is easy. Success breeds overconfidence and overconfidence leads to losses. Here is a variant of that, shown in **Figure 12.1**.

I thought I could trade and make millions! I had a few successful trades with General Electric, Pfizer, and Coca-Cola, and decided to invest my money in China Agritech (CAGC).

My first four trades with CAGC were very successful, and I managed to make around $2,000 in just a few days. I thought the good fortune would continue, so I put all of my money into the stock and bought shares worth $13,604.

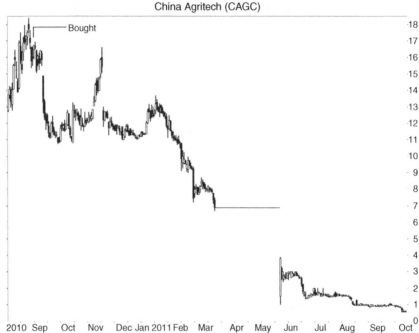

FIGURE 12.1   An example of buying high and holding on until almost nothing is left.

I also convinced my mother to open a Roth IRA and put all of her retirement money into the stock, a total of $11,788, bought on August 27, 2010 [shown]. She also bought over $18,300 worth of shares for her individual account.

As I write this, all three investments are down over 95 percent. I have lost almost all of the money in our portfolios.

I can't believe I did not sell it early and cut my losses when I had the chance, but it is always the hope of it going up. One is paralyzed to act.

Two big lessons I take from this are to never put all of your eggs in one basket, and to always use a stop order to minimize any future losses.

THREE NEWSLETTER DISASTERS

Any newsletter or software is expensive if it costs you money. Here are some emails I received that tell how bad they can be.

I had a subscription to a newsletter that auto-traded my account. They supposedly had a wonderful track record, but happened to have a particularly bad time during my subscription.

The same thing happened with a gold mining subscription a year before that, which had a perfect record of seven consecutive winning years of 100 to 300 percent [gains] for each year in stocks. After I subscribed that year, it lost 92 percent and I lost $20,000.

Here is the second tale.

I started trading stocks in 2004. My very first trade lasted a few days and made me a nice profit. I watched [the stock] go up and when it started to change direction, I exited in what was similar to a narrow, rounded top. That was before I knew anything at all about trading, not to mention technical analysis.

Later I subscribed to dozens of newsletters, looking for the right one, and they were all bad, especially in options. In total, I lost over $50,000 (and that's beside the price of the newsletters, which cost thousands of dollars). All of the expensive software I bought was also worthless.

I have been trading this Forex account for three years, but started being profitable only in the last few months. During those three years, I managed to "nuke" my account five times.

I think one needs a lot of will power to go on after failing so many times and a large amount of money to start with. Many times, I just gave up in desperation, only to start again.

Later, with Forex, I could experiment and learn without risking so much money and yet trade on a real account (which is much better, I think, than paper trading). In the end, I found out that the only way to make money was to listen to my own advice. You also need to learn and learn and learn nonstop and try a lot of things until you find something that works for you.

Here is one more.

I'm writing you from Italy, and it is the second try to start living as a trader. The first time was in 2001, and I blew out my account on 9/11 with covered warrants.

The second time, I started this year investing in U.S. stock options and I've lost 40 percent of my account by subscribing to a newsletter at $400 per month. When we had a draw down, [the newsletter owner] told us to stay disciplined on positions that were losing 40 percent, then 70 percent, then 80 percent!

After that, I stopped my subscription and started buying option books and reading forums where I understood that what I needed was to be good at direction (technical analysis) and volatility, two things where I was totally lacking.

I subscribed to Dan Zanger's website, which I think is the real deal in this world of snake oil vendors. He is very serious and generous. I paper traded his picks and had good results, but I feel very unsatisfied with myself. I know that I'm not a trader until I will be able to create my [own] strategy: search, buy, sell.

Now I've gone back to work because I need money to support my family. My wife feels I've deluded her a little bit with the time I've lost at the computer, but I like this game, and I know that I'll find a way to be profitable sooner or later.

THREE OPTION AND WARRANT DISASTERS

As I read these emails, I see a common thread among them. Many are using options or warrants to erase a good portion of their net worth. If a scenario like the one in the movie *Brewster's Millions* happens to you (where Brewster had to spend $30 million in 30 days without accumulating any assets before he could inherit $300 million), then try options. Careless use of leverage is one sure way to blow out your account.

In early 1987, I took a major portion of my savings, about $25,000, and after spending a lot of time reading, researching, and paper trading, decided to get into the market. I had a personal computer and stock charting software—this in the days of 5¼-inch floppy disks. I had a little radio receiver that got actual real-time market pricing for any stocks I programmed in.

In about six months, I had turned the original $25,000 into a bit over $75,000. Almost all of that was in options trading. I had visions of a career, even a fund solicited from family and friends.

I was fully invested at the close on Friday, October 16, 1987. As usual, I had most of my money in the expected market direction, long at the time, and a few "hedge" investments the other way, in puts, that day.

On Monday, October 19, the crash of 1987 started. Stocks didn't even open—this was back in the day when human market makers were supposed to step in and make an "orderly" market by taking the opposite side when orders in their stocks were in serious imbalance.

I started trying to get my broker on the phone before 10 a.m. In those days, there was no web trading. When I finally got him on the line that afternoon and tried to salvage a few shreds of my portfolio, he said, "Picture standing at the bottom of an elevator shaft and at the very top someone tips over a barrel of sell orders. How many of them, do you think, you can grab and process?"

He told me he would put in any orders I wanted, but it was unlikely that anything would be executed. He was right.

With young children and a wife to support, I refocused on job/career in business for most of the next 20 years. I kept my retirement accounts in secure bonds and missed the entire tech bubble. Only in the past few years have I stuck a toe back into equity investments.

I cannot forget that there is always what we now call a "black swan" or "fat tail" out there.

I told him my story of the crash: "I remember having my IRA money in a mutual fund for five years, ending 1987, and made 1 percent a year as a result of the crash. The fund was a dog, but the 1987 crash killed the animal."

Here is another trade in warrants. As I write this, expiration has not come yet, so there is still hope of salvaging the trade. Refer to **Figure 12.2**.

I had attended a conference on the Canadian markets a week before the purchase, and a well-respected technician was very bullish. I was

FIGURE 12.2   This trader bought the stock near a peak and has not seen it recover.

75 percent in cash because I had sold in December, so I was just itching to get back into the market.

I was looking for something that was undervalued and would rise with the tide, as all boats float in a rising market. I had been doing some surfing on the Internet and found a warrant of a gold company with a host of formidable directors and board members. The warrant was in the money with 18 months before expiration, so I thought that it should move dollar for dollar with the stock.

On Monday morning, I was in front of the computer watching the major gold stocks gap up at the open. I wanted in and figured I had a couple of minutes before needing to attend to Lucy (my dog— all night long, it seemed, I was outside with her, and something was coming out one end of her or the other). Usually I trade with a risk/ reward ratio of 1 to 4 and hadn't figured it out with the warrant, so bought what I could lose and still sleep at night.

Thursday morning was the next time I looked at my warrant purchase. %$#! It was down 25 percent. One may think sometimes it can happen...BUT even if I had thought to place a stop loss, I realized it was trading about 2,500 shares a day, slightly more than I purchased. The volume is really an unknown as it only began trading two months ago! I still own them at a 35 percent loss and the plan is to sit on them and learn. Their expiration is September 2012.

When I wrote to you, "Up all night with sick dog and no stop loss," I accepted that I was tending to a loved one all night and sometimes we should just give ourselves a break. In this business, it is about minimizing risks and mistakes. I am learning that flogging myself hinders my confidence and impedes my ability to learn. Preserving my mental capital is becoming as important as preserving my portfolio. The other lesson: Cash is a position!

Here is another story with an unusual funding twist.

In late 2006 and early 2007, I blew up two accounts, with $300 left, for a total of $14,700. The dollar amount might not sound too offline for many, but what makes this unusual is how I funded those accounts.

Funding: I balance transferred a total of $15,000 from two credit cards. They offered 0 percent APR Balance Transfer rate for 12 months with a 3 percent transaction fee. You do not have to have an existing balance to transfer from them. You can directly deposit the money to your own checking account then do whatever you want with it. What I did was to set up two trading accounts and off I went

to make money. As long as my return is higher than 3 percent within 12 months, I am covered, *I thought.*
   I traded put options on housing stocks.
   The rest of the story is standard. I had enough knowledge to do the maximum damage, with zero risk management in place.
   I still reflect upon this experience from time to time. What type of person am I who is capable of such behavior? I love all types of movies, but horror? I guess I have a version of my own.

TWO MISSED OPPORTUNITIES

I think most traders have looked back at their trades and said, "If only I held on longer." Here is an example, shown in **Figure 12.3**.

I had been watching Interclick decline from its July 6, 2011 [point E] high of $8.93 to bottom on September 6 at $4.98 [F]. It rallied back to $6.22 [G] on September 20 and then put in another bottom at $4.94 on October 4 [H]. By my lights, it had formed a double bottom pattern.

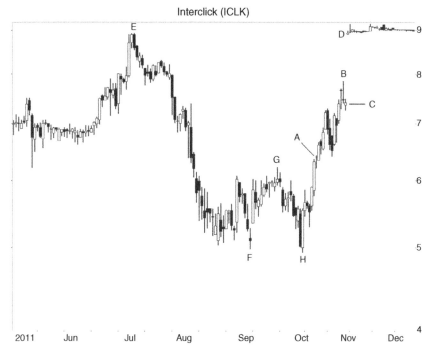

Interclick (ICLK)

FIGURE 12.3 The day after selling, the stock jumped on a takeover offer.

On 10/11, the stock had a big up day and broke above the 50-day EMA [exponential moving average, not shown], the 200-day EMA, and the double bottom entry price of $6.22. I had been reading Stan Weinstein's book at that time, and it looked to me as if the stock broke out of a stage 1 consolidation complete with a double bottom pattern.

So, in I go (big time for me) on 10/12 at $6.41 per share [A]. Sixteen days later [B], on October 28, it closed at $7.47, but it formed a gravestone doji. I was worried about the doji, but I was up 17 percent in two weeks. October 28 was a Friday and as the market drew to a close, I decided to keep ICLK over the weekend. This gave me the opportunity to fret about this over the weekend, and I concluded that if ICLK opened down on Monday, I would exit the position.

Sure enough, it opened down on Monday morning [C]. I exited at $7.35 for a 15 percent gain. Tuesday morning, the very next morning, ICLK gaps up to $8.91 [on a takeover offer from Yahoo!] and closes at $8.94. Had I not stewed over that gravestone doji, I would have been up 40 percent.

Initially, I was astonished at my bad luck. You know, you work so long to find these opportunities, and to have the stock take off one

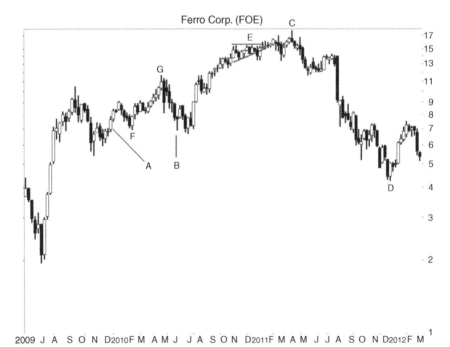

FIGURE 12.4 This trade saw profits soar to 137 percent and then dive to a loss of 43 percent.

lousy day after I sold was so disappointing. I always try to find a lesson in each trade—both winning and losing trades. In this one, I concluded that when a candlestick pattern is known to be essentially random, well, random is random so don't hang your hat on it.

The following trade is another missed opportunity, but unlike the last one. I show it in **Figure 12.4** on the weekly scale.

I started watching Ferro in mid 2008, but chickened out of buying the stock because I expected the market to drop. That's what happened during the 2008 bear market. The stock flew as well as an airliner after a bird strike snuffs out the engines. It crashed from a high of over 24 in September 2008 to a low of 81 cents in March 2009, a 97 percent plunge!

By year-end 2009, it was flying back up to 9. I liked the stock because the chemical industry was doing well, so I bought 1,000 shares at 7.60 in mid December [point A]. I had visions of seeing this soar to 10 then 14 and eventually 20. At 17 overhead resistance began [not shown], and at 20, the resistance was as thick as mosquitoes on a summer's day at the lake. Twenty was my target.

The stock climbed to over 11 before settling back down at a cruising level of about 7. In June 2010, I bought another 1,000 shares at 7.42 [B]. Together, I had $15,000 in the stock. I was averaging down and saw an unconfirmed double bottom [bottoms F and B, confirmed when price closes above peak G].

In January, the stock broke out downward from an ascending triangle [E], but I wasn't worried. My target was 20, and the stock had climbed to "only" 15.50.

I had doubled my money. Wasn't that enough profit? Noooo! I had to hold on for the last few bucks.

The pilots regained control after the triangle, and the stock increased its altitude to almost 18 before hitting turbulence again. Still, the stock wasn't at 20, so I held on. Big mistake.

The stock started dropping. I was busy with other things and with a portfolio of 30 or 35 stocks, it's easy to ignore those easing lower week by week.

At first, it was just a retrace of the up move. It will recover, I thought. It always has. Then it kept dropping. Soon, I had given back too much profit to sell.

I watched the stock drop from a 137 percent gain at the peak [C] to a loss of 43 percent [D]. It has recovered somewhat, but news out of the company says that the stock is going lower. I better alert the airport to foam the runway.

THE $1 MILLION SURPRISE

Many times, traders blame market makers for manipulating stocks. "The market maker forced the stock to hit my stop" is a common refrain. Here is a story from the market maker's viewpoint.

In 1983, I was an independent market-maker on the floor of the CBOE [Chicago Board Options Exchange]. I was backing a trader in the TXN pit [Texas Instruments]. He had a number of out-of-the-money (worthless) puts that I decided there was no reason to cover, but let them run out to expiration and expire worthless. (Greed!) After all, we knew that $140 stocks didn't drop like rocks.

After the close on Friday, June 10, TXN announced quarterly earnings. [See **Figure 12.5,** *point A].*

The psychological cost was high because I knew after the close on Friday that TXN was going to be down on Monday, but not by how

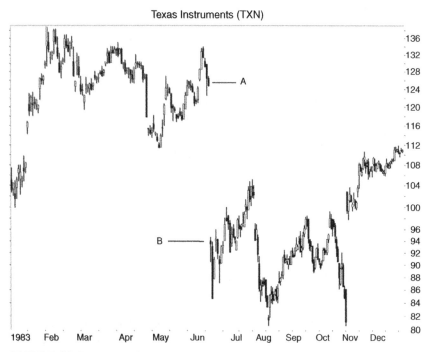

Texas Instruments (TXN)

FIGURE 12.5   The stock dropped after a quarterly earnings announcement, causing a massive loss.

much. I, being a worrier, thought the worst and assumed that I was going to be broke.

In the 1980s, we traded in tinnies (1/16 of a dollar). All of the puts I was short were offered at one-tinny before the announcement. The worst ones to go against me were the 120 puts. TXN closed at 124.75 on Friday and reopened at 94.10 on Monday. The 120 puts for June expiration (which was coming a week later) probably went from one tinny to $30 (because of the high demand from many people wanting to buy them back). That's roughly a $3,000 loss per short option. When you're short hundreds of them, it adds up to real money, quickly.

I remember the mob scene when the options opened for trading with many traders buying them back or shorting stock to go flat. Other traders were selling puts because, of course, there had to be a bounce in the stock. I flattened out as quickly as I could and went to the bar to lick my wounds.

When I knew I wasn't going broke, I was somewhat happier (if one can be happy losing $1,000,000). I was also up a million for the year when this of all happened, so I eventually looked at it as working for the year up to that point for nothing.

TXN closed Monday about where it opened, 94. The next day, it closed at 84, where I would have been broke! All in all, not a good trade, but not the end of the world.

A few days later, I was showing a friend around the floor and took him over to the TXN pit. I said, "I know you can't see them, but in that pit are what were going to be my next house and car!"

After beating myself psychologically for maybe a couple of weeks (about how stupid I was), I set a goal of "finding the guy out there with my money and getting it back." I don't think I made all of the million back that year, but I think I put a big dent in it.

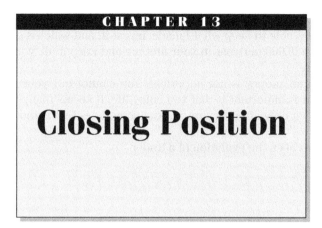

CHAPTER 13

Closing Position

I started investing in stocks near the beginning of a bull market, so I was fortunate. I used fundamental analysis to make my stock picks, and I pocketed a lot of money.

In later years, I became disenchanted because I repeatedly watched handsome gains turn into ugly losses. I did not know when to sell a buy-and-hold position.

I taught myself technical analysis and started position trading. I did not throw away the fundamentals; I just added timing mechanisms. Some of those position trades turned into swing trades as bear markets came and went, and I grew fearful of losing profits.

I experimented with day trading, but grew to dislike it. I do not like sitting before a screen, watching my money grow and die with each new candlestick. My guess is that day traders burn out quickly because of the stress of seeing their next mortgage payment appear and vanish.

A fund manager I know made a leveraged bet that went bad and put him out of business. His clients lost tens of millions. Trading for a living is not an easy life.

After the 2008–2009 bear market, I pumped money into the stock market and rode the bull to prosperity. Now, four years later, I have turned cautious. Some of the buy-and-hold positions that I held since the bear went into hibernation have been sold to lock-in profits. New positions will be shorter duration, so it is back to position and swing trading, sprinkled with buy-and-hold and maybe some day trades.

As I look back at my life, the point is not that I made a lot of money. Rather, I was able to keep what I made, invest it, and watch it grow. If you make only $20,000 per year in your lifetime and keep it all, you can retire a millionaire.

Of course, money is not important. You cannot buy your way out of death. What is important is that you enjoy life. It seems that people begin to realize that only after they retire. And sometimes that is too late. Think about it.

This has been the evolution of a trader.

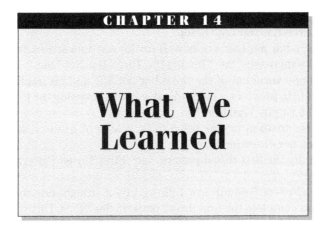

CHAPTER 14

What We Learned

T his chapter lists all of the discoveries I shared with you in these pages, sorted by chapter.

Chapter 1: Introduction to Swing Trading

- ☐ Range trading is buying and selling as price bounces between highs and lows. See "What Is Swing Trading?"
- ☐ A trend trade buys near the swing low and sells near the end of a short-term trend (or the reverse: sell high and buy low). See "What Is Swing Trading?"
- ☐ Swing trading is best suited for people who are accustomed to using stops and like to follow the markets daily. See "Who Should Swing Trade?"
- ☐ The Exxon Mobil Corp. trade started with the breakout from an ascending triangle and ended using a stop. See "A Swinging Example."

Chapter 2: Swinging Techniques

- ☐ Price drops faster than it rises. See "Quick Review: Support and Resistance."
- ☐ Making money is almost as easy as determining where support and resistance are. See "Quick Review: Support and Resistance."
- ☐ Trendlines work on all time scales. See "Trendline Trading."
- ☐ For trendline trading, see "Trendline Trading Tips."
- ☐ For channel trading, see "Trading Using Channels."

☐ The three-bar net line is a visual way to determine a trend change. See "The Three-Bar Net Line Setup."

☐ The three-bar net line works well for longer time scales, but the hold time loss increases. See "Testing the Three-Bar Net Line."

☐ The Guppy variation of the three-bar net line and his implementation of scaling in provides a methodical way of increasing the position size. See "The Guppy Variation."

☐ Decrease position size as price rises, scaling it to the risk of a trend reversal. See "Position Size."

☐ To identify the first thrust pattern, see "First Thrust Pattern for Swing Trading."

☐ Use the lowest 6-month low followed by a straight-line run up and a pause to complete the first thrust pattern. See "First Thrust Testing."

☐ The first thrust pattern creates an entry signal, not a sell signal. See "First Thrust Testing."

Chapter 3: Swinging Chart Patterns

☐ Price throws back after a straight-line run 78 percent of the time. See the introduction.

☐ Pullbacks occur 69 percent of the time after a straight-line run down from the breakout. See the introduction.

☐ Cut the failure rate of high and tight flags (HTF) to 19 percent by waiting for price to close above the top of the flagpole. Otherwise, the failure rate is 33 percent. See "HTF Trading."

☐ *Always* wait for price to close above the top of the HTF before buying. See "HTF Trading."

☐ Shallow sloping price trends leading to the start of the HTF result in better post-breakout performance. See Table 3.2.

☐ For high and tight flag trading tips, see "HTF Trading Tips: What I Use."

☐ The section "Fishing for Inverted and Ascending Scallops" discusses identification guidelines.

☐ See Scallop Trading Tips for details on how to profit by trading scallops.

☐ See Twice Is Nice: Eve and Eve Double Bottoms for identification tips.

☐ See Trading Eve and Eve for trading tips.

☐ Symmetrical triangles have a tendency to double bust—breakout in one direction, reverse, and reverse again to resume the original break-out direction. See "Symmetrical Triangle."

☐ Ascending triangles often see price rise by small amounts before reversing. See "Ascending Triangle."

☐ See "Support or Congestion" for tips on how to trade those areas.

☐ Flags can be half-staff patterns. The move before the flag mirrors the one after. See "Flag."

☐ Use the linear scale when searching for flat bases. See "Flat Base."

☐ The breakout from a flat base can take months before it occurs. See "Flat Base."

☐ Midway through a rounding turn, price tends to jump upward only to ease back down to near the launch price. See "Rounding Bottom."

☐ Watch for a descending scallop to develop instead of completing a rounding bottom. See "Rounding Bottom."

☐ If price breaks out downward from a descending triangle, reverses, and then closes above the top trendline, it busts the pattern and can lead to a powerful upward move. See "Busted Descending Triangle."

☐ A busted symmetrical triangle can lead to a powerful move providing it does not double bust. See "Busted Symmetrical Triangle."

☐ An ugly double bottom highlights a trend reversal from down to up. See "Ugly Double Bottom."

☐ Throwbacks see price gain an average of 8 percent in five days. See "Swinging Throwbacks and Pullbacks."

☐ Pullbacks lose 9 percent in six days. See Table 3.3.

☐ Table 3.4 shows a frequency distribution of time and gain/loss for throwbacks and pullbacks.

☐ Half of throwbacks and pullbacks occur within four to five days of the breakout (respectively) with moves of 4 to 10 percent being common. See "Swinging Throwbacks and Pullbacks."

☐ Consider waiting for a throwback or pullback to complete and for price to resume the breakout direction before trading. See "Trading Example."

☐ Waiting for a throwback or pullback to complete can setup a low risk, high reward trade. See "CNO Throwback Entry."

☐ Use the measure rule to predict how far price is going to move. See "Measuring Swings."

☐ Combine the measure rule for chart patterns with overhead resistance to determine how far price is going to move *before* taking a trade. See "Measuring Swings."

☐ Check the longer-term chart for tradable patterns. See "FTO Trade."

Chapter 4: Swing Selling

☐ Sometimes selling for tax reasons can be a mistake. See the introduction.

☐ Determine how far price is likely to move before selling a holding or shorting a stock. See "Selling Ideas."

☐ If support is closer than 5 percent, a downward breakout may push through it. See "Selling Ideas."

☐ The decline one month after a breakout is often small and tends to lessen because price rises over time. See Table 4.1.

☐ Identify diamond tops and bottoms: see "Diamond Tops and Bottoms."

☐ Price may overshoot or undershoot the entry to a chart pattern. Ignore it when determining whether the chart pattern is a top or bottom. Instead, use the primary price trend as the direction of entry. See "Overshoot, Undershoot, and Identifying Diamonds."

☐ Many diamond patterns tilt to one side and can appear irregularly shaped. See "Overshoot, Undershoot, and Identifying Diamonds."

☐ Quick declines sometimes follow quick rises. See "Diamond Price Behavior."

☐ A pullback may end the decline if the industry or market are trending higher. See "Diamond Price Behavior."

☐ See "Diamond Trading Tips" for, well, trading tips.

☐ See "Complex Head-and-Shoulders Top" for identification guidelines.

☐ See "Trading a Complex Head-and-Shoulders Top" for trading tips.

☐ If price forms a 2B top in a swing trade, then sell. See "2B."

☐ Sometimes using a profit target exit makes sense. See "Hit Target."

☐ See "Overhead Resistance" for selling tips.

☐ If price rises by 5 to 20 percent or more in one session, consider selling. See "Inverted Dead-Cat Bounce."

☐ If a risky stock doubles in price, then sell it or sell a portion of it. See "Double Your Money."

☐ Look at how other stocks in the same industry behave. They may show the same chart pattern. See "Chart Pattern Trend Change."

☐ Avoid buying and consider selling stocks in stages 3 or 4. See "Weinstein's Approach."

☐ Improve your trading skills instead of focusing on the money. See "Weakness."

☐ If the fundamentals change, then consider selling. See "Fundamentals."

☐ Diversify your holdings so that any one position does not dominate your portfolio. See "Diversification."

☐ If price pierces support, expect a swift decline. See "Support Pierced."

☐ Symmetrical triangles can make for good exit signals. See "Symmetrical Triangle."

☐ Try to sell at the top of the dead-cat bounce. See "Dead-Cat Bounce."

☐ Sell if overhead resistance looks like it will reverse a trend. See "Resistance."

☐ Wait for bearish chart patterns to confirm before selling a stock. See "Head-and-Shoulders Top."

☐ Try to predict how far price will move, set a target, and use a stop to protect profits. See "Trading Example: The Teradyne Exit."

☐ A 2B top is often a temporary peak but sometimes it indicates a lasting reversal. See "Trading Example: Exiting Forest."

☐ An inverted dead-cat bounce presents a selling opportunity. See "Trading Example: Swinging CNO."

Chapter 5: Event Pattern Setups

☐ The best performance comes when price trends down before announcement of the common stock offering, but the breakout is upward. See "Common Stock Offerings Setup."

☐ Price tends to make lower highs for a few days, so trail a buy stop a penny above the lowest high until buying the stock. See "Common Stock Offerings Setup."

☐ Price bottoms or peaks quickly. In 2 weeks or less, 65 percent reach bottom after a downward breakout and 49 percent peak after an upward breakout. See "Common Stock Offerings Setup."

☐ The median recovery time for the stock to return to the pre-announcement close is 29 calendar days. See "Common Stock Offerings Setup."

☐ For a trading setup on common stock offerings, see "Trading Offers."

☐ The event decline of a dead-cat bounce sees price drop an average of 32 percent in six days. See "Surviving a Dead-Cat Bounce."

☐ The bounce phase sees price rise an average of 27 percent in 19 days. See "Surviving a Dead-Cat Bounce."

☐ The postbounce drop averages 29 percent in 40 days. See "Surviving a Dead-Cat Bounce."

☐ The larger the event decline, the larger the bounce. See "Surviving a Dead-Cat Bounce."

☐ Another dead-cat bounce follows the first one between 29 percent and 42 percent of the time within three to six months. See "Surviving a Dead-Cat Bounce."

☐ Avoid buying a stock showing a dead-cat bounce within the past six months. See "Surviving a Dead-Cat Bounce."

☐ The belief that the event decline is oversold creates buying demand that pushes price higher for a time. See "DCB Example."

☐ Price averages a drop of 18 percent below the event decline low. See "Trading the DCB."

☐ Price in an inverted dead-cat bounce jumps up by 5 percent to 20 percent or more in one session. See "The Inverted Dead-Cat Bounce Setup."

☐ If you bought at the closing price the day before the Dutch auction's announcement and sold at the tender price, you would make money 85 percent of the time. See "Trading Dutch Auction Tender Offers."

☐ After the auction ends, price often trades outside of the auction's high-low price range within the first month. See "Trading Dutch Auction Tender Offers."

☐ Nearly all of the time (95 percent), price drops below the tender price within three months of the auction's end. See "After the Auction."

☐ Price rises above the tender price 79 percent of the time within three months of the auction's end. See "After the Auction."

☐ Buybacks more than 14.6 percent of shares outstanding tend to see price decline after the auction ends. Small buybacks tend to see price rise. See "After the Auction."

☐ For tips on selecting and trading earnings surprises, see "Earnings Surprise Setup."

☐ Price peaks three weeks after the announcement of good earnings. See "Earnings Surprise Setup."

☐ Review the section "Bad Earnings" for the scoop on identifying and trading a bad earnings event pattern.

☐ After a bad earnings announcement, price drops and continues lower for two to three weeks before rebounding somewhat and then continuing lower. See "Bad Earnings."

☐ See "Earnings Flag Setup" for identification details on the earnings flag.

☐ For tips on trading the earnings flag, see "Earnings Flag Example."

☐ Ignore stock upgrades in a bear market. See "Stock Upgrades and Downgrades."

☐ Downgrades in a bull market tend to be less effective than downgrades in a bear market. See "Stock Upgrades and Downgrades."

☐ For a list of trading tips, see Stock "Upgrades and Downgrades."

☐ Neither a forward nor a reverse stock split has any effect on the value of a holding. See "Stock Splits."

☐ Stocks gain 3 percent during the month before a stock split, climbing higher than the S&P 500 index 62 percent of the time. See "My Results."

☐ Three months after a reverse split, price is down 55 percent of the time, losing an average of 35 percent. See "Reverse Stock Splits."

☐ For better performance, only buy stocks with a rising price trend in the month before the reverse split. See "Trend Filter."

Chapter 6: Swinging Tools and Setups

☐ The chart pattern indicator helps determine when the market changes trend. See "The Chart Pattern Indicator."

☐ The narrow range 7 pattern predicts higher volatility ahead and the breakout gives the direction. See "The NR7."

☐ The chart pattern indicator is a daily ratio of bullish and bearish NR7s in hundreds of stocks. See "The CPI Equation."

☐ Do *not* use the chart pattern indicator as a trading tool, but as a sentiment indicator. See "The CPI Equation."

☐ A new signal is often set three days after it occurs. See "The CPI Equation."

☐ Use the swing rule to help predict how far price might rise. Measure a drop from peak to valley and project that height above the peak to get a target price. See "The Swing Rule."

☐ For up trends, price tends to exceed the swing rule target rather than fall short of it. See "The Swing Rule."

☐ The swing rule for up trends works best in a bull market. See "The Swing Rule."

☐ The swing rule works best when the decline used in the measure is less than 10 percent. See "The Swing Rule."

☐ The swing rule for downtrends works best for small swings (less than 10 percent) in a bull market. See "Swing Rule for Downtrends."

☐ Above-average breakout day volume does not mean substantially better performance. See "Pump Up the Volume or Not."

☐ Chart patterns with above-average breakout volume fail twice as often as do those with below-average volume. See "Failure Rates by Volume."

☐ Throwbacks and pullbacks are three times more likely to occur after a high volume breakout. See "Throwback and Pullback Rates by Volume."

☐ For the best performance, look for the relative strength line to reverse from falling to rising from the day before the start to the day before the breakout of a chart pattern. Avoid chart patterns with a relative strength line that turns from rising to falling. See "IRS Study."

☐ For the best performance from downward breakouts of chart patterns, look for a reversal in the relative strength line from the day before the start of the chart pattern to the day before the breakout. See "IRS Study."

☐ For various trading setups using ascending triangles and rectangles, see "Three Swing Trading Setups."

☐ "Trading Setup: Simple Moving Average Tests" use a moving average to test rectangles.

☐ A smile pattern is a rounding bottom. Enter a trade after the stock has bottomed and is moving up. Avoid buying a stock when price is still moving down. See "The Smile and Frown Setup."

☐ Buy smiles not frowns. See "The Smile and Frown Setup."

☐ Categorize your trades into smiles and frowns to see if your results might improve by concentrating purchases during smiles and sales during frowns. See "Smile and Frown Testing."

☐ Use a line chart to show smiles and frowns. See "Smile and Frown Trading Tips."

☐ For historical price charts, offset a simple moving average to the left by half the moving average length (for example, offset a 200-day moving average by 100 days). See "Smile and Frown Trading Tips."

☐ For real-time charts, do not offset the moving average. See "Smile and Frown Trading Tips."

☐ Do not go long in a bear market. Wait for the bear market to end (about 1½ years old). See "Smile and Frown Trading Tips."

☐ When searching for smiles, avoid stocks that have been declining for over a year. See "Smile and Frown Trading Tips."

☐ Look for a sharp decline in a stock over a week or two that leads to a smile pattern. See "Smile and Frown Trading Tips."

☐ When searching for frowns, look at the shape of prior peaks. Are they narrow or wide? Expect a similar shaped peak during the frown. See "Smile and Frown Trading Tips."

☐ Practice paper trading smiles and frowns. See "Smile and Frown Trading Tips."

☐ Do not smile/frown trade stocks within six months of those stocks showing dead-cat bounces. See "Smile and Frown Trading Tips."

☐ Try using the weekly chart to find stocks for swing trading using smiles and frowns. See "Smile and Frown Trading Tips."

☐ Use Figure 6.8 as a template for how a trade should progress. Buy at C (as close to B as possible) and sell at F (as close to E as possible). See "Smile and Frown Trading Tips."

Chapter 7: Introduction to Day Trading

☐ Day trading is opening and closing a position within the same day.

☐ Day trading can reduce, but not eliminate, single stock risk.

☐ See "Is Day Trading for You?" for a checklist.

☐ See "What Are the Problems of Day Trading?" for a checklist.

Chapter 8: Day Trading Basics

☐ Just 4 percent of traders make over $50,000 annually. See "Managing Expectations: How Much Can You Really Make?"

☐ To make $60,000 annually from trading requires a portfolio valued at $546,000, based on the S&P's average annual return of 11 percent. See "Managing Expectations: How Much Can You Really Make?"

☐ If you want to become a day trader, keep your expectations realistic, your living expenses low, and be well capitalized. See "Managing Expectations: How Much Can You Really Make?"

☐ See "Building the Home Office" for tips on creating your own trading space.

☐ Creating a home office need not cost a lot of money. Start small and add equipment as necessary. See "Office Setup Cost."

☐ "Pattern Day Trading Rules" outline the regulations for day traders.

☐ The wash sale rule only postpones a loss. See "Wash Sale Rule."

☐ Look for stocks with a 10-day average volume of at least 1 million shares. See "Trading Volume."

☐ Select stocks with a large ($1 to $5) high to low daily trading range. See "Trading Range."

☐ Avoid trading stocks below $10. Low priced stocks show higher volatility. See "Stock Price and Volatility."

☐ Avoid stocks that are too volatile or not volatile enough. See "Stock Price and Volatility."

☐ If you have difficulty making money, try switching to a longer time scale (from 1 minute to 5 minute, for example). See "Time Scale."

☐ Select stocks that trend. Avoid choppy stocks. See "Trend."

☐ Select stocks with tradable price trends after the breakout from chart patterns. See "Tradable Chart Patterns."

☐ Look at the difference between the bid and ask prices. If they are wider than a penny or two apart, consider looking for another stock to day trade. See "Bid/Ask Spread."

☐ Build a core list of stocks that you trade each day. See "Building Core Holdings."

☐ Avoid taking a position during the first minute of the trading day. See "Price Reversal Times Revealed!"

☐ Price is most likely to reverse direction a minute after the hour, a minute after the half hour, and 51 minutes after the hour. See "Price Reversal Times Revealed!"

☐ The reversal times are the same regardless of price trend (up or down) and market condition (bull or bear). See "Price Reversal Times Revealed!"

☐ Price trends more often in the morning session than the afternoon. See "Price Reversal Times Revealed!"

☐ Most often, stocks set the day's high (10 percent) or low (9 percent) within the first minute of trading. See "What Time Sets Intraday High and Low?"

☐ Within the first and last hour of trading, stocks post the day's high or low between 66 percent (for lows) and 68 percent (for highs) of the time. See "What Time Sets Intraday High and Low?"

☐ Price will tie the day's high or low 38 percent of the time, on average, sometime during the day. See "What Time Sets Intraday High and Low?"

☐ Should you use Level II quotes? See "Inside Level II Quotes."

☐ Clockwise movement from shrinking bids to expanding offers suggests a falling stock. Counter-clockwise movement of bids and offers means a rising stock. See "Level II Games."

☐ ECNs that cater to day traders can signal market direction, providing others follow their lead. See "Level II Games."

☐ Bids or offers further down the list help identify technical turning points. See "Level II Games."

☐ Watch for market markers to manipulate the Level II display with numerous small sized bids or offers. The market will move in an unexpected direction, trapping players on the wrong side. See "Level II Games."

☐ Use the market maker ID to identify participants that frequently manipulate the stocks you commonly trade. The ID may vary from stock to stock because a different individual from the same firm may handle the other stock. See "Level II Games."

☐ The speed of the time and sales ticker shows the stock's liquidity. See "Heartbeat of the Market: Time-and-Sales Ticker."

☐ A slowing time-and-sales ticker can indicate a coming price reversal. See "Heartbeat of the Market: Time-and-Sales Ticker."

☐ See "Pre-Market Checklist" for a shopping list to help profit from the day's trading.

☐ Did each trade follow the trading plan? See "After-Market Analysis."

Chapter 9: Opening Gap Setup

☐ Bull or bear markets have almost no influence on the closure rate of opening gaps. See "Do Bull or Bear Markets Matter?"

☐ In stocks, 72 percent of opening gaps (either up or down) closed by day's end. See "Do Bull or Bear Markets Matter?"

☐ ETF opening gaps (either up or down) closed just 56 percent of the time. See "Do Bull or Bear Markets Matter?"

☐ The closure rate for full and partial gaps is similar: 77 versus 79 percent, respectively. See "Closure Rate for Full and Partial Gaps."

☐ The closure rate for *up* gaps increases if the prior day's open to close price trend was also up. See "What Gap Size Works Best?"

☐ The closure rate for *down* gaps increases if the prior day's open to close move was downward. See "What Gap Size Works Best?"

☐ For fading the opening gap, the prior day's price trend is less significant than the gap being below the 50-day simple moving average. See "Use a Simple Moving Average?"

☐ Fade only when price gaps below the 50-day simple moving average (it works for both up or down gaps). See "Use a Simple Moving Average?"

☐ There is a 28 percent chance that price will close a gap on the second day and 18 percent on the third day. Holding a trade open for an additional day and hoping for the gap to close is a mistake. See "Should You Hold Longer Than a Day?"

☐ Fading the gap and holding on for additional gains until the day's close works 47 percent to 48 percent of the time. See "Gap Closes. Hold On or Sell?"

☐ Expect one to two minutes of price continuing in the gap direction before a reversal begins. See "Trade Entry Details."

☐ Tall upward opening gaps tend to see price reverse quicker than short ones. See "Trade Entry Details."

☐ Few gaps taller than 1 percent close within the first minute. See "How Many Gaps Close in First Minute?"

☐ If the gap closes before entry, skip the trade. See "Trade Anyway If Gap Closes?"

☐ If price stalls one-third, midway, or two-thirds of the way across an opening gap, then sell. See "Trade Exit: Five Popular Selling Prices."

☐ Fading the gap, if done carefully, can lead to profitable trades. See "Opening Gap Setup Rules."

Chapter 10: Day Trading Chart Patterns

☐ Review each chart pattern for specific trading setups.

☐ For bearish chart patterns, use the measure rule to predict how far price may drop. Compute the height of the chart pattern and subtract it from the lowest price in the chart pattern to get a price target. See "Day Trading Double Tops."

☐ Watch the clock to be sure you have enough time to complete the trade before the day's close. See "Day Trading Double Tops."

☐ If a pullback occurs, consider adding to an existing position or entering a new one. See "Day Trading Double Tops."

☐ After a strong move up, look for the stock to remain just above the launch price. See "Day Trading Double Tops."

☐ Use historical price movement to help gauge if there is enough time to complete a trade by day's end. The slope of the trend before and after a chart pattern can help determine if price will reach the target before the close. See "Do You Have the Time?"

☐ A reversal chart pattern needs something to reverse. After a small rise leading to a reversal chart pattern, expect a small decline after the breakout. See "Day Trading Triple Tops."

☐ After a straight-line run forms (three consecutive lower highs and lower lows), trail the stop lower by placing the stop a penny above the prior bar's high. Lower the stop as price drops, but do not raise the stop. See "Day Trading Symmetrical Triangles."

☐ If the neckline slopes downward in a head-and-shoulders top, use the right armpit's low as the breakout price. See "Day Trading Head-and-Shoulders Tops."

☐ If the neckline slopes upward in a head-and-shoulders bottom chart pattern, then use the right armpit as the breakout price. See "Day Trading Head-and-Shoulders Bottoms."

☐ The measure rule target often serves as a minimum price to which the stock moves. See "Day Trading Triple Bottoms."

☐ If you are having trouble making money day trading, try trading ETFs based on a major market index. See "Other Trading Tips."

☐ Trade using the 5-minute scale. See "Other Trading Tips."

□ Use the chart pattern indicator to show market sentiment. See "Other Trading Tips."

□ Run the calculation to predict tomorrow's close. See "Other Trading Tips."

Chapter 11: Opening Range Breakout

□ Before an upward breakout, look for price to hug the top of the range more than it does the bottom of the range. Before a downward breakout, look for the reverse: Price should hug the bottom of the range most often. See chapter introduction.

□ Prices ending with zero (round numbers) make good profit targets. See chapter introduction.

□ The quicker you enter a range breakout trade, the better. See "What Is Best Range Time?"

□ The shortest opening range (five minutes) results in the best profit for opening range trading. See "What Is Best Range Time?"

□ Trade with the trend. In a bear market, downward breakouts tend to make more money than upward breakouts in intraday trading. In bull markets, upward breakouts make more money. See "What Is Best Range Time?"

□ For upward breakouts, trade only those situations where price closes above the middle of the opening range most of the time. See "Price Should Hover near Breakout."

□ Downward breakouts from the opening range do best when price resides below the range's midpoint most often. See "Price Should Hover near Breakout."

□ Do not use a short moving average with the opening range breakout. See "Ten-Period EMA."

□ Do not delay entering a trade. See "Offset Entry by 5 Cents."

□ Round numbers, those ending in zero, are support and resistance areas that make good price targets for day trades. See "Round-Number Exit."

□ Range breakouts that use an initial stop perform worse but limit losses. See "Initial 10-Cent Stop."

□ A trailing stop can help trim losses and salvage profits. See "Trailing Stop."

□ The three-bar exit resulted in larger losses. See "Three-Bar Exit."

Visual Appendix of Chart Patterns

Broadening Bottoms

Broadening Formations,
Right-Angled and Ascending

Broadening Formations,
Right-Angled and Descending

Broadening Tops

Broadening Wedges, Ascending

Broadening Wedges, Descending

Bump-and-Run Reversal
Bottoms

Bump-and-Run Reversal Tops

Cup with Handle

Cup with Handle, Inverted

Dead-Cat Bounce

Dead-Cat Bounce, Inverted

Diamond Bottoms

Diamond Tops

Double Bottoms, Adam & Adam

Double Bottoms, Adam & Eve

Double Bottoms, Eve & Adam

Double Bottoms, Eve & Eve

Double Tops, Adam & Adam

Double Tops, Adam & Eve

Double Tops, Eve & Adam

Double Tops, Eve & Eve

Flags

Flags, High and Tight

Gaps

Head-and-Shoulders Bottoms

Head-and-Shoulders Bottoms, Complex

Head-and-Shoulders Tops

Head-and-Shoulders Tops, Complex

Horn Bottoms

Horn Tops

Island Reversals, Bottoms

Island Reversals, Tops

Islands, Long

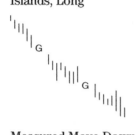

Measured Move Down

Measured Move Up

Pennants

Pipe Bottoms

Pipe Tops

Rectangle Bottoms

Rectangle Tops

Rounding Bottoms

Rounding Tops

Scallops, Ascending

Scallops, Ascending and Inverted

Scallops, Descending

Scallops, Descending and Inverted

Three Falling Peaks

Three Rising Valleys

Triangles, Ascending

Triangles, Descending

Triangles, Symmetrical

Triple Bottoms

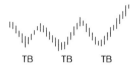

Triple Tops

Wedges, Falling

Wedges, Rising

Bibliography

Active Trader Staff. "Intraday Swing Extremes." *Active Trader* 12, no. 5 (May 2011).

Bandy, Howard. "Scaling Out as an Exit Technique." *Active Trader* 10, no. 9 (September 2009).

Bandy, Howard. "Scaling In as an Entry Technique." *Active Trader* 10, no. 10 (October 2009).

Bulkowski, Thomas. "A Trend Channel Trade." *Technical Analysis of Stocks & Commodities* 14, no. 4 (April 1996).

Bulkowski, Thomas. *Encyclopedia of Candlestick Charts.* Hoboken, NJ: John Wiley & Sons, 2008.

Bulkowski, Thomas. *Encyclopedia of Chart Patterns*, 2nd ed. Hoboken, NJ: John Wiley & Sons, 2005.

Bulkowski, Thomas. *Getting Started in Chart Patterns.* Hoboken, NJ: John Wiley & Sons, 2006.

Bulkowski, Thomas. *Trading Classic Chart Patterns.* Hoboken, NJ: John Wiley & Sons, 2002.

Bulkowski, Thomas. *Visual Guide to Chart Patterns.* Hoboken, NJ: John Wiley & Sons, 2013.

De Bondt, Werner F. M., and Richard H. Thaler. "Further Evidence on Investor Overreaction and Stock Market Seasonality." *Journal of Finance* 42, no. 3 (July 1987).

Desai, H., and P. Jain. "Long-Run Common Stock Returns Following Stock Splits and Reverse Splits." *Journal of Business* (1997).

Fama, Eugene F., and Kenneth R. French. "The Cross-Section of Expected Stock Returns." *Journal of Finance* 47, no. 2 (June 1992).

Fama, Eugene F., Lawrence Fisher, Michael C. Jensen, and Richard Roll. "The Adjustment of Stock Prices to New Information." *International Economic Review* 10 (February 1969).

Farley, Alan S. *The Master Swing Trader.* New York: McGraw-Hill, 2001.

Fischer, Robert, and Jens Fischer. *Candlesticks, Fibonacci, and Chart Pattern Trading Tools.* Hoboken, NJ: John Wiley & Sons, 2003.

Fosback, Norman G. *Stock Market Logic: A Sophisticated Approach to Profits on Wall Street.* Fort Lauderdale, FL: The Institute for Econometric Research, 1976.

Frost, A. J., and Robert R. Prechter. Jr. *Elliott Wave Principle: Key to Market Behavior.* Chichester, England: John Wiley & Sons, 1999.

Garcia de Andoain, Carlos and Frank W. Bacon. "The Impact of Stock Split Announcements on Stock Price: A Test of Market Efficiency." *Proceedings of ASBBS* 16, no. 1 (2009).

Glass, Gary S. "Extensive Insider Accumulation as an Indicator of Near Term Stock Price Performance." PhD diss., Ohio State University, 1966.

Grinblatt, Mark S., Ronald W. Masulis, and Sheridan Titman. "The Valuation Effects of Stock Splits and Stock Dividends." *Journal of Financial Economics* (1984).

Guppy, Daryl. "Matching Money Management with Trade Risk." *Technical Analysis of Stocks & Commodities* 16, no. 5 (May 1998).

Guppy, Daryl. "Exploiting Positions with Money Management." *Technical Analysis of Stocks & Commodities* 17, no. 9 (September 1999).

Hall, Alvin D. *Getting Started in Stocks*, 3rd ed. New York: John Wiley & Sons, 1997.

How to Invest in Common Stocks. The Complete Guide to Using The Value Line Investment Survey. New York: Value Line Publishing, Inc., 2007.

Ikenberry, David, G. Rankine, and E. K. Stice. "What Do Stock Splits Really Signal?" *Journal of Financial and Qualitative Analysis* (1996).

Investopedia.com. "Keep Your Eyes on the ROE." www.investopedia.com/articles/fundamental/03/100103.asp.

Jaenisch, Ron. "The Andrews Line." *Technical Analysis of Stocks & Commodities* 14, no. 10 (October 1996).

Kaplan, Peter. "Finding the Value in Losses." *Stocks, Futures and Options*, September 2006.

Kaufman, Perry J. *A Short Course in Technical Trading.* Hoboken, NJ: John Wiley & Sons, 2003.

Knapp, Volker. "Top Stop Exit." *Active Trader* 9, no. 9 (September 2008).

Knapp, Volker. "Insider Buying." *Active Trader* 9, no. 10 (October 2008).

Knapp, Volker. "Insider Selling." *Active Trader* 9, no. 11 (November 2008).

Lakonishok, Josef, Andrei Shleifer, and Robert W. Vishny. "Contrarian Investment, Extrapolation, and Risk." *Journal of Finance* 49, no. 5 (December 1994).

Landry, Dave. "Trading Trend Transitions." *Active Trader* 11, no. 12 (December 2010).

Lynch, Peter, and John Rothchild. *One Up on Wall Street: How to Use What You Already Know to Make Money in the Market.* New York: Penguin Books, 1990.

Mamis, Justin, and Robert Mamis. *When to Sell: Inside Strategies for Stock-Market Profits.* New York: Cornerstone Library, 1977.

Martell, Terrence F., and Gwendolyn P. Webb. "The Performance of Stocks that Are Reverse Split." New York: Baruch College/The City University of New York, 2005.

McClure, Ben. "Keep Your Eyes on the ROE." www.Investopedia.com/articles /fundamental/03/100103.asp.

Nicholson, S. Francis. "Price-Earnings Ratios." *Financial Analysts Journal 16*, no. 4 (July–August 1960).

Nilsson, Peter. "Money Management Matrix." *Technical Analysis of Stocks & Commodities* 24, no. 13 (December 2006).

O'Hare, Patrick. "Looking for Bottoms in Individual Stocks." *Stocks, Futures & Options* 3, no. 5 (May 2004).

O'Higgins, Michael, and John Downes. *Beating the Dow.* New York: HarperCollins, 1992.

O'Shaughnessy, James. *What Works on Wall Street.* New York: McGraw-Hill, 1997.

Patel, Pankaj N., Souheang Yao, and Heath Barefoot. "High Yield, Low Payout." *Credit Suisse*, August 2006.

Pugliese, Fausto, "Daytrading Rule 1: No Overnights." *Technical Analysis of Stocks & Commodities* 30, no. 7 (June 2012).

Rogoff, Donald T. "The Forecasting Properties of Insider Transactions." PhD diss., Michigan State University, 1964.

Sperandeo, Victor, with Sullivan Brown. *Trader Vic—Methods of a Wall Street Master.* New York: John Wiley & Sons, 1991, 1993.

Stowell, Joseph. "Teacher, Trader Still Teaching: Joseph Stowell." *Technical Analysis of Stocks & Commodities* 13, no. 7 (July 1995).

Subach, Daniel. "Stock Analysis and Investing for the Small Investor." *Technical Analysis of Stocks & Commodities* 24, no. 13 (December 2006).

Tweedy, Browne Company LLC. "What Has Worked in Investing: Studies of Investment Approaches and Characteristics Associated with Exceptional Returns." Revised 2009.

Vakkur, Mark. "The Basics of Managing Money." *Technical Analysis of Stocks & Commodities* 15, no. 9 (September 1997).

Vakkur, Mark. "New Tricks with the Dogs of the Dow." *Technical Analysis of Stocks & Commodities* 15, no. 12 (December 1997).

Vince, Ralph. *The Handbook of Portfolio Mathematics: Formulas for Optimal Allocation & Leverage.* Hoboken, NJ: John Wiley & Sons, 2007.

Weinstein, Sam. *Stan Weinstein's Secrets for Profiting in Bull and Bear Markets.* New York: McGraw-Hill, 1988.

Wisdom, Gabriel. *Wisdom on Value Investing.* Hoboken, NJ: John Wiley & Sons, 2009.

OTHER SITES OF INTEREST

www.Activetradermag.com—website for *Active Trader* magazine.

www.ThePatternSite.com—Mr. Bulkowski's website.

www.traders.com—website for *Technical Analysis of Stocks & Commodities* magazine.

www.Yahoo.finance.com—a general finance website.

About the Author

Thomas Bulkowski is a successful investor with more than 30 years of experience trading stocks. He is also the author of the John Wiley & Sons titles:

- *Visual Guide to Chart Patterns*
- *Getting Started in Chart Patterns*
- *Trading Classic Chart Patterns*
- *Encyclopedia of Candlestick Charts*
- *Encyclopedia of Chart Patterns, Second Edition*
- *Evolution of a Trader: Trading Basics.*
- *Evolution of a Trader: Fundamental Analysis and Position Trading*

Bulkowski is a frequent contributor to *Active Trader* and *Technical Analysis of Stocks & Commodities* magazines. Before earning enough from his investments to retire from his day job at age 36, Bulkowski was a hardware design engineer at Raytheon and a senior software engineer for Tandy Corporation.

His website and blog are at www.thepatternsite.com, where you can read over 500 articles and the latest research on chart patterns, candlesticks, event patterns, and other investment topics, for free, without registering.

Index

Printed and bound by CPI Group (UK) Ltd, Croydon, CR0 4YY

16/04/2025

14658449-0004